D1617322

Division of Labor and Welfare

THE LIBRARY OF POLITICAL ECONOMY

POLITICAL ECONOMY is the old name for economics. In the hands of the great classical economists, particularly Smith, Ricardo and Marx, economics was the study of the working and development of the economic system in which men and women lived. Its practitioners were driven by a desire to describe, to explain and to evaluate what they saw around them. No sharp distinction was drawn between economic analysis and economic policy nor between economic behaviour and its interaction with the technical, social and political framework.

The Library of Political Economy has been established to provide widely based explanations of economic behaviour in contemporary society.

In examining the way in which new patterns of social organization and behaviour influence the economic system and policies for combating problems associated with growth, inflation, poverty and the distribution of wealth, contributors stress the link between politics and economics and the importance of institutions in policy formulation.

This 'open-ended' approach to economics implies that there are few laws that can be held to with certainty and, by the same token, there is no generally established body of theory to be applied in all circumstances. Instead economics as presented in this library provides a way of ordering events which has constantly to be updated and modified as new situations develop. This, we believe, is its interest and its challenge.

Editorial Board

Andrew Graham, University of Oxford
Keith Griffin, University of Oxford
Geoffrey Harcourt, University of Cambridge
Roger Opie, University of Oxford
Hugh Stretton, University of Adelaide
Lester Thurow, Massachusetts Institute of Technology

Volumes in the Library

Dangerous Currents: The State of Economics—Lester Thurow
The Political Economy of Nationalism—Dudley Seers
Women's Claims: A Study in Political Economy—Lisa Peattie and Martin Rein
Urban Inequalities under State Socialism—Ivan Szelenyi
Social Innovation and the Division of Labour—Johnathan Gershuny
The Structuring of Labour Markets: A Comparative Analysis of the Steel and Construction Industries in Italy—Paola Villa
Monetarism and the Labour Market—Derek Robinson
Agrarian Impasse in Bengal: Institutional Constraints to Technological Change—James K. Boyce
Does Aid Work?—Robert Cassen and Associates

Division of Labor and Welfare

An Introduction to Economic Systems

Louis Putterman

OXFORD UNIVERSITY PRESS
1990

Oxford University Press, Walton Street, Oxford OX2 6DP

Oxford   New York   Toronto
Delhi   Bombay   Calcutta   Madras   Karachi
Petaling Jaya   Singapore   Hong Kong   Tokyo
Nairobi   Dar es Salaam   Cape Town
Melbourne   Auckland

and associated companies in
Berlin   Ibadan

Oxford is a trade mark of Oxford University Press

Published in the United States
by Oxford University Press, New York

British Library Cataloguing in Publication Data
Putterman, Louis
    Division of labor and welfare: an introduction to economic systems. –
    (The Library of political economy).
    1. Economic systems
    I. Title   II. Series
    330.12
    ISBN 0-19-877299-8
    ISBN 0-19-877298-X (pbk)

Library of Congress Cataloging in Publication Data
Putterman, Louis.
    Division of labor and welfare: an introduction to economic systems/Louis Putterman.
    (Library of political economy)
    Includes bibliographical references.
    1. Division of labor.   2. Welfare economics.   3. Comparative economics.
    I. Title.   II. Series.
HD51.P88   1990   306.3'68--dc20   90-7035
ISBN 0-19-877299-8
ISBN 0-19-877298-X (pbk)

Typeset by Best-set Typesetter Ltd
Printed in Great Britain by Bookcraft Ltd, Midsomer Norton, Avon

*To my parents, who have set an example
by their generosity, caring, and optimism*

Preface

This book provides a brief introduction to the study of economic systems. It revolves around a conceptual framework which gives centrality to the idea that modern economic systems represent different ways of grasping the productive advantages of complex divisions of labor, and of dealing with the accompanying problems of economic coordination, of distribution of burdens and benefits, and of changes in social relationships and in the conditions of individual development. An introductory chapter sets the tone of the book by illustrating the ways in which economic arrangements matter not only to societies' economic performances and to their members' pocketbooks, but also to virtually all aspects of people's lives. The Introduction also takes up the questions of whether economic systems should be viewed as objects of choice by societies as collectivities, and of whether it is possible to understand them in a manner free of ideological bias.

The basic approach is introduced in Chapter 1, which begins by defining economy and economic system, then explains what is meant by division of labor and why it is both useful and problematic; the chapter ends by suggesting some criteria for evaluating the success of economic systems in solving the problems raised by division of labor. Chapters 2, 3, and 4 take up in turn three ideal or archetypal economic systems—capitalism, centralized socialism, and decentralized workers' self-management—viewed as alternative solutions to those problems. Each system is defined by a few basic institutions, but is also characterized by an articulated rationale as a solution to the problems of division of labor. The suitability of each system is examined first under ideal conditions; for capitalism, for example, these conditions include perfect competition, while for centrally planned socialism, they include the assumption that the state represents the interests of the vast majority of the people; the systems are then looked at under increasingly realistic, and more adverse, conditions. Finally, proposals for reform, and modified versions of the systems, are considered. The fifth and last chapter includes a discussion of the comparative performance of societies operating under differing economic systems,

and takes up some remaining questions about economic organization: How does our discussion of economic systems apply to less
developed countries? Are there alternatives to markets and planning? How crucial (or universal) is self-interest? and : Is scarcity a
permanent and unavoidable fact of human existence?

This book does not provide a complete introduction to the subject
of economic systems, but rather, it attempts to supply a conceptual
framework to complement more detailed materials on the institutions, histories, and performances of economies representing the
different system types; it tries also to supplement materials dealing
with relevant analytical techniques such as the method of input-
output analysis, linear programming, or the theory of labor-
managed firms. As such, the book may serve as a companion to
textbooks or course materials, in courses on comparative economic
systems at both undergraduate and graduate levels. (A draft of this
material has served successfully in that role in my courses at Brown
University over the last several years.) Readers should also find the
book of interest apart from a course setting.

As for the choice of systems to be discussed in depth, the selection
of capitalism and centrally planned socialism will raise few
questions in view of their dominance of the industrialized world
today.[1] Devoting equal attention to workers' self-management, a
choice more likely to be questioned, is justified by the desirability of
considering at least one alternative to the two dominant systems, by
the sustained interest in this particular system in the comparative
economics literature of the last twenty years, by the existence of
cooperative sectors and forms of partial self-management in a great
many countries, and by the fact (demonstrated, it is hoped, in the
pages that follow) that as cogent and distinct a case can be made for
this, as for the other two systems, as a solution to the problems of
division of labor. Although variations on the themes of capitalism
and centrally planned socialism are of great interest in their own
right, self-management seems unique in these respects as a system in
and of itself.

It is fair to warn that no attempt has been made to ensure that the
book will find favor with all instructors of this subject. Rather than
being a consensus approach, the framework adopted by the author is
only one of a great number of different ways of viewing the subject of
economic systems, and it is certain to be liked by some and disliked
by others now teaching in this field. Methodologically, the emphasis

is on theoretical argumentation, rather than empirical observation; yet that argumentation is eclectic in approach, and little of it is mathematical or what economists think of as 'formal' in character. As a statement of a particular way of conceptualizing economic systems, the book is also intended to address a readership additional to that of the economics student, and it is hoped that it will prove stimulating to the thinking of students and scholars in a variety of disciplines. While the technical level of the discussion is therefore kept suitable to the advanced undergraduate student, throughout, the attempt has been made to do so without sacrificing substance of potential interest to these other audiences.

Acknowledgments

This book has taken shape over a number of years. In preparing it, I have benefited from the assistance, forbearance, and support of individuals and institutions too numerous to name. Special mention must be made of the teachers who introduced me to the field of comparative economics—John Michael Montias, the late Raymond Powell, and Steven Sacks—and of the students at Brown University on whom the approaches presented here have been tried out over a number of years. Thanks are due to the editors, to the advice of unnamed readers for the latter, and to Frederic Pryor and Keith Griffin, whose encouragement provided the necessary final impetus to complete the work. I am also grateful to Avner Ben-Ner, David Ellerman, Randy Kroszner, Marilyn Rueschemeyer, Gil Skillman, Rajiv Vohra, and Steven Smith, for comments and suggestions on particular issues or portions of the book, to John Burkett and Frank Durgin for their comments on the entire manuscript, and to Jeanne Carroll for research assistance, especially with respect to section 5.2. As always, I wish to thank my wife, Vivian Tseng, for her unfailing support and understanding.

Notes

1. While I had thought this statement uncontroversial when writing the initial draft, one more recent reader wondered whether the Soviet-type economy as it has been known from the late 1920s to the present might not in fact soon be a thing of the past. If the reforms now sweeping the socialist world progress rapidly enough, it is true that much of what

follows on that system will be of more interest as intellectual history than as interpretation of a living form of social organization. Some possible results of socialist reforms, and some reasons why change may be slow, are considered in Chapter 3.

Contents

Table and Figures

Introduction

The Importance of Economic Arrangements

The central role of economic organization in determining the character of societies and the prospects of human beings as individuals, families, social groups, and nations, is difficult to deny. Some have gone so far as to argue that economic forces represent a kind of foundation or basis upon which most social institutions are built, and that the culture and world-view of the individual and group are largely derived from the nature of their economic environment and from their particular positions in that environment. Although the most deterministic variants of this argument ought probably to be rejected, and while causality may quite often flow in more than one direction, at least some aspects of that view of human reality are compelling.

Contrast the lives of the Jones family of Akron, USA, and of the Ivanov family of Minsk, USSR. In his early twenties Mr. Jones found a job in a tire manufacturing plant that was sufficiently well paid to permit the family to buy a three-bedroom home in a residential neighborhood, where Mrs. Jones began to attend to the raising their three children. The family lived in this fashion for a dozen years, making mortgage payments on their home, owning one and eventually two private automobiles, and building up a small amount of savings. In the early 1980s recession and foreign competition led Mr. Jones's employer temporarily to shut down operations. After a period of unemployment, Mr. Jones found work as a delivery man for a consumer products firm, where he earned slightly over half his previous wages; Mrs. Jones took a job working behind the check-out counter of a large retail chain store. With two jobs, the Joneses were able to continue their mortgage payments until Mr. Jones's plant reopened and he got back his old job. However, the Jones's neighborhood has in the meantime begun to deteriorate, as they see it—declining standards of upkeep, rising crime and drug use, a 'lower class' of resident—and they feel that a move to a better neighborhood is really what is needed to maintain their standard of living; but houses in such neighborhoods have become unaffordable, even if Mrs. Jones continues to work. In their late teens, their children are beginning to take part-time jobs, and the Joneses wonder about the prospects that *they* will face in the working world.

In Minsk, Mr. Ivanov works on an assembly line manufacturing automobiles, while his wife works in the upholstery shop of a furniture enterprise; the enterprises that employ them are controlled by their government, rather than by individual owners. They share a two-bedroom apartment with their three children, and travel to their work and shopping rounds by public transportation or on foot. Their salaries are modest, but their housing and transportation costs are low, owing to subsidies, and their jobs are secure and provide health and other benefits, and pensions. The neighborhood in which they live is clean, but drab. The lives of most of their neighbors and relatives are quite similar to their own, and with education, job training, and help in job placement provided by the state, they have had reason to expect the same for their children. Of late, though, amid grumblings about an inefficient and stagnant economy, the government has spoken of radical changes, the consequences of which are hard for the Ivanovs to gauge.

Although the Joneses feel that maintaining their living standard is becoming more precarious, they appear in most ways to be economically far better off than the Ivanovs. For example, the Joneses purchase a large variety of frozen, canned, dry, and fresh foods, including fruits grown in California, Mexico, and elsewhere, in any of several supermarkets in their vicinity. The Ivanovs' diet is plainer. Their food is obtained with much greater difficulty (including frustrating waiting for rationed or unavailable items) and is less varied, and they spend more time on preparing their meals from unprocessed ingredients, unassisted by some of the appliances, like a microwave oven, that the Joneses take for granted. While the Joneses struggle with high medical insurance premiums and deductibles, the quality of medical care which they enjoy is considerably higher—in terms of cleanliness of facilities, availability of advanced equipment, and waiting time—than that of the care available to the Ivanovs without charge. The Joneses own three television sets, a cassette player, a stereo, and a Polaroid camera, and have two telephones in their home, while the Ivanovs own one television set, a monaural record player, and a camera that would be considered old-fashioned in the United States, and they share a telephone with several neighbors. The Joneses eat out in a family restaurant once or twice a month, and are able to purchase a wide array of clothing, cosmetic and drug supplies, and home needs, in a variety of shopping centers, whereas the Ivanovs always eat at home or with relatives, and face a limited selection of clothing and supplies.

The significance of other comparisons is harder to assess. While the Ivanovs have the sense that most people (one exception being high officials) live more or less as they do, the Joneses are aware of the existence of more inequalities. Parts of their city contain large numbers of abandoned buildings and severely run-down residences, are served by inferior schools, and generate distressing rates of juvenile deliquency, drug dealing, and crime. Local news features stories about the city's homeless and hungry, and Mr. Jones knows the approach of panhandlers and the sight of people sleeping on heating grates as a reason to prefer the suburban shopping malls to the inner city. Often paralleling these economic problems are the racial strains conveyed to the Joneses both by local and national news media, and by changes impinging on their own community. Furthermore, in his recent employment, Mr Jones frequently made deliveries to more affluent neighborhoods where he saw homes far larger and better appointed than his own, wives staying at home and enjoying the assistance of hired domestic workers, landscaped properties, and expensive automobiles. He knows that the people in these homes eat in expensive restaurants, take vacations at fine resorts, travel to foreign countries, and have a far greater likelihood than he of sending their children to good colleges. He might also observe that their manners of speaking are different from his and his family's, just as their own language differs from that of the people in the city slums. Mr. Jones buys lottery tickets two or three times a week and lets himself dream of joining the ranks of the more privileged. At the same time, he anxiously watches news stories about families like his own reduced to dire circumstances by regional economic slumps or by medical crises. The Ivanovs, who have long been told that these inequalities and tensions are signs of the anarchic character of capitalism, are more vaguely aware of similar problems in their own society, which until recently had received little attention in their press. Although now jolted by reports of violence over conflicting nationalisms, controversies over political freedoms, and denunciations of past leaders of their country, the Ivanovs' lives had until recently tended to be both less hopeful and more stable than those of the Joneses.

Beyond the 'life chances' and living standards determined by the economic systems and the positions within them occupied by these two families, other aspects of their attitudes and experiences are influenced by the economic institutions of their respective societies. This is obvious with regard to the education of their children, which is of similar content[1] with respect to training in basic mathematics, literacy, and sciences, but rather different in their history lessons, the nature of civic values taught, and the concepts of justice communicated. Other influences, transmitted through news and cultural media, convey differing messages: for example, consumerism and material aspiration is promoted by private advertisers in the media reaching the Joneses; patriotism, the evils of capitalism, and fraternity with socialist nations are stressed in the more publicly controlled media reaching the Ivanovs. The Joneses, of course, are also exposed to patriotic messages and are influenced by anti-Communist attitudes permeating their society. They pay occasional attention to political events, but only Mrs. Jones regularly bothers to vote in state and national elections. The Ivanovs are not Communist Party members and see politics as something quite uncontrollable by them, yet capable of having immediate consequences; thus it is often a topic of heated conversation among family and friends. Differences in their attitudes and values are also reflected in their views of inequality. Mr. Ivanov is concerned that unfairness would result if economic reforms allow workers in more profitable enterprises to earn more than those in less profitable ones who work equally hard, and he agrees with official propaganda that the wide gaps separating rich and poor in the West are unjust. Mr. Jones's view of those who become rich not only by hard work or superior skills, but also by better luck, is one of envy without any feeling of resentment or sense of injustice. Jones opposes measures that might reduce the scope for personal enrichment, feeling that the fact that just about anyone can become rich, however remote the chance, is part of his country's greatness.

These particular examples only begin to suggest the influence of economic organization in people's lives. That influence is felt by way of differences in the prosperity of the nation and the availability of consumer goods; in the individual's and family's status in the workplace, society, and in the distribution of income; in income and employment security, or the lack of it; in the quality of the physical environment, and the prevalence of health risks in the workplace and living space; in the presence of feelings of inadequacy resulting from economic failure, or of moral disquiet resulting from knowing of the deprivations of others while one's own family enjoys comfort; in fear of the economic consequences of illness, or of the physical consequences of limited available care; in freedoms to seek a better job, invest in one's enterprise, move to a new location, participate in political activities, or practice religion, or lack of such freedoms; in levels of community cohesiveness or of social tension, of security or crime, of neighborliness or prejudice, of satisfaction or frustration, of belonging or alienation.

To bring these influences to a concrete and personal level, consider the economic consequences for the family should Mr. Jones suffer a lengthy, incapacitating illness requiring expensive medical care and home nursing just when he is unemployed and without private health insurance; the possibility that one of their sons starts a successful business that grows to employ other family members; the consequences of both senior Joneses losing their jobs in a new economic downturn; the prospect of their daughter becoming an attorney and bringing the family a new level of economic security and pride, but perhaps also new social strains; the impact of losing a family member to a cancer that is found to be caused by contamination of the local water supply. Likewise, consider the possibility that Mr. Ivanov falls victim to alcoholism, which is prevalent in his society, or is maimed in a bus crash caused by the negligence of traffic officials or by the alcoholism of a driver; imagine that Mrs. Ivanov needs an operation and can have one in good time and by an experienced surgeon only through payment of a bribe that taxes the family's limited means, or that she dies after her operation because of unsterile conditions common in hospitals where resources are short and morale is low; that a son becomes a party official and gains access to scarce imported and high quality goods that benefit the family; that a daughter marries a man with heterodox political views, putting the family under suspicion by the authorities; and so on. Some of these events could happen in either family's society, but the likelihood that they will occur, and their economic and personal implications, are clearly linked to the nature of each family's socio-economic environment, the rules of the economic system under which each lives, and each one's position in that environment and system.

The examples just employed are also limited in the sense that comparisons of members of the least advantaged strata, or of the most advantaged groups, or of persons in very different occupations, within the societies that the Joneses and Ivanovs inhabit, would generate different contrasts from those just explored. The influences of an economic system and of individuals' positions within it are illustrated, for example, by contrasts within the same society. That these influences go beyond effects on consumption standards is demonstrated by the fact that socio-economic background correlates with school performance, preferred forms of recreation, views on social issues, and so forth. To take an example from the health field, in the United States of the 1980s, cigarette smoking and obesity were more common among lower-income working people, while something called 'chronic fatigue syndrome', although suspected of having a viral origin, disproportionately afflicted young professionals. A more pointed example of not strictly 'economic' influences on both political views and life chances is provided by American society in the late 1960s, when young men of middle- or upper-middle-class backgrounds were likely to be opponents of their country's military intervention in Vietnam, and to find ways of avoiding military service, while their co-generationists from working families of more modest means were likely to serve in that war, sometimes at the cost of their lives. From one standpoint, such differences between social groups may be viewed as natural outcomes of irreducible economic inequalities, with analogues in most if not all societies. But the existence of different forms of economic organization, and the differences in resulting socio-economic structures, suggest that they should also be seen as manifestations of particular institutional frameworks, and as illustrations of the influence of such frameworks not only on how much cash we carry in our pockets, but also on who we are, and on our likelihoods of living full and meaningful lives.

Of course, economic organization is not the sole force shaping people's lives. If we are to assess the influence of economic organization, we should filter out, from our comparisons, the separate influences of different political histories, of different levels of economic development, of different cultures and religious backgrounds, and so on (although these factors may be influenced by, and may influence, economic organization, if an appropriate time frame is considered). To do that, we will need a clearer sense of what is meant by economic organization or economic system. But a proper definition will be left to Chapter 1.

Economic Systems as Alternatives

Before beginning our discussion of the nature of economic systems, it may be useful to raise critical issues of two kinds. First, to what extent should economic systems be studied as objects of choice by societies and their members? Second, given the highly controversial nature of judgments about economic institutions, can economics be counted upon to inform us about those institutions without introducing ideological biases? The first question is addressed in the present section, and the second is discussed in the next and final section of this Introduction.

The notion that the major economic systems of the modern world are in some sense alternative ways of organizing economic life might suggest that the purpose of studying economic systems is to permit informed choice among these alternatives. The menu of existing alternatives consists not only of the great embattled world systems of private enterprise market capitalism and centrally planned state enterprise socialism, but also of a great variety of points in the middle ranges of the capitalist–socialist spectrum, and of others defying this dichotomous classification. This very variety suggests that there can be smaller but meaningful choices in the realm of economic systems—for example, movements towards government planning and coordination within the general framework of capitalism, towards the use of markets in planned socialism, or towards the establishment of networks of enterprises based on worker or community decision-making in any decentralized system. However, in reading the record on the nature and experiences of differing systems of economic organization to obtain greater awareness of social possibilities, including the possibilities for one's own society, there is also a danger of grossly oversimplifying the complex historical processes from which present systems have emerged. Statements such as 'The United States has chosen to organize its economic life on the basis of free enterprise capitalism' attribute unity and personality to a complex social entity, an amalgam of interacting individuals having differing beliefs, stores of knowledge, values, and interests, not to a single mind. A 'society's choice' of economic system, and its members' choices between apples and oranges, or among modes of transportation, cannot be put on the same plane.

Some may argue that the notion of social choice of economic systems does have meaning at least in countries with democratic political institutions. For example, Americans or Europeans may be said to choose between different variants of capitalism and even socialism when they go to the polls to elect national representatives and leaders. Such political acts do indeed lend concreteness to the notion of system choice, relating the systems implemented in these societies to the manifested preferences of citizens. There are, however, reasons to be cautious about interpreting the outcomes of even democratic political processes as measures of a collective, rational will. Fundamental difficulties and paradoxes exist that prevent sets of individually rational choices from adding up to collectively rational choices with any assurance.[2] Also to be taken into account are: the importance of historically-evolving norms of justice and economic rights, the forces influencing the messages that citizens receive about the ramifications of choice, and the economic and political power concentrations skewing political outcomes toward particular interests. The ways in which wealth, influence, talent, ambition, and other characteristics are distributed in a population affect not only individual choices, but also the determination of which economic and political questions will lie within the domain of choice. Choices that are voluntary at the level of the individual add up to 'social choices', such as the choice to have a system of large hierarchical corporate enterprises (the result of investor and worker decisions) or a shantytown in a Latin American city (the result of rural migrants' decisions), that may or may not represent well the collective interests of those involved.

Although one might reject the view that economic systems represent rational choices made by societies between different ways of organizing economic and related dimensions of social life, this need not imply that some kind of historical determinism (for example, a simplistic Marxist notion of inevitable stages of history) or else blind chance, are man's masters in matters of social order. Understanding the organization of economies is important precisely because we do have some potential to will changes in (or preservation of) our institutions. Even as we treat the idea of picking and choosing between systems with caution, we therefore reject both the view that prevailing economic systems in democratic countries must be optimal given their ratification by individuals and society, and the schematized Marxist doctrine that social orders progress according to inevitable historical mandates, unalterable (except perhaps in pace or detail) by human will. Human understanding of the forces set in motion by human wills is always imperfect. Still, human wills make a difference. Therefore it is reasonable (and even, one can argue, the most socially responsible course) to strive to improve our understanding, to know better our situation, in order to see a bit more clearly what the consequences of change, or of maintaining the status quo, might be.

Knowledge or Ideology?

The subject matter of economics often impinges upon matters of public policy, and probably none of these is so fundamental as the question of how society is to organize its economic affairs in the most general sense. Although economic theory is frequently presented as a matter of factual, scientific analysis, the critical student must ask where impartial analysis ends and personal conviction begins. Before we use the insights of economics to investigate the question of society's choice among economic institutions, it is worth pausing to consider whether the apparatus of investigation does not contain built-in biases.

The social sciences by their nature pose difficult questions of epistemology, that is, of determining the truth or falsehood of our hypotheses and observations. Some scholars in the social sciences have claimed that by virtue of our own humanness, social scientists have an advantage over physicists, chemists, and astronomers: they can understand the persons who are the subjects of inquiry through empathy and introspection, methods that are closed to scientists who study things.[3] The opposite point of view may be taken, however: our very involvement with our subject may suggest that the social sciences, including economics, can never be objective in the same sense as their sister natural sciences.

One reason why involvement presents dangers in economics is that there is rarely, if ever, uniformity of interest among members of a society who occupy different positions in the spectra of property ownership, employment status, family size, and skill. In addition, whether correlated with their personal positions or not, individuals have differing views about the desirability of equality, about the trade-offs between work and leisure and between material and nonmaterial goods, about the value of economic growth, about the importance of environmental preservation, and so on. As a result, and because many issues are resistant to easy resolution by means of empirical observation, there exists a danger that economic description and analysis will be used as weapons with which to win others over to one's personal beliefs about the nature of man and of the best possible social arrangements.

Economic analysis must always be ideological in at least one respect—that it produces material useful for the fashioning of ideas about the social order. Adam Smith's conception that unregulated competitive markets tend to harmonize the pursuit of private profit with the fulfillment of social needs was at one and the same time a hypothesis of economic analysis and the cornerstone of a political philosophy sanctioning private property rights, free domestic and international trade, and a limited economic role for government. Thomas Robert Malthus's hypothesis that rapid population growth combining with more sluggish growth of output from a non-augmentable natural resource base would mean a perpetual tendency of workers' incomes to remain at basic subsistence levels, was also the central element of a social-philosophical polemic against the Enlightenment notion of the perfectability of man and the possibility of a world without poverty and inequality. David Ricardo's theory of value and distribution identified landlords—the heirs of feudal aristocracy—as the enemies of social and economic progress, and it supported his advocacy of measures (such as the repeal of the protectionist Corn Laws) that he thought would favor the interests of non-landlords. Karl Marx's theory of value, on one level a scientific analysis of the conditions for economic growth or 'expanded reproduction' that anticipated modern input-output theory, was linked to a normative theory of exploitation that sought to demonstrate that capitalism's days were numbered by identifying trends in the levels of capital expenditures per employed worker, the concentration of capital ownership, and the rate of profit.[4]

It can be argued that contemporary Western economic theory, although on the surface cleansed of such unscientific references to social controversies, is haunted by the ghosts of its past. As a synonym for price, we continue to use the word 'value', although this calls forth old connotations of 'intrinsic worth' or 'just price'. We build theories upon the assumption that economic agents seek to maximize 'utility', a concept that in the nineteenth century was viewed as something measurable and capable of comparison across persons, and that still conjures up an underlying view of man as hedonist, of wealth and objects as 'goods' and of work as 'bad'. And we continue to speak of 'social welfare' as something that can be inferred from the 'utility' achieved by each of society's members.[5] The argument can also be turned around, if we note that even efforts to make economics more objective or scientific are not necessarily free of evaluative implications, and that such efforts may be more successful when those implications are conformable to academic fashion. 'Utility' may provide an excellent example here, as well. A major twentieth-century innovation in economic theory was to drop the assumption that utility levels can be summed up or compared among individuals. The old idea that that *could* be done, when combined with the concept of declining marginal utility, implied that 'social welfare' rises when a dollar is taxed from a rich man, for whom it has low utility, and given to a poor one, to whom it has high utility. While most economists view the innovation just mentioned as an advance of their discipline towards a more scientific approach, a few dissenters have wondered whether the change was not readily adopted for another reason: perhaps it was found attractive by the defenders of the liberal social ethic of untrammeled pursuit of property and happiness because it avoided an unwanted implication of the concept of declining marginal utility of income.[6]

To take another example, economists often seem careless about making the conceptual leap from the idea of marginal factor products and factor incomes under competitive market conditions, to concepts of factor *rewards* or *returns*, which seem implicitly to endorse a particular system of property rights as if it were a natural facet of human social life. In this respect, contemporary economics may be hardly less open than that of a century ago to the critique that 'It is an enchanted, perverted, topsey-turvey world in which Monsieur le Capital and Madame la Terre do their ghost-walking as social characters and at the same time directly as mere things.'[7]

But finding ideology lurking in economics should not lead us to conclude that economics is *only* ideology. The social sciences cannot help but be ideological, in the sense that they are capable of justifying particular social policies; and to say that a theory or idea sometimes functions as ideology cannot logically be taken as implying that it is a false idea. Whatever are our values and ideological commitments, we have a need to know more about reality. We can seek facts and clarity by critically questioning the intellectual constructs of ourselves and others, by asking how well a proposed theory stands up to testing against empirical observations, and by being clear about what our values are and how they affect our views of social issues.

Notes

1. If by some accounts superior in mathematics and science on the Soviet side.
2. See Chapter 3, section 3.6.2.
3. This view was held by some members of the 'Austrian school' of economists, and was especially championed by Ludwig von Mises. See Mises 1981.
4. See Smith 1985; Malthus 1970; Ricardo 1951; Marx 1967*a*. A basic overview of their theories is provided by Barber 1967; a more intensive treatment is that of Blaug 1978. The view of the relationship between ideology ('economic philosophy') and economic analysis developed in this paragraph is close to that of Joseph Schumpeter 1955; see pp. 34–43. On Marxian economics and input–output, see Morishima 1973.
5. These remarks follow the classic discussion by Myrdal 1961.
6. See Cooter and Rappaport 1984.
7. Marx 1967*b*, p. 830. For a contemporary critique, see Ellerman 1986.

1.
The Nature of Economic Systems, and Some Criteria for Evaluation

1.1 Economic Systems

1.1.1 The Economic System and its Context

In the Introduction we indicated that for purposes of comparing economic systems it is desirable to separate those systems, at least conceptually, from the other factors that interact to determine economic and social outcomes. For example, when we compare the United States with the People's Republic of China, it clearly would be misleading to suggest that the former country is rich and the latter poor solely, or even primarily, because the one has a market capitalist economy and the other a planned socialist system. Although the effects of the system difference on recent progress may well be substantial, the case for caution in such a comparison should be obvious, just as it is when we question the claim that the German Democratic Republic (East Germany) is rich and that Honduras is poor because the former but not the latter has a Soviet-type economy. Both comparisons involve countries with enormously different histories of economic development and stores of skilled manpower, among many other differences not to be explained primarily on the basis of their current economic systems. Not only for purposes of comparison, but also simply in order to comprehend the nature and characteristics of economic systems, we should distinguish between the system and its historical, geographic, cultural, and social contexts.[1] What, then, do we mean by economic system?

1.1.2 Defining 'Economy'

It is useful to break this compound term into its constituent parts. Although the first member of the term, 'economic', seems familiar enough, from the standpoint of our particular approach (and perhaps of the comparative systems field, as a whole), it is worth pausing to look at two rather different definitions, each of which has some currency. On the one hand, the 'economic' is that which pertains to 'the allocation of scarce resources among competing ends'. Especially if the word 'rational' (as in 'rational allocation') is added, this definition, which has been favored by general economics textbooks in the years since its proposal by Lionel Robbins in 1932, emphasizes the idea of 'economizing' in the use of scarce factors or goods. There is another definition of 'economic', however, which is closer to popular usage, and is the first one given by my college dictionary. It is 'pertaining to the production, distribution, and use of income and wealth'.

Although both definitions are relevant to our subject matter, and we may not be forced to make a strict choice between them, there are some arguments to be made for adopting some variant of the seemingly less technical, second definition. First of all, not all that goes on under the rubric of 'economizing' has much to do with the economy as we generally understand it. For example, when scientists try to find materials that maximize ability to withstand stress and extremes of temperature while minimizing weight, when a poet seeks to give full expression to an emotion using a minimal number of words, or when a politician tries to maximize his appeal to moderate voters while minimizing his loss of support among a smaller, more ideologically committed constituency, the problems facing each may be analyzed under the rubric of economizing, but their activities do not principally fall into the sphere of social life ordinarily described as economic. In this respect, the 'economizing' definition is too broad.

On the other hand, are all of the activities in the economic sphere of life economizing in nature? Clearly, the answer is no, in so far as the actions of most economic agents are not economizing all of the time: they are sometimes wasteful, inattentive, inefficient. Indeed, some economic institutions, even, may be 'uneconomical' in their behavior or consequences. Modern free market economists often allege this to be the case with Soviet-type central planning; radical economists, in turn, argue that firms in market economies waste social resources on duplicative investments in research and facilities, on advertising, and on supervision which would be unnecessary in less hierarchical production units; and some modern observers would be reluctant to describe as 'economizing behavior' the actions of Kwakiutl Indians competing to destroy property in their potlatch ceremony, or of Egyptian or Chinese emperors being buried together with the vast treasures of their households (including many useful goods, animals, and sometimes persons). To suppose that all economic activity is economizing in nature may be to put the cart before the horse in the sense of prejudging economic institutions according to their apparent degree of rationality.[2]

Since 'economizing' as a concept is too widely applicable and fails to delineate the boundaries of the economy as a particular sphere of social life, it seems better to lean towards what economic anthropologist Karl Polanyi (whose arguments have just been paraphrased) called a 'substantive' definiton of the economy.[3] The substantive definition of the economy that we will adopt in this book is 'the sphere of social activity in which people produce, distribute, and consume their material requirements and wants'. In addition to delineating clearly what activities are to be considered as falling under the heading 'economic', this definition has the advantage of avoiding the potential bias of suggesting that only such actions and institutions as are 'economizing' in nature or intention should be considered to belong to the economic realm, a bias that could be particularly problematic in comparing different economic arrangements or institutions.

1.1.3 Defining 'System' and 'Economic System'

Turning to the second half of the term 'economic system', a standard dictionary definition is 'a set of regularly interacting items or things'. To apply this definition to *economic* systems, we need to specify what the relevant items or things are, and the ways in which they regularly interact. Happily, this seems easy enough, provided that we can include human beings and groups of people among the 'items or things'. In that case, our list of the latter could begin with human agents (consumers, laborers, resource owners, traders, government planners, and so on). That list could also count material resources (such as plots of land, pieces of machinery, factory buildings and houses), and could finally consider organizations such as firms (which are collections of individual agents, as well as being systems in their own right, and thus 'subsystems' of the economic system as a whole). The 'interactions' among these items and things include, prominently, production, exchange, and consumption. They also include the relationship among persons, and between persons and things, that we call 'ownership', or the formation and maintenance of 'property rights'. (This interaction is in a sense prior to the others mentioned, since the existence of property rights usually precedes their 'exercise' in the processes of exchange, production, and consumption.) Finally, we should probably include among interactions group decision-making processes such as the public determination of the levels of taxes and government expenditures, voting by the share-holders of a corporation, and the construction of an economic plan in a government ministry.

When we study an economic system, we focus on the types of interactions that regularly occur among its different elements in the course of producing, distributing, and consuming the material requirements and wants of the members of the society in question. In fact, it is in identifying the nature of the recurring interactions that we most clearly isolate the economic system from the rest of the economic environment, which, for its part, may be identified with a complete listing of who the interacting agents, and what the interacting things, are. The distinction shows why an economic system is to some degree an abstraction. A nation's principal industries, its level of development, who its international trading partners are, and other such features, may be critical to the performance of its economy, and may be much influenced, especially in the long run, by its economic system; but these are not features of the economic system as such. This means that a given economic system may be observed under different cultural and social milieux, and with varying details of practice, in different countries. Indeed, it will sometimes be useful to identify some basic features of the system as its pure or ideal type, although this 'model' may not be precisely observed in any existing country.

1.1.4 Identifying Particular Economic Systems

This book deals primarily with three economic systems or system types, and with some of their variants. Having defined economic systems in general, what procedure will we use to identify a specific economic system, and to distinguish it from others?

Just above, we said that in studying an economic system we focus on the types of interactions that regularly occur among its constituent members and elements. It seems natural, then, to say that when two economies differ in that the types of interactions that regularly occur among the elements of one are distinctly different from the types that occur among the elements of the other, they have different economic systems. The economic system of each can therefore be identified by isolating the prominent, recurring forms of interaction that distinguish it from economies with other economic systems. These interactions can also be called 'institutions', and we may say, then, that we identify different economic systems by their different, characteristic economic institutions.

For example, we earlier identified relations of ownership or property rights as one of the central types of interaction that occur in economic systems. It is well known that in capitalist economies, private individuals own most of the land, capital goods, and other resources used in producing goods and services, whereas in socialist economies of the Soviet type, the corresponding resources are owned by the state. Therefore, we may identify private ownership of productive factors as one distinguishing feature of capitalism, and state ownership of such factors as a distinguishing feature of Soviet-type socialism.

To take another example, the interactions between production units and consumers in a capitalist economy usually fall under the general heading of market exchanges. That is, products are transferred from firm to firm, or from firm to consumer, in the context of voluntarily entered exchange transactions. In the ideal model of a centrally planned socialist economy, on the other hand, products and resources are transferred from enterprise to enterprise as part of the implementation of a centrally devised economic plan, and without any bilateral agreement between the parties directly involved. Hence we may say that market exchange is a characteristic institution or form of interaction in capitalist economies, whereas resource allocation by central plan is a characteristic institution of the type of socialist economy considered in this comparison.

In Chapters 2, 3, and 4 we will define each of the three basic economic systems to be examined by listing distinctive and characteristic institutions or forms of economic interaction associated with that system. Although later we will also discuss performance features of these systems, and examine them with reference to certain criteria of evaluation, it should be kept firmly in mind that the systems are defined by their institutions, not by their performance or success in meeting a set of evaluative standards.

1.2 The Division of Labor and its Benefits

1.2.1 How 'Division of Labor' is Used in this Book

As our title indicates, this book puts the division of labor at the center of its approach to understanding economic systems. There are other candidates for this honor (none of which will be entirely ignored in our discussion), for example: some studies of economic systems are organized around the question of how information is gathered and transmitted in an economy;[4] others give pride of place to property rights.[5] But to focus on the division of labor is itself hardly novel. Both the spiritual father of free market economics, Adam Smith, and the man who founded 'scientific socialism' a century later, Karl Marx, identified the division of labor as a central phenomenon of economic life. Our treatment of the subject will draw on the insights of both men.

By division of labor, we refer in the broadest sense to specialization in economic activity. This covers specialization (in function, skills, tasks, and equipment) of the workers, shops, and departments within enterprises or production units; and it also covers specialization (for example, in activities or product lines) of production units in the larger economy of which they are a part. In addition, it covers not only specialization of persons, but also that pertaining to all resources—for example, the specialization of land to different uses by the farmer or developer, or the specialization of capital to different ends by the investor, who determines whether it will take the form of a screw-threading machine, a word processor, or an oil tanker.

Our approach to economic systems and the division of labor borrows informally from the approach of the 'cost-benefit' analyses which are familiar from management science and from the evaluation of public projects. After noting the pervasiveness of complex divisions of labor in modern economies, we will recognize that the phenomenon of division of labor carries both pluses and minuses for human well-being. This will lead us to consider that there are different ways of organizing economic life, each of which has some advantages and some disadvantages with respect to its ability to maximize the benefits, and to minimize the costs, of the division of labor. Each system will accordingly be conceptualized as a set of social arrangements that could be proposed as a solution to that cost-minimizing, benefit-maximizing problem.

1.2.2 Division of Labor Illustrated

The correlation between the complexity of the division of labor, and the degree of modernity or industrialization of the society, is easy to illustrate, even if, like most correlations, there exist departures from the trend. Compare, for example, the 15 million or more rural inhabitants of Tanzania, in eastern Africa, with roughly the same number of residents of the state of New York, in the eastern United States. The vast majority of the rural Tanzanians are small-scale farmers, who grow the bulk of what they eat, and eat the bulk of what they grow. Most of their homes are made of local materials, principally mud, wood, and thatch, and most of their families build their own homes, with the help of neighbors and friends, each of whom is familiar with most of the skills needed to complete the job. Many household items, such as containers, straw mats, twine beds, and wooden furniture, are also homemade or made by neighbors using only a few relatively unspecialized tools. Most Tanzanian women bear their children in the village, rather than a hospital, and know how to assist other women of the village in that process.

Among the Americans, only a small fraction are farmers, but even they illustrate well the difference in the extent of division of labor, since almost all of what they grow is intended for sale, and since the greater part of what they eat is purchased with some of the cash thus earned. Their farming involves substantial use of purchased chemicals, fertilizer, hybrid seeds, and machinery, and their products are destined for mechanized processing and packaging before being purchased by other households. The great majority of the remaining Americans, in this and other industrial states, specialize in small parts of complex production processes. As individuals, in fact, they often do not produce anything identifiable as a finished product. Not only do typical members of their society know little about how their food is grown and processed, how their automobiles are manufactured and what makes them run, how the furnace that heats their homes in winter or the air conditioners that cool them in summer operate. They are also generally unable to carry out the full set of steps involved in producing the end product of the very industry in which they directly labor, or even to state exactly what those steps are. (Consider, for example, a worker who has a role in assembling telephones for an electronics company, tends the machine that affixes labels to the packages coming off the conveyer belt of an automated bakery, or processes paperwork for the home mortgage department of a bank. Such a worker cannot make or sell to you a telephone or commerical-standard cake, or personally offer you a mortgage.) And quite unlike her rural African counterpart, the typical American woman will see different specialists for general medicine, gynaecology, and obstetrics, may attend a course in childbirth, and will likely be attended by nurses and doctors having several different levels and types of training when she gives birth in a modern hospital filled with complex and expensive equipment.

From this comparison, a glimpse of the costs and benefits of specialization comes immediately into view. If conditions force the members of a Tanzanian family to move, with only a bag of corn, some digging sticks, and two or three hoes, to a different part of their country having a similar climate, they can immediately begin building a new house, can plant the crops they need for their survival, and can even continue the process of building their family. A counterpart American family, by contrast, could scarcely begin constructing a shelter at anything like the standard of their society, and, deprived of a source of money income, would be quite unable to feed themselves. (Even so ordinary a component of their diet as spaghetti is produced by the coordinated efforts of processors, packers, and truckers, of the farmer, the seed breeder, the manufacturer of chemical fertilizer, the designer and manufacturer of tractors and farm implements, the combine driver, and many other specialized workers.) Yet the second family is vastly richer in material goods, its members have a 42 per cent longer life-expectancy (they can expect to live 75 rather than 53 years, on average) and 90 per cent lower infant mortality rate (10, versus 108 deaths, per 1000 births before age 1),[6] and they are spared the backbreaking drudgery of laboring long hours with crude tools, and of carrying wood to their stoves and water to their houses.

Much of the difference in the levels of economic development of their societies can be attributed to differences in the quantity and quality of physical and human capital—that is, of both equipment, buildings, and physical infrastructure, and of knowledge and the infrastructure to develop and transmit it—with which their members work. But the types of capital used are bound up with the extent of the division of labor in the two societies, and the quantities of capital that the societies have accumulated are also ultimately linked to division of labor, which makes possible productivity capable both of meeting subsistence needs in consumption, and of devoting substantial resources to producing things to produce things.[7]

1.2.3 How Division of Labor Raises Productivity

How does division of labor raise productivity, thereby making possible both higher consumption and the accumulation of still more productivity-raising capital? Two principal mechanisms can be distinguished, the first involving increasing complexity of the production process or division of labor in the factory, the second entailing increasing specialization among enterprises and thus a more complex division of labor at the level of the society or economy as a whole.

The mechanism of division of labor within the production enterprise is highlighted in the famous pin factory example in Adam Smith's *The Wealth of Nations*. There, Smith claimed that an individual workman not specialized in the tasks involved might be capable of making a maximum of twenty pins in a day, whereas a factory specializing in making pins only, facing an effectively unlimited market for them, and employing ten workers each specializing in one small detail of the pin-making process, could produce as many as 48,000 pins in a day, or 4,800 pins per worker—240 times the daily output of the lone workman. The reasons given by Smith for the increase in productivity are (1) the increased skill each workman gains in performing a specialized task repeatedly, (2) the time saved from laying down and picking up tools, due to elimination of the need to move from one task to another, and (3) the impetus to the development of more specialized tools (such as a particular kind of plier for drawing the wire of the pin shaft) stemming from the division of tasks, and the higher productivity from the use of such tools.

The productivity-enhancing powers of division of labor within the production enterprise can be said to derive from 'economies of scale', since by having ten people join together to produce pins, the average productivity of each worker rises. However, it is not merely the scale of the activity that has changed, but also the methods used. Complexity and sub-specialization, rather than scale alone, thus account for the productivity-enhancing outcome. With merely physical economies of scale, on the other hand, productivity increases simply by changing the quantity or size of the inputs, with no change in organization. The classic example is that of batch production of steel, chemicals, or wine, in large vats. To double the amount of the product handled by the vat, it is necessary to double its volume; but because volume increases more rapidly than surface dimensions, this involves increasing the amount of material incorporated in the vats by a factor of less than two. Similarly, it is likely to take less than twice the original amount of labor to tend the production process in the larger as opposed to the smaller vat. So output can be doubled using less than double the inputs, hence at less than double the cost, when the scale of production increases. In this case, the complexity of the production process is not itself affected.

How, if at all, are such physical economies of scale, which involve no change in the division of labor from the standpoint of the operations being performed, to be related to our discussion of the division of labor? They are related in that achieving physical scale economies inside the factory depends on the division of labor in society as a whole for its feasibility. To take Smith's example, so long as a village is isolated and the transportation of products in or out of it is prohibitively costly, only the services of one blacksmith are needed; thus, since it is impossible to keep ten workers busy each with a different specialized aspect of the pin-making process, the cost of pins can be no lower than what is commensurate with the blacksmith's productivity at part-time pin making. However, suppose that the building of roads or canals, the development of new modes of transportation, or the more effective suppression of highway robbers permits the opening of trade over a broader, more populous region. In that case, there arises the possibility that the blacksmith can organize sixteen villagers to engage in specialized pin making while buying their horseshoes, nails, and food from other specialized producers with the cash earned. (If they and the other specialized producers compete to sell their wares at lower prices, unspecialized blacksmiths and part-time pin makers will gradually be driven from business because their costs are too high.) It is this same extension of the market that permits the manufacturing of wine, steel, and chemicals to take place on a larger scale, thus reaping the technological economies discussed in the previous paragraph. While the latter economies are not results of the division of labor in a sense *internal* to the production processes which are involved, they are certainly, therefore, products of the division of labor external to those processes. In other words, the specialization among groups of people and localities leads each to give up some of the more varied activities they would carry on in a less economically complex society, and to concentrate on a particular activity, exchanging the resulting outputs with others in order to obtain their final consumption needs. All of this makes clear the meaning of Adam Smith's famous phrase 'the division of labor is limited by the extent of the market'.[8]

The points made by Smith regarding the benefits of division of labor in the pin factory also extend to specialization *across* factories or production units. As the activity of blacksmithing gives way to a large number of distinct industries, and as other industries (in manufacturing, processing, building, and so forth) also break down into more specialized trades, specialization of enterprises among industries, and of workmen among professions, both increase. This process creates more possibilities for refined skills to be mastered, for facilities, and producers' attentions, to be concentrated on more specialized activities, and for methods and tools more precisely appropriate to particular uses to be developed, invested in, and employed. So the factors emphasized by Smith operate both within firms, and at the level of 'the division of labor in society' (that is, among firms).

Another potential source of benefits from division of labor can arise from an appropriate allocation of differing individuals to different tasks. While Adam Smith tended to treat workmen as being of roughly equal capability, and thus emphasized the benefits of refinements in skill that are to be gained through practice, other economists have placed more emphasis on the parallel benefits that may flow from the more refined sorting of workers, each having his or her particular skills and propensities, among tasks.[9] One person, they point out, has a special ability to perform fine manual operations, another is good at lifting heavy objects, a third has the steadiness required for concentration on a certain delicate task, a fourth is a good decision-maker and likes managing subordinates, a fifth has strong intellectual abilities but enjoys working independently, and so forth. Without division of labor, they all will do a little of everything, and have few opportunities to excel, or to benefit others, through developing their abilities to do that for which they have special aptitude or interest. Hence, in so far as people differ from one another, division of labor makes it possible for the productivity of all to rise, by 'assigning them' (through the working of competitive markets and self-selection, through the management decisions of superiors in a hierarchical enterprise, through the instruction of state planners, or by some other means) to the most appropriate tasks. This benefit of division of labor occurs through specialization both within enterprises (in deciding who will draw out the wires, who will attach the heads to the pins), and among industries (in determining who will be a horseshoe maker, who a nail maker, and so forth).

Finally, those benefits of specialization which can be traced to pre-existing differences in the skills and propensities of different producers have a parallel in the area of differences in non-labor resource endowments. In Adam Smith's Scotland, it might be desirable that each village specialize in one or a few lines of production so as to pursue those activities on a scale benefiting from technological economies and from the productivity-enhancing division of labor within the enterprise, even if there were no particular reason for village A to specialize in industry X and village B in industry Y, rather than the other way around. However, additional benefits from specialization arise if village A is relatively better endowed with the natural resources, locational advantages, etc., for expanding industry X than is B, which is in turn better endowed with the resources needed to develop industry Y. In that case, by each pursuing its own comparative advantage and engaging in exchange, people in both villages can benefit not only from scale economies and more complex internal divisions of labor, but also from the fruits of a more specialized use of differentiated resources. This is none other than the classical argument for free trade, and the mechanism concerned should also be included among the gains from division of labor. As was the case with workmen, the benefits here arise from assigning resources to the uses to which they are better suited from the standpoint of productivity.

Figure 1.1 summarizes our discussion of the sources of productivity gains from the division of labor. Division of labor within enterprises raises productivity by promoting increased skills, better allocating individuals to jobs, fostering the development of specialized tools, and reducing set-up time. Division of labor among enterprises raises productivity by permitting enterprises to grasp physical economies

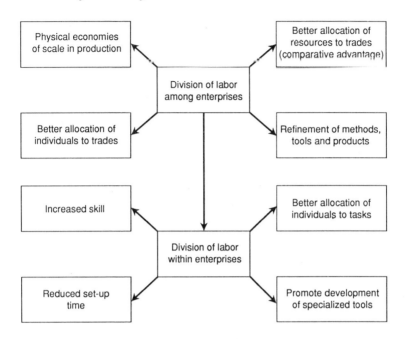

FIG. 1.1.
Schematic summary of sources of productivity gains from division of
labor

of scale, by encouraging an appropriate allocation of individuals to
trades, by fostering more refined methods, tools, and products, and'
by permitting resources to be allocated to industries according to
comparative advantage. The arrow from the upper to the lower
rectangle indicates that division of labor among enterprises also
raises productivity by making possible more division of labor *within*
them.

1.2.4 *Comments and Provisos*

These basic points about the division of labor having been laid out,
some further remarks ought to be added. First, it should be pointed
out that in Adam Smith's example it is the market, or the voluntary
exchange of goods in the search for individual benefit, that makes
possible both division of labor within the factory, and the larger
scale of production that is facilitated by division of labor among

enterprises. However, the advantages of division of labor that are identified in the examples can, hypothetically, at least, be grasped by some other form of organization that permits large-scale, specialized production. The most obvious example is that of a centrally planned economy, such as that imagined by Marx, in which the state owns all means of production and issues instructions to factory managers on what is to be produced. Here it is by following the instructions of the plan, rather than pursuing their interests in the market, that economic agents transfer outputs onwards to other enterprises requiring them as inputs, or to final consumers. Yet, the scale effect is in principle the same as that resulting from a large market: specialized enterprises can establish complex internal divisions of labor, and production can take place on a scale that benefits from technological economies. Likewise, the benefits of specialization of workers, industries, and tools, whether due simply to perfection through practice, or instead to appropriate assignment according to existing propensities, abilities, or endowments, might be captured, at least hypothetically, in a society where planners, rather than market forces, coordinate a complex division of labor.

Our second comment concerns the evolution of complex divisions of labor, and the illustration with which we began this section. What must be borne in mind is that, while it is convenient to imagine that human societies have smoothly progressed from those with virtually no division of labor, little social complexity, and low levels of productivity and scientific knowledge, to those with complex divisions of labor, great social complexity, and high levels of productivity and scientific knowledge, there is no evidence of a society, past or present, entirely lacking in the division of labor, and there could well be exceptions to the rule that greater complexity is associated with higher productivity, greater scientific sophistication, etc. Thus, while helpful in imagining the effects of an increasing division of labor, the notion of an isolated individual in a mode of subsistence can hardly be viewed as the starting point, in any historical sense, from which more complex societies evolved. Anthropological evidence suggests, rather, that man has always been a social being; and no known society is entirely lacking in specialization within the band, clan, or other social grouping, whether in collective action to secure basic needs, or in economic relations of distribution, reciprocity, or exchange.[10] Also, we should not fall into the trap of imagining that every step towards a more complex division of labor represents progress in the improvement of human welfare; as our framework implies, costs may well outweigh benefits.

The comment just made regarding the ubiquity of divisions of labor may be amplified with reference to the illustration with which we began this section. While seventeenth- and eighteenth-century thinkers such as John Locke, Jean Jacques Rousseau, and Adam Smith were free to draw examples from imagined 'early and rude states', or to speak of 'states of nature' or 'noble savages', students in our own day are constrained to greater realism. The example with which we illustrated the idea of division of labor in section 1.2.2, that of peasant farmers in Africa, was not really one of a society without a division of labor. Although we can and did argue that its division of labor is less complex than that of the American comparator, the point was somewhat exaggerated by our intentional neglect of the African country's urban sector, and of the fact that most of its rural households grow some cash crops or work for wages in order to purchase modern mass-produced goods such as matches, sugar, salt, tea-leaves, kerosene, cloth, and for the slightly better off, radios and bicycles. Moreover, some of the latter goods are produced using equipment made in America, while some of the coffee, sisal fibers, and cotton produced by the Tanzanian farmers will probably make their way into the shopping baskets of American consumers. And, for their part, the Americans engage in a great deal of non-monetized production within their households, providing themselves with cleaning, laundry, cooking, and child-rearing services outside of the stream of market exchange (but not, to be sure, without practicing an internal, usually sexual, division of labor). Thus, the more complex reality behind our illustration is one in which the division of labor operates on an international scale, and manifests both subsistence and exchange elements in the activities of *all* who are involved.

1.3 Costs of the Division of Labor

1.3.1 Overview

So far, we have stressed the benefits of the division of labor, and neglected the costs and problems that a complex division of labor poses.

One such problem, already mentioned in passing, is: by reducing the self-sufficiency of the individual and family, and increasing its interdependence with others, a complex division of labor may make people more vulnerable to the actions of others, and to decisions over which they have little control.

Another potential drawback of a complex division of labor was noted by Adam Smith and Karl Marx. Both worried that carried to its logical conclusion, the sub-division of tasks to the point at which each worker repeats the same simple operation throughout the working day would render him, in Smith's words, 'as stupid and ignorant as it is possible for a human creature to become'.[11] Marx remarked that '[s]ome crippling of body and mind is inseparable . . . from division of labor',[12] and quoted a contemporary (Urquhart) who wrote, 'To subdivide a man is to execute him.'[13] Smith's main concern was with the ability of workers to be citizens, and to contribute to technical progress; Marx argued that, under the employment of a capitalist, work is alienating.

Both Smith's and Marx's comments appear to recognize that man is not only the creator, but also the product, of economic arrangements. As regards skills and abilities, Smith saw people as much the same by nature, but as becoming differentiated through their different roles in work and society—a differentiation that could carry costs, as well as benefits. Marx emphasized the differentiation of society, under a capitalist market economy, into antagonistic classes of owners of means of production, and laborers. Once rendered 'unfitted to make anything independently', Marx argued, 'the manufacturing laborer develops productive activity as a mere appendage of the capitalist's workshop'.[14] Other economists, by no means all of them social radicals, have seen value changes, such as the advent of consumerism, as at best mixed blessings of a competitive market system. Defenders of capitalism, on the other hand, see the worst danger as lying in the replacement of its system of voluntary exchanges by one of centralized coordination, which, in their view, would shackle human liberty. These and other issues will receive further attention as we consider relevant criteria for judging economic systems, later in this chapter, and as we take up the defenses and critiques of individual systems, in Chapters 2, 3, and 4.

In the sections that immediately follow, we will focus on two potential problems of economic systems having complex divisions of labor. The first is that a mechanism, or mechanisms, must be found for coordinating the actions of the many interdependent agents in the complex economy. Each of the main candidates for this role, voluntary exchange in markets, and incorporation into a hierarchical or bureaucratic organization, has its advantages and disadvantages. In so far as no coordination mechanism is perfect, the need to accept one or both of these may be counted as a cost of complexity.

In the second section, we consider the inequalities that exist in complex economies, and the fact that not all people may benefit, and that some usually benefit more than others, from the division of labor. In particular, we emphasize that the need to provide incentives to each agent to play his or her part in the complex economic system effectively may place constraints upon the set of possible outcomes of economic activity, such as dictating a more unequal distribution of income, or of control over wealth, than might be considered desirable on social or ethical grounds.

1.3.2 Coordination and Hierarchy

Much of economics deals with the problem of coordination posed by complex divisions of labor. Both the problem of coordination *among* producing and consuming units, on which neoclassical economics has focused, and that of coordination *within* the enterprise, emphasized by Marx and by several strands of recent economics literature,[15] belong to this set of issues. The general question is this: if each individual tends only a minute aspect of one (or a few) particular production process(es), and if each enterprise produces only a small number of specialized goods, what is to assure that individual goods are properly completed, that the total output of society contains the various goods in appropriate proportions to one another for consumption and as production inputs, and that the right goods get to the right places when they are needed? The (Adam) Smithian and the contemporary neoclassical answer, which will be reviewed in some detail in the next chapter, is that the coordination mechanism is implicit in atomistic profit-seeking itself; but not all economists have agreed. Marx labeled markets as 'anarchic' and compared their 'a posteriori' regulation of the division of labor unfavorably with the 'a priori' organization of production in the factory; Malthus worried about gluts of goods; Keynes saw wastage of labor and plant capacity in unemployment; Galbraith argues that corporate capitalism creates artificial wants and underproduces public goods; and modern conservationists are concerned with the unresponsiveness of markets to demands for environmental quality. If spontaneous coordination is inadequate, public agencies may act to oversee coordination in the public interest; but where economic decision-making is completely centralized, coordination turns out to be a complicated and to some degree intractible problem (as we will see in Chapter 3). 'Market socialists' (as we will also see there) seek to marry public or social ownership with decentralized revenue seeking, while controlling undesired externalities of markets via social compacts, regulations, and other mechanisms.

While economists have proposed and have sometimes helped to implement a variety of solutions, including *laissez-faire*, or leaving the market to do the job, nearly all economists agree that there is, at least conceptually, a coordination problem in complex economies. This includes the proponents of the 'invisible hand', who see the market's strength precisely in its ability to solve the coordination problem without a central bureaucracy, information gathering, and collective decision-making; and it includes centralizers, who hold the opposite view. Most economists of both of the latter persuasions, however, see the only alternatives for coordinating a complex economy as either markets, or planning. (Another approach would be to eliminate complexity and have a subsistence economy.) A specialized economy, therefore, is taken to leave open only a very limited number of alternative methods of coordination,[16] which can be counted a cost of specialization to the extent that neither market nor plan is viewed as an entirely desirable institution.

Compared to the coordination of the relations among the various units of an economy, coordination within enterprises has, until recently, received much less attention from economists. As some recent commentaries have pointed out, the conventional theory of the firm treats that unit as if it were a spontaneous, multilateral exchange of inputs, cash, and goods among a group of entirely independent agents. Yet enterprises are generally highly organized, centrally-directed, long-term associations of economic (and social) actors. What this means is that, as Ronald Coase argued in 1937, capitalism does not differ from centralized socialism by being devoid of spheres of planning; rather, it differs in that the size of those units that do cohere on the basis of centralized direction is determined by a market process, not as a constitutional feature of the economic system.[17] The point that the capitalist market system uses a combination of markets and internal plans to solve its coordination problem, further developed in Oliver Williamson's celebrated book, *Markets and Hierarchies*,[18] was clearly recognized over a century earlier by Marx, who distinguished between 'division of labor in society' and 'division of labor in the factory', and in typically caustic fashion, wrote that 'in a society with capitalist production, anarchy in the social division of labour and despotism in that of the workshop are mutual conditions the one of the other'.[19]

The fact that the problem of coordinating the actions of the many agents interacting in production enterprises is conventionally resolved, in both capitalist and centrally planned economies, by the establishment of a planning hierarchy within the firm, does not in itself prove that hierarchy and authority make the only satisfactory solution to that problem. Focusing on profit sharing and on workers' participation in decision-making, recent studies in the field of comparative economic systems have questioned the necessity of strict hierarchy in the workplace, and, with reference to existing examples, have discussed the possibility of alternatives to it.[20] It seems clear that the internal division of labor in firms or enterprises does not, in many cases, admit the same alternatives—market, or plan—as does the division of labor among firms, since fully spontaneous exchange relations among so many agents are incompatible with the technical and organizational requirements for the smooth production of goods and provision of services. However, a relevant choice may none the less exist between planning by a hierarchy, to which the personnel of the enterprise are unambiguously subordinated, and planning by representatives of those personnel, or by a management chosen by them and answerable to them.

While the character of market interactions have been variously depicted as, on the one hand, voluntary and free, and on the other, chaotic and effectively coercive of those disadvantaged by virtue of their limited control over resources, the character of the planning entities that are the main alternative to markets have also been contrastingly described: on the one hand, as dictatorial and inefficient, and on the other, as rational and responsive to real human needs. Moreover, the contrasting attributes of markets and plans need not be a matter of perception only. Markets may be either competitive or monopolistic, and their benefits may be more or less broadly distributed, depending on the distribution of control over resources, and of final income. Planning entities, for their part, may be more or less responsive to the interests of those under them; indeed, the planning pyramid could, theoretically, be inverted, so that those at the bottom, from the standpoint of implementation, may collectively be the masters in the ultimate setting of policy and selection of leaders. In addition, at least for small units, it may be possible to reduce hierarchy even at the implementation stage, replacing it with more teamwork and participatory action. Which sides of markets are more likely to be manifested, and whether planning and democracy are in practice compatible, are questions that will be explored in later chapters.

1.3.3 Distribution and Incentives

Just as individuals take on more specialized roles in complex economies, including the assumption of decision making roles by some and the acceptance of decision implementing positions by others, so people may also be more differentiated in such economies in terms of the shares of the total product of society that each receives. Indeed, differentiation of roles and of incomes in modern societies appear to be closely related.

Economic theory, in its theory of the consumer, shows that the manner in which income is distributed affects both the distribution of personal welfare, and the composition of demand for goods and services. The theory of factor markets shows, on the other hand, that income distribution is generated by individual abilities and choices, by access to resources, and by the rules governing such access; and these determinants of income distribution in turn affect people's incentives to work, spend, invest, and so forth, thus influencing the level of output. Clearly, distribution and production are closely connected facets of the economic process.

Capitalism, for example, is characterized on the one hand by largely unrestricted private ownership and alienability of goods and non-labor resources, and on the other hand, by inalienability of the individual's right to dispose of his or her labor, except within the limits of the employment relationship. Personal endowments of wealth, whether derived from earlier privilege or pillage, from hard work and entrepreneurship, or from bequests, are respected under its system of property rights. As workers and resource owners seek out activities providing more returns for less trouble and risk, more economic rewards flow toward resources that are scarcer in terms of the balance between demand and availability.

The link between income distribution and economic growth was at the center of the analytical approach of the classical economic writers. In early capitalism, as viewed by Smith, Ricardo, Malthus, and Marx, capital was relatively scarce, labor relatively plentiful. Despite variations, all derived from this configuration of relative scarcities and from the assumption of capitalist property rights the theorem that wages are never far above subsistence level. From the assumptions that capitalists channel their growing earnings into investment, and that at least some resources are in fixed supply, they derived also the notion of a falling rate of return on capital as capital accumulation proceeded. To Malthus, especially, the irreplaceable necessity of grain and the non-augmentable fixity of land spelled an increasing siphoning of output to landlords, stalling the process of economic growth and leading to a steady state of widespread modest living if not outright poverty. Marx, from a mid-nineteenth-century vantage point, accorded only a peripheral role to land; and, rather than a steady state, he saw capitalism as heading for complete collapse as a result of industrial strife and economic instability. None the less, all of the classical economists, including Marx, saw trade-offs between the income shares of the various classes. All tended to see a ceiling on the welfare of workers under capitalism, and all worried about the sustainability of capital accumulation.

Although the depression of the western industrial economies in the 1930s prompted John Maynard Keynes too to worry over capitalism's viability, the neoclassical school of economics which has enjoyed overall intellectual dominance from the late nineteenth century to the present, has tended to play down or ignore such issues of income distribution and dynamic development, instead focusing on the timeless concept of a general economic equilibrium such as that depicted by the mathematical economist Leon Walras in the 1870s. Conflicts of interest of the types that concerned Marx or Ricardo were replaced by a peaceful vision in which each agent in the economic marketplace received from it exactly what his or her participation in the system added to overall output—his or her marginal product. In spite of the ethical reassurance which writers such as John Bates Clark (1899) drew from this approach, however, the technical tool kit of neoclassical economists allowed a sharpened perception of the relations between distribution and scarcity.

In the neoclassical model of the economy, any given distribution of resources, when combined with a set of personal preferences (utility functions) and technical possibilities (production functions), implies some definite distribution of incomes as a consequence of the mathematical relationship of these elements, uninfluenced by social conventions or normative considerations. Assuming them to be determined by marginal product alone, however, there is nothing to prevent the wages that accrue to a plentiful labor force from falling *below* the subsistence requirements of laboring households, except for the long run consideration that the starving will die off, emigrate, or take up arms, leading to a reduction of their numbers. While the market can therefore be said to have the virtue of supplying consumers with goods in the quantities and varieties demanded, demand and need are separated by the intervening variable of purchasing power. The distribution of the latter is as much dependent upon initial endowments, which remain arbitrary (from the standpoint of neoclassical theory), as upon willingness to contribute and to risk resources.

Incentives: The Impact of Distributive Rules on Output and Growth   Our discussion must not treat the distribution of income and goods independently of their production. Through their influence as incentives, the rules of access to resources, the rights to dispose of, invest, or bequeath income and wealth, and the payment schemes adopted by enterprises, determine both the level of composition of social product, and its distribution among individuals. For example, allowing an entrepreneur to earn large profits by correctly anticipating mass demand for a new consumer good is an effective way to bring about the allocation of resources to a use in which their value is particularly high, as judged by market demand; but in the process, the entrepreneur who guesses correctly becomes wealthy, thereby acquiring greater influence in his own role as a consumer, which may mean that some resources flow from the production of foodstuffs and simple clothing into that of his preferred luxury goods, in the next period. There will also be social ramifications if the entrepreneur becomes an employer of domestic workers, if his limousine and swimming pool engender envy in those less privileged, or if he uses contributions to political candidates to gain influence over government policies. Of course, it is not necessarily the case that material rewards, and those only, determine economic behavior; but the effects of reward structures on such behavior can scarcely be ignored. Hence, in assessing the properties of a system, the levels of output, productivity, and welfare, must be assessed alongside their distribution, as the two emerge from a single process.

Nor can we treat distribution as solely a matter of division among current members of the community. The division of social output as between consumption and production goods is at least as fundamental an issue as is its distribution among individuals; the distributive effects of this division are partly intertemporal, even intergenerational. For a given level of efficiency in their allocation and use, the higher the proportion of producers' goods (such as machines and factory buildings) in the composition of each period's output, the greater the rate of growth of a society's total output. In principle, therefore, reduced consumption today ought to translate into increased consumption in the future.

However, the problem of savings is at one and the same time one of distributing income between generations, and of distributing it within each generation. With capital accumulation a necessary condition of economic growth, the question is: who shall be charged with the function of accumulating capital, and who can and ought to be so charged. If households with higher incomes are inclined to turn most of their income in excess of consumption requirements into more capital goods, then one solution is to entrust them with the responsibility of accumulating capital on behalf of the society as a whole. The advantage of such a solution becomes clear if it is found that those with low incomes have a high propensity to consume rather than invest any additional incomes alloted to them. Such a finding would however imply that, at least in a capitalist economy, the more unequal the present distribution of income, the higher the rate of economic growth. If, therefore, one in fact desires both a more equal distribution of income, and a high rate of savings, this may constitute grounds for preferring that the role of capital accumulation be turned over to the state, as advocated by socialists.

Since the preferences of wealthier individuals have a greater impact on production, and since those individuals are likely to have greater ratios of savings to consumption because the marginal utility of consumption declines as the level of an individual's consumption rises, the analysis of modern economists is descriptively consistent with the classical expectation that unequal income distribution may be needed to sustain high rates of savings. But contemporary welfare economics provides no reason for preferring either a high level of savings or an unequal income distribution, as such. The normative question for contemporary western economists is not whether an economic system produces a high enough rate of savings, but whether its level of savings is properly consistent with the preferences of the society's members, and which economic institutions are more conducive to such consistency.

Of course, one could argue, against this approach, that even a savings level perfectly matched to the wishes of today's population is less than ideal from the standpoint of the 'overall' welfare. This would be done by asserting that the interests of individuals yet unborn should be counted in that welfare, but are not counted in the procedure just described. Exactly how one is to discern the interests of the unborn, how those interests are to be weighed against those of the living, and who will be counted on to do both of those things, and with what incentives, are questions to be addressed later on.

Division of Labor and the Perception of Distributive Justice   We began our discussion about the implications of the division of labor for income distribution by noting that differentiation of economic roles appears to be correlated with differentiation of incomes. We will close it by considering the possibility that the perception and interpretation of inequality may be influenced by the complexity and mode of organization of an economic system.

Some writers have suggested that the complexity of the division of labor in a market economy may make it more difficult for market participants to interpret the inequalities that they observe, and may even thereby create a tolerance for outcomes that would otherwise be perceived as unjust. For example, Marx, noting that the set of goods consumed by a typical worker on a typical day are produced using a certain number of hours of labor in each of a large number of industries, and calling the sum of those hours the 'socially necessary labor time' for producing the worker's consumption bundle, contended that those who work more than that necessary labor time and earn only enough to consume the typical bundle are being exploited, while those who work less but earn more than enough to purchase that bundle are engaging in exploitation. Commenting on this, John Roemer writes:

Because of the social division of labor, [a worker] has no clear conception of the amount of labor that is necessary to produce the goods he consumes. Thus, the social division of labor—the arrangement by which no worker in modern capitalism produces all the goods that make up his consumption bundle—obscures the relation of exploitation between capitalist and worker.[21]

Roemer attributes this effect specifically to the market or commodity system, in which people produce goods to be exchanged, rather than consumed directly; but if the phenomenon is real it is of interest to ask whether there are or are not alternative ways of grasping the benefits of a complex division of labor that make it less difficult to discern injustice in the distribution of income. Moreover, since labor is not after all homogeneous and the world is in fact more complex than the simple model considered by Marx, the question arises as to whether a complex division of labor does not make it difficult even to define *in principle* what exactly a just distribution of income is.

1.4 Economic Goals and Criteria of Evaluation

1.4.1 Why Evaluate?

In the foregoing discussion and in this book's title, the relationship between the nature of a society's economic arrangements, and the well-being of its members, have been emphasized. Whether economic growth, for example, is or is not to be considered a universal goal of economic systems and hence a criterion for evaluating their relative performance, is one of a larger set of questions that we wish to address in the remaining portion of this chapter, the purpose of which is to lay out a set of criteria for evaluating the strengths and weaknesses of different economic systems. If an economic system is seen as a set of ways in which economic agents, resources, and organizations interact to supply the needs and wants of individuals in society, and if modern economic systems share the common goal of grasping the benefits of a complex division of labor while minimizing unwanted costs, it should be possible to measure the success of each system against some common set of standards.

But why, some may ask, do we attempt any judgments at all? Is it not the purpose of science to analyze and predict, leaving evaluation to ethics and aesthetic? In the author's view, there are three basic arguments for explicitly laying out criteria of evaluation as we begin a survey of alternative economic arrangements. First, while the aspiration to observe and analyze objectively may be laudable, the fact of the matter is that in a subject of such great social controversy as the present one, one's choice of topics, frames of reference, and even one's vocabulary, are always and necessarily colored by underlying value judgments, and the influence of such judgments may be made most plain, thereby aiding objectivity, by making them more explicit. Second, there is already at least one set of evaluative tools—namely, the Pareto criteria of efficiency—so deeply embedded in the language and analytical structure of modern economics, that it is virtually impossible to use economic analysis without referring to it. But once any one set of normative criteria have found their way into our discussion, we are forced to justify the inclusion or exclusion of others, since to ignore them is also a value-reflecting choice. There is a third, more affirmative reason for considering explicit criteria of evaluation: rather than being an embarrassment, as it seems to be to some who are intent on making of economics a pure science, the tradition of normative analysis that has been bequeathed to us by a succession of economic writers can be viewed as a strength of the discipline, in the absence of which economic discourse would be impoverished.

In practice, it is already conventional for comparative economic studies to take into consideration a variety of evaluative criteria, including not only allocative efficiency, but also the rate of growth of per capita income, the rate and direction of change in factor productivity, the distribution of income, performance with regard to basic indicators of development such as literacy and life expectancy, and environmental quality. By comparison with this list, allocative efficiency or Pareto optimality, which is the dominant concern of the formal field of welfare economics, is a rather narrow concept. Our discussion of evaluative standards begins with a review of this concept of efficiency.

1.4.2 Allocative Efficiency: Production, Distribution, and Output Mix [22]

The concept of allocative efficiency can be boiled down into a set of three attributes or properties. The first of these properties may be referred to as *efficiency in production*. An economy is efficient with respect to production if resources are allocated among industries in such a way that output of a good cannot be expanded except by reducing the output of some other good. The reader who is familiar with basic economic analysis will recognize that this means that the set of outputs produced lie on the production possibility frontier, in an output-output diagram, and on the contract curve, along which the isoquants of different industries are tangent to one another, in an Edgeworth box diagram where the dimensions are input quantities and the diagonally opposite origins are the zero input points of each industry.[23] An important point to be added here is that *allocative* efficiency in production, with which this type of analysis is concerned, usually takes for granted the achievement of *technical* efficiency—that is, that inputs are used effectively from an engineering standpoint to produce the maximum amount of a given output consistent with current technical knowledge. We may follow this convention by treating technical efficiency in production as implicit in allocative efficiency, and therefore as a necessary but not sufficient condition for the latter to hold.

The second dimension of efficiency is referred to as *efficiency in distribution*. An economy is said to be efficient with respect to distribution if it is impossible to reallocate consumption goods in such a way that the welfare of some individuals would be improved without harming that of any others. This is shown formally, in the standard case, by a situation in which the allocation of goods between any two consumers lies on the contract curve, along which their indifference curves are tangent, in the Edgeworth box diagram, the dimensions of which are quantities consumed, and the diagonally opposite origins of which are the zero consumption points of the two consumers.[24]

The third and last aspect is that an economy is efficient with respect to the *mix of products* if the set of things produced cannot be altered so as to make any individual better off without making at least one individual worse off. In terms of economic analysis, the idea here is that while there is an infinity of points on the production possibility frontier that satisfy efficiency in production, not all are equally good from the standpoint of consumer satisfaction. The efficient mix of outputs corresponds to the point on the production possibility frontier at which one of 'society's indifference curves', an aggregation of its members' preferences 'weighted' by the prevailing distribution of income or of influence over the choice of outputs, is tangent to the frontier.[25]

Despite a high degree of consensus about the technical meaning of efficiency, just how the efficiency criteria are to be applied in the context of economic system evaluation remains subject to some uncertainty. The most straightforward approach is to use the three criteria to judge two sets of economic arrangements, call them A and B, by asking whether one but not the other satisfies all of the criteria, taking its institutions as given. But if no system fully satisfied all three criteria, it would be difficult to compare any two systems in this way. One response might be to put aside the three efficiency properties as such, and to substitute the Pareto-style rule that system A is better than system B if every member of the society in question enjoys at least as high a level of welfare under A as he would under B, and if at least one person enjoys higher welfare under A. However, this procedure also requires a rather strong ranking (for example, we cannot say that the American economic system is more efficient than the Soviet, by this standard, unless each and every Russian, without exception, would be better off under the American system). A final alternative would be to go back to the original three criteria, and look for some way of assessing not simply whether each criterion is met fully, but also how far short of meeting it each system tends to fall.

1.4.3 Limitations of the Efficiency Concept

One reason that the Pareto criteria have been attractive to economists is that, once one assumes that human well-being is fundamentally desirable, there seems to be every reason to accept them, and no reason to object to them, especially if other considerations can be set aside by invoking the familiar assumption that 'all else is equal'. In fact, their 'unobjectionableness' has led some into the fallacy of viewing the Pareto criteria as non-normative—that is, as not entailing any value judgments. Such a view must be rejected, when further thought is given to the matter, if only because the premise of the desirability of well-being is itself a value judgment. Equally important is the very real possibility that satisfying the Pareto criteria may in some circumstances be in conflict with other desirable ends, forcing a judgment of their relative importance. In view of this possibility, the decision to employ the Pareto criteria alone as measures of institutional fitness cannot be held to be value neutral.

Two aspects of the value-specific nature of the Pareto criteria deserve special mention. The first concerns the way in which human welfare is judged when the criteria are applied. The problem here is that how one determines who is 'better off', and so on, is open to ambiguity. Many people would consider it reasonable to measure how well off others are by looking at the degree to which their needs for food, clothing, and shelter are being met; others might add security, dignity, and the like. To use the first set of criteria would require a determination of what are adequate levels of, say, food, while to add the second would further require the discovery of acceptable proxies for the less tangible components (for example, dignity). Moreover, if comparisons are to be made of states in which the individual has more food with others in which he has more clothing, some kind of weighting system must be provided.

Economists generally reject these approaches and define a person's welfare as higher when consuming bundle X as opposed to bundle Y (of goods and activities) if he or she selects X over Y when both are attainable or affordable. This approach has the advantages of relying on actions, rather than on statements of preferences or needs (which may be misleading), and of avoiding the problem of constructing independent standards and weights. But it is principally on philosophical grounds (and thus, arguably, as a reflection of another value judgment) that it has been justified: deducing what makes the consumer better or worse off from his or her own decisions reflects the philosophy of liberalism, since it enshrines free choice as the arbiter of value; it is also non-paternalistic in letting A judge him- or herself better off with one set of goods than with another, even if the preferred set consists of cigarettes, whiskey, and shooting pool, while the one rejected consisted of healthful foods and recordings of Mozart.

A second sense in which value judgments are least implicitly embodied in the Pareto criteria is that they tend to push questions of the *distribution* of well-being out of consideration. This happens because under the Pareto criteria two differing distributions of welfare can be compared with one another only when each and every individual whose welfare differs in the one and in the other, experiences the same qualitative change (either an improvement, or a deterioration). If some persons are better off under arrangement A than B, while others are better off under B than A, no comparison can be made, even under the most extreme conditions. For example, let situation A be one in which 1,000 families are malnourished and one family eats such a rich diet that its members suffer from obesity and clogged arteries. Let situation B be one in which the rich family loses half of its income, which causes its members to eat well but to put on weight and clog their arteries more slowly, while the income foregone by them is transferred to the 1,000 poor families, who with this supplement are able to reach some recommended nutrition standard. So long as the rich family prefers its situation under A, and the poor prefer theirs under B, the two are Pareto-noncomparable. (Note, by the way, that if paternalistic evaluations were permitted, even an observer with no concern about equity could judge B to be better, on grounds that both the poor families and the rich family are 'objectively' better off in B.)

If a greater range of judgments about equity, non-subjective measures of needs fulfillment, or other factors are to be considered, it is clear that the Pareto criteria are not enough to do the job of evaluating economic arrangements. On the other hand, this does not imply that we need to throw those criteria away. If we place value on equality of incomes, for example, we may still agree that more efficiency is desirable for any given level of equality. Our choice, then, might be to give both equality and efficiency dimensions of economic performance appropriate weights in evaluation. The proponent of equality could then judge the arrangements leading to situation A to be better than those leading to B, above, although they are simply not comparable by the Pareto criterion alone.

1.4.4 *Five Standards for Evaluating Economic Systems*

How, then, ought we to proceed? Basically, we start out from the premise that evaluation is a legitimate and important part of the study of economic systems, and from the recognition that 'value-free evaluation' is a contradiction in terms. We select our list of evaluative criteria broadly, where possible in conformity with widespread practice. Finally, we leave open the issue of relative weightings of the various criteria, by not attempting to sum them into any overall index. Our criteria fit into five general types of expectations of what economic systems might be asked to achieve: (1) satisfaction of basic material needs; (2) equitable distribution of economic outcomes; (3) efficiency in production, distribution, and product mix; (4) favorable (or at least acceptable) impact on the satisfaction of social and nonmaterial needs; and (5) environmental

stewardship and resource and technology bequest to future generations. In the remainder of the chapter, we discuss each criterion in
turn, adding remarks on the relationship between them where
helpful.

Criterion 1: Provision of People's Basic Material Requirements This first
desideratum derives immediately from our definition of an economy
as the set of activities through which people meet their needs and
wants in society. In the first half of this chapter, we focused on how
the division of labor can raise productivity, thus at least making it
possible for people to acquire food, clothing, shelter, and other
goods more easily, despite the scarcity of productive resources. It
seems reasonable, therefore, to judge an economic system as more
successful than another when, everything else being equal, it is
demonstrably better at allowing people to achieve these ends.
Indeed, an economy's ability to satisfy people's material wants is
related to what we aim to capture when using what is in practice the
most favored welfare index, Gross National Product per capita. But
the latter may not be well correlated with basic needs satisfaction for
a country's people as a whole, if, for example, a large part of its
population receives a very small share of its total income. Why the
conjunction of equity and efficiency, which will be our second and
third criteria, do not suffice to assure satisfaction of basic material
requirements, which is our first, is a question that we leave to
answer later in the chapter.

Although measures of consumption are in practice widely used
to assess societies' levels of economic development, and although
limited supplies of consumer goods are frequently held up as
evidence of the failure of one or another economic system or set of
policies, the concept of 'basic needs', which in recent years has been
adopted by such international organizations as the World Bank,
meets criticism from some neoclassical economists. These economists argue that any attempt to distinguish between 'basic needs' and
'mere wants' must lead to distinctions which are arbitrary,
inherently paternalistic, and potentially dictatorial. Yet, in spite of
its cautionary merits, their position is undercut by widespread
agreement, for example, among health professionals, on at least a
rough set of core nutritional, medical, and other requirements for
securing satisfactory levels of health, capacity to work and engage in
non-work activities, and life expectancy. This is not to say that even

so simple a question as the required daily nutritional intake of an average-size man in Milan, Italy or Mysore, India, has been established beyond all controversy. However, it is for our own purposes unnecessary to decide upon the exact standards in calories, rooms, or lengths of cloth, by which needs satisfaction will be measured. It is sufficient that we keep the idea of material needs satisfaction in mind as we examine alternative ways of organizing economic life; the criterion can be left in an imprecise and elastic form, potentially reinterpretable by the individual analyst according to his or her own understanding of the issues.

One more possible objection ought to be anticipated. Using 'satisfaction of basic needs' as a criterion for evaluating economic systems may seem to imply the view that individuals have an unconditional right to be cared for by society (the collectivity of individuals including themselves). This should *not* be read into our use of the criterion. A better way of stating it might be that an economic system can be evaluated according to its provision or safeguarding to individuals of opportunities or means to meet their needs. This implies that, while people may choose collective provision of some services out of considerations of efficiency, the society is obligated to care for its members' needs directly only if it has prevented them from organizing joint provision or denied them individual access to the necessary means of self-provision of those requirements. None the less, actual attainments of material welfare remain an appropriate indicator of the availability of opportunities to meet these needs, and thus a measure of success with respect to this first criterion.

Criterion 2: Equitable Distribution of Economic Outcomes   While the criterion of equity is, like the previous criterion, best introduced in a relatively elastic fashion, the decision to consider the dimension of equity follows almost as a matter of course if heed is given to the expressed sentiments and values of contemporary societies.

The term 'equity' is intentionally chosen over the contending idea of 'equality'. Certainly, exact equality of incomes is not a consensus demand made of economic systems; equity, or fairness, which *is* widely demanded of social and economic institutions, is more often thought of in terms of equality of opportunities and, sometimes, equality of outcomes for equal behaviors or inputs—for example, equal pay for equal work. Under the heading of fairness, there are also competing considerations. For example, while equality of returns to inputs is itself a demanding objective (since in an uncertain world, its attainment by a market economy might require the kind of comprehensive social insurance that would be incompatible with enterprising behavior, and therefore deleterious to high productivity) one can question whether it is a sufficiently fair standard. One could point out, in particular, that input-contributing capabilities, including the skills, strength, and endurance of workers, can themselves be viewed as arbitrarily distributed, and that consumption needs are unequal. (For example, those afflicted with disabilities may require more medical and therapy resources to achieve the same level of well-being as those not so afflicted.) Needs also appear to be uncorrelated—or maybe even negatively correlated—with ability to earn income.

This brief sketch suffices to suggest that agreement on a specific equity standard for economic systems is bound to elude us. Yet the passion with which alternative positions are advocated, and the near universality of adherence to one equity concept or another, provide ample reason for the inclusion of some such criterion, open to whatever interpretation suits the preferences of the analyst. The discussion could be concluded here, then; however, two further remarks on current practice and on a possibly more universalizable interpretation of the concept of equity will be offered.

The first comment concerns the widespread use, in equity discussions, of measures of inequality such as the Gini coefficient and various percentile ratios,[26] which if based on accurate data and properly computed, record nothing more than the distribution of income or wealth, without, that is, any reference to labor or other contributions, or to 'needs'. This practice suggests that distribution itself, or in other words equality, is (after all) widely regarded as an adequate proxy for equity, since no resolution of the various conceptual and philosophical problems in the definition of equity is in fact sought or viewed as necessary by many who employ such measures.

Use of equality or inequality measures as tests of equity may, of course, reflect pragmatism in the face of difficult statistical problems and unresolvable philosophical questions. However, another possibility is that inequality is of direct concern to ordinary people, and that part of what one is trying to get at in including equity in the list of criteria by which to judge economic systems, is that the distribution of the economy's burdens and rewards should be widely enough acceptable for the social order to be preserved and the economy to remain viable over time. (This kind of viability might alternatively be purchased by means of armed force, but such measures probably introduce their own negatives, which would enter into evaluation under our fourth criterion.) This suggests looking at equity as a socially-specific concept, the test for which, in a given society, can only be administered by the members themselves.

Criterion 3: Allocative Efficiency The three components of the efficiency concept of neoclassical economics have already been stated and tentatively accepted as one set of standards by which we will judge economic systems. Essentially, they boil down to the intuitive view that, all else being equal, it is better not to waste resources that can contribute to people's well-being, whether by failing to combine them properly or to put them to their most valued uses in production, or by failing to permit mutually advantageous trades to be carried out prior to consumption.

Since the efficiency concept is widely misunderstood, especially by non-economists, a few words on what it does *not* mean, intended to show that even a humanist can affirm efficiency, may be warranted here. First of all, efficiency does not mean that 'only results' are important, and that what goes into achieving those results is to be ignored. Increasing the intensity and duration of drudgery, reducing (to anticipate the next criterion) the autonomy and self-respect of workers, or adding (likewise) to the impersonality of life in a complex society, for example, are not to be counted as nothing in a drive to get maximum physical output from given piles of raw materials, stocks of machinery, and barracks full of human sinew, in the name of efficiency. If the moderation of drudgery, the nurturing of self-respect in labor, and humane social institutions are desirables to a society's members, then they are to be sacrificed for physical productivity only to the extent that they are traded off for more highly valued increments of other desirables, including output, income, or economic growth, and that the choices are in fact unavoidable.

Similarly, the sense of strain and struggle that may be stirred up by the thought of always striving to avoid waste, to do things in the most economical manner, etc., is to be rejected as not necessarily intrinsic to efficiency. For, in so far as the mental effort of calculation, observation, and decision-making is itself a cost, the efficiency rule does not say 'spare no effort to avoid waste'; rather, it says: 'make all such efforts to avoid waste as can be expected to return benefits greater than their own direct disutility' This point is clear as regards the trade-off between income and leisure, the intangible good that economists most consistently remember to consider. It is recognized that a country's welfare could increase even as its GNP declined, if the loss in output were more than compensated by a desired increase in leisure. There should be no problem, then, with extending the same principle to mental drudgery. In principle, a society that values freedom from concern with detail could, with perfect efficiency, purchase such freedom in a manner that reduces the productivity of inputs other than attention and calculation, provided that it continues to maximize the returns on its resources, including the attention and calculation that it still commits to economic matters, to the extent that remains feasible.

Restated, then, the efficiency principle says (at least by way of illustration) that for given inputs of material resources, foregone consumption, drudgery, hierarchy, etc., we should produce as much food, as many clothes, as many houses, etc., as technology permits; that we should let Joe and Sam swap apples for oranges if they both feel better off as a result; and that we ought to produce less millet and more wheat, if everyone is at least as happy and one or more people happier that way. But it equally says that drudgery together with income, or alienating working arrangements with income, should be reduced where that makes people better off.

A special note is required on the relationship of efficiency to the other four evaluative criteria adopted in this essay. It is that in so far as society may reach frontiers at which more equity, or more satisfaction of material needs, or more long-term growth, can only be obtained by implementing policies or establishing institutions whose side effect is that some resources may be misallocated, thus violating the requirements of 'efficiency' as more narrowly defined, then the various objectives should themselves be traded off efficiently against one another. That is, given some scale for measuring the relative importance of these objectives to society as a whole, only so much 'efficiency' should be sacrificed to achieve a given increment in equity, or in basic needs satisfaction, or in growth, or in the nonmaterial dimensions of the life of the community, as is in fact necessary for doing this; one objective should be traded off against another up to the point at which the marginal loss in the first dimension just equals the marginal gain in the second, so that social welfare is maximized; and an optimum has not been reached unless the full bundle of achieved objectives can not be transformed into some other bundle that is more desirable to some and no less desirable to any. For example, if the only way to increase equity is to levy a tax on profits and on high personal incomes, and if such a tax tends to shift resources into activities of lower economic value to society, then if society values both equity and efficient resource allocation, it may be 'big E' efficient to implement such a tax, knowingly trading some 'little E' efficiency for some equity; but the level of the tax should be geared to balancing the value of the two objectives being traded, at the margin. What this means is that beyond Pareto-optimality in resource allocation one may define a 'meta-efficiency' at the level of the objectives competing with and including Pareto-optimality. However, for terminological clarity, this book will usually use the word 'efficiency' in the narrower sense in which it represents one of five standards of evaluation, and not in this broader sense of a principle for trading off those standards against each other.

Criterion 4: Impact on the Satisfaction of Social and Nonmaterial Needs   Our earlier emphasis on the link between economic systems and aspects of life quality, values, social environment, etc., has the implication that attention to the provision of such material needs as food and shelter may produce an incomplete measure of what economic systems deliver to their members or allow them to enjoy. Here again, there will be substantial controversy over how to rank, and even whether to admit, various candidates to the list of social and non-material needs. Autonomy, personal expression, non-alienation, spiritual nurturance, cultural development, and opportunities for 'self-actualization', may be listed by some and not by others. Libertarians are inclined to introduce the value 'liberty' into their evaluative comparisons of economic and social systems, whereas traditional radicals tend to focus on alienation and power, Gandhians on self-sufficiency, and so on. However, once it is recognized that the nature of an economic system is intimately connected with the nonmaterial features of social life and of the environment in which personal development takes place, some such dimension of evaluation has to be admitted as relevant; debates between alternative constructions only serve to underscore this dimension's importance.

Leaving specific applications of these criteria to the chapters that follow, two questions arise here with regard to the place of this category in the present list. First, why do we list 'social and nonmaterial needs' separately from 'material needs', and second, what, if anything, is implied by the order of listing? The two questions can be answered together: according to our definition, the satisfaction of material wants and needs is the immediate aim of economic activity (with this factor being what distinguishes the economic from other types of social activity), and so the effects of economic arrangements on the psychological well-being of the individual, and on the social character of the community, are necessarily viewed in our framework as by-products, however great their importance may be. We know that 'man does not live by bread alone', and the evolution of economic institutions may often have moved down one path, rather than another, in order to protect or create valued social institutions, rights, and so on. Even so, it is conceptually convenient to view economic arrangements as ways of producing and getting bread into the hands of men and women, in the first instance, with social effects taken into account as important further consequences, rather than to view social objectives as the primary forces behind those arrangements, and the production and distribution of bread as *their* side effects. No comparative ranking of the two types of needs by intrinsic importance should be inferred from the order of listing, however. While food and water may be more critical to short-term endurance, a sense of self-worth, belonging, or purpose may be equally critical to the quality of life, and even, in some sense, to the ability to live.

Criterion 5: Stewardship and Growth   Whereas the concept of static efficiency is defined in terms of the well-being of society as contemporaneously constituted, economic systems will also impinge upon the nature of the physical environment, capital stock, and level of technological knowledge bequeathed to future generations. Assuming that the analyst places some weight on the welfare of those later generations, and of now-living individuals at future points in time, performance of the economic system with respect to environmental stewardship, capital accumulation, technological change, and so forth, from this dynamic and long-term point of view, belongs among the basic criteria of evaluation.

Once again, the precise nature of standards cannot be stated independently of the values of the analyst. For example, while some may bring to bear on this domain a presumption that current generations are obliged to sacrifice so that the motherland, the free (alternatively: socialist) world, or simply posterity, may be prosperous, others may follow the *laissez-faire* philosophy to its logical conclusion that the present generation ought to do whatever it likes, with unregulated, spontaneous savings behavior and resource use determining what future generations happen to inherit. While the latter view might seem to amount to rejection of the criterion itself, an alternative interpretation is that the current members of the community reveal their personal weightings of the importance of the future through their savings and other relevant behaviors. Rather than eliminating the rate of savings as an evaluative criterion, the *laissez-faire* approach as thus interpreted provides its own standard for judging an economic system's performance. (For instance, Soviet-style socialism will be judged to perform poorly when it forces a high level of savings on a reluctant population.) As before, we can proceed to consider system performance with respect to this dimension without embracing in advance any particular interpretation of the criterion.

1.4.5 Interrelations among the Five Criteria

We may conclude with a few comments on the interrelations of the five criteria. A question posed earlier, to which our answer has been deferred, concerns the possible redundancy of at least one of the first three of our criteria. In particular, it was suggested that an economy that makes efficient use of its resources is bound to succeed in satisfying its members' material requirements, unless it is marked by a highly unequal distribution of income. Therefore the conjunction of criteria 2 and 3 seems to suffice to cover any problems that might arise under criterion 1.

One possible response is that if resources are extremely scarce, or known technologies are of low productive potential, then even efficient production and egalitarian distribution cannot guarantee the satisfaction of basic material needs. However, this is not a very good example, since it suggests no obvious link between the cause of poverty and the nature of the economic system, and it is not, therefore, of particular relevance to system evaluation.

A more relevant point is that with the definition of equity left open, it is conceivable that a distribution of income could be judged equitable even if it left some members of a society below subsistence levels or in dire poverty, while enough people lived far enough above their minimum needs that poverty could be eliminated through redistribution. For example, under a certain ideology, it might be considered to be equitable that each individual should receive an income equal to the value of the marginal product of his or her labor and the other factors that he or she contributes to production. Unless special allowances are made or sufficient voluntary transfers of income occur, persons lacking other factors of production and unable to work because of physical incapacity may end up living in extreme poverty, even if the society as a whole is quite prosperous and uses its resources very efficiently. Under the prevailing definition of equity, the society would then have both an efficient and an equitable economic system, but one that failed to satisfy the basic material needs of a portion of its population.

It is also worth pointing out that we have defined efficiency independently of the assignment of control over resources, and of the preferences or objectives of those who end up having such control. Consider, for example, a Soviet-type society with centralized control over the means of production. If the leaders formulate objectives which assign priority to the growth of the producers' goods and military industries, efficiency requires only that the available resources produce the maximum amount of each targeted output subject to the production of each other good; that the planners are not able to increase anyone's welfare without hurting someone else's (or their own) by producing more of one good (say, food) and less of another (say, steel mills); and that people are free to exchange final goods. Conceivably, such an economy could operate efficiently, and the distribution of income within it could be judged equitable (for example, if planners and party members made the same sacrifices as other consumers for the sake of growth, and if income were distributed quite equally). Yet some basic material needs of the current generation might go unmet, owing to the planners' high valuation of growth.

The fact that efficiency is defined entirely in terms of the relationship between resources, techniques, and objectives, and does not say which objectives are good or bad, provides another reason for distinguishing between criterion 3 and criterion 1. The latter, but not the former, assumes that people have objective material needs, independent of anyone's subjective preferences. To take an extreme example, imagine a free market economy in which, partly under the influence of advertising, consumers who could otherwise afford at least a basic standard of nutrition, clothing, and shelter, spend a large fraction of their incomes on cigarettes, liquor, and even, perhaps, narcotics (which in an extreme free-market environment might be unregulated). The economy might be quite efficient in transforming its resources into the products that the consumers demand, and the distribution of income could even be such that everyone attains a roughly equal consumption standard. Yet an objective observer might find the population to be malnourished, and as a consequence to suffer from high levels of disease, and a low life expectancy. Criterion 1 judges not only how much but also what is produced and consumed by an economy, not on the basis of subjective preferences only, but also on the basis of objective criteria of welfare. It could lead to the judgment that the economic system just described is unambiguously inferior to a modified variant of the same system in which narcotics sales are banned, warning labels and consumption taxes are attached to cigarettes and liquor, and the government devotes the resulting tax revenues to educating citizens about health risks and dietary issues. Without criterion 1 there would be no basis on which to reach such a judgment.

Looking at the last two paragraphs together, a careful reader might notice that, since we define efficiency as being independent of whose objectives are given weight, and since our first criterion focuses on *needs*, assumed to be objectively identifiable, it is possible that our five evaluative standards will pay no attention whatsoever to whether the *desires* (or wants) of the people in the society are being satisfied, and to whether they are made happy by the uses to which their society's resources are put. There are two ways of dealing with this legitimate concern without adding another criterion. First of all, we could draw more inclusively on our definition of an economy as the set of activities through which people meet their needs and wants in society when establishing our first criterion, so that at least some weight would be given to wants, and not all of it to needs. The other possibility is to make use of three other criteria: those of equity, efficiency, and social dimensions. With these in mind, we could point out that a liberal economist's inclination to give higher marks to an economic system in which consumers are able to purchase goods suited to their tastes, can be read as a preference for interpreting the equity dimension as requiring a fairly broad-based distribution of income, the social dimension as requiring that people be free to spend their incomes as they wish, and the efficiency dimension as requiring that resource allocation responds appropriately to consumer demand. If people have purchasing power, if economic institutions allow them to exercise it freely, and if the production sector successfully supplies what is in demand, then no additional standard is needed to assure that the economy is responsive to people's wants. (The example is not meant to rule out the possibility that non-market social arrangements could also respond to what people want, although whether that possibility can be realized in practice will have to be considered at a later point.)

1.5 Conclusions

To understand and compare economic systems, it is important to distinguish between the cultural, historical, and other factors which influence a country's economic life, and its economic system as such. Defining the economy as the sphere of social activity in which people produce, distribute, and consume their material requirements and wants, and a system as a set of regularly interacting elements, we identified economic systems as the sets of interactions among people, and between people and economically useful things, that occur regularly in the course of the production, distribution, and consumption of their material requirements and wants. Individual systems are distinguished from one another by the different characteristic forms of interaction, or economic institutions, that occur with regularity in the economies practicing them.

In this book, we use the term 'division of labor' to refer to economic specialization in all its forms, including that pertaining to resources other than labor *per se*. We say that the division of labor is increasing when the activities of individuals, and the uses to which productive factors are put, become more specialized and differentiated, and when, therefore, the interactions between them become more complex. A difference in the degree of division of labor was illustrated by comparing a rural society in an underdeveloped nation, in which most of the economic activities of most households are directed at the immediate satisfaction of their own consumption needs, with a highly industrialized society, in which most individuals are engaged in highly specialized activities, and purchase the bulk of their material requirements from others, using incomes earned as wages or factor payments. While households in the first society have a more versatile array of skills and are far more self-reliant, households in the second society enjoy a much higher living standard, which may be related to the complex and specialized organization of their economy, as well as to its accumulation of physical and human capital, itself aided by past specialization.

Division of labor is thought to raise human productivity by means of specialization within and among production activities, and the increased scale of those activities. Specialization within or among activities (or production enterprises) takes the forms of task and tool specialization, which raise productivity through learning effects; through reduced set-up costs or costs of moving between tasks; through the stimulus given to the development of more specialized tools and their higher productivity, compared with general tools; through the allocation of workers among tasks according to abilities and skills; and through the action of the principle of comparative advantage as applied to immobile resources. Production on a larger scale, apart from directly facilitating division of labor internal to the production unit, often exhibits economies of scale which are due to the physical characteristics of production technologies. We view these effects as belonging among the overall results of the division of labor, because large-scale production is not functional until different enterprises and localities can specialize in different product lines, which is made possible by market or planned exchange and the resulting division of labor among units.

Although the division of labor can bring enormous benefits, it also has potential disadvantages. Overspecialization of tasks can breed boredom, alienation, and ignorance among workers. Specialization means interdependence, which in turn means vulnerability to the potentially hostile actions of others. A complex, specialized economy requires a coordination mechanism, and the known candidates (markets and planning, where the latter includes hierarchy at the workplace) may each have their drawbacks. Differentiation of tasks and roles appears to be associated with differences in incomes, social status, and economic and political power, and ethically or socially preferred rules of equitable income distribution may be in conflict with the need for incentives to work and invest. Also, complex economies appear to be capable of fostering economic growth, but either large income differences or state intervention may have to be used if that capability is to be realized in practice.

Evaluation seems almost unavoidable in discussions of our topic. It is also implicit in the vocabulary of economics, and although it can lead to bias if left hidden, it is potentially part of the richness of that vocabulary. While efficiency (which has a precise technical definition distinct from everyday usage) is the criterion central to formal welfare economics, we argued that other evaluative criteria, some of which appear more frequently than others in the writings of economists, need also to be considered, as each represents a value in its own right, and since there may be trade-offs among them.

Given the definition of an economy as a set of activities geared to the satisfaction of material needs and wants, we adopted the level of such satisfaction, especially of needs that may in principle be objectively identifiable, as a first criterion. The second criterion that we will employ is equity in distribution, a concept permitting a number of different definitions. After efficiency, we listed the effects of economic arrangements on nonmaterial aspects of social and personal well-being, such as liberty, sense of community, and satisfaction from work, as a fourth standard for evaluation. Fifth and last, we listed the effects of the economic system on the economy's performance with respect to the stocks of capital and resources, the technological capabilities, and the state of the physical environment, that it passes on from one generation to those that succeed it. We concluded by pointing out the complementarities and distinctions between these standards, in part by raising and then arguing against certain suspicions of redundancies or oversights.

Notes

1. A similar point is made by Montias 1976, who stresses the importance of distinguishing between system and environmental factors when evaluating the effects of the system on economic outcomes.
2. It is possible to construct a sophisticated defense of the economizing approach, according to which virtually all behavior is economizing once it is accepted that the ends in question can vary without limit and are not themselves to be judged when characterizing the activity. Also, departures from what would be rational in a world of perfect rationality and costless calculating abilities may be rational, when seeking information, and processing it, are costly in terms of time and of physical

and psychic energy. The concern that 'economizing' has a normative thrust that may interfere with the study of economic institutions is worth bearing in mind even if these qualifications are valid, however.

3. Polanyi 1957.
4. See Hurwicz 1971; Neuberger and Duffy 1976.
5. See, for example, Furubotn and Pejovich 1974.
6. Data are from the World Bank, *World Development Report 1988*, and refer to 1986.
7. A complicating consideration is that the developed condition of America and the underdeveloped condition of Tanzania may in some part result from the fact that the one has historically benefited from extracting resources from the other in the context of colonial and post-colonial relationships. While a discussion of this point would take us away from our main concerns at the moment, it might be pointed out that, rather than requiring the rejection of our general approach, reference to the colonial phenomenon can be viewed as an example of the division of labor—in this case, an example in which it is obvious that not all those affected need be beneficiaries. As will be seen shortly, we by no means rule out inequalities and relationships that may be interpreted as exploitative, under the rubric of division of labor.
8. Smith 1985, Book I, chapter 3.
9. See, for example, Williamson 1980.
10. This may be because division of labor is linked to biological specialization in reproduction, to the prolonged dependence of human young upon their mothers, or to other life-cycle phenomena. Perhaps labor specialization and collective action also result from advantages of banding in hunting and defense, and from the ability of groups to sustain individuals through spells of injury and illness. In view of these advantages, the evolutionary forces of differential survival may have acted to preserve individuals inheriting propensities to gregariousness and sociability, and groups culturally inventive in the ways of cooperation.
11. Smith 1985, Book V, chapter 1, part 3, article 2.
12. Marx 1967a, p. 362.
13. Loc. cit.
14. Marx 1967a, pp. 360–1.
15. Much of the latter begins with an article by Coase 1937, and has sometimes styled itself 'the new institutional economics'. More mathematical theorizing on incentives in teams, 'principal-agent' models, tournaments, and so forth, may also be noted. For some samplings of work in these areas, the reader may consult Pratt and Zeckhauser (eds) 1985; Putterman (ed.) 1986, or Nalebantian (ed.) 1987, among other collections.
16. See, for example, the essays by Paul Samuelson and by Assar Lindbeck

in Lindbeck 1977.

17. Coase, op. cit.
18. Williamson 1975
19. Marx 1967a, p. 356.
20. References to this literature will be provided in Chapter 4.
21. Roemer 1988, pp. 46–7.
22. This subsection, and subsection 2.2.2 of Chapter 2, are probably the only parts of the book that will be found to be too technical by readers who have not had at least an introductory course in (neoclassical) economic theory. An appendix is provided at the end of the book briefly to introduce such readers to the concepts involved, but interested readers who have had no other exposure to the technical apparatus used may also wish to consult a more detailed exposition, such as that of Scherer 1966, which the present discussion draws on, or any of a number of different intermediate micro-economics texts.
23. See Figures A.2 and A.3 in the Appendix.
24. See Figure A.2, and its reinterpretation, in the Appendix, in the section headed 'Distributive Efficiency'.
25. See Figure A.3 and discussion.
26. Some of these measures are introduced in Todaro 1989, pp. 145–53, and in other widely available textbooks on economics systems or economic development.

2.
Capitalism

2.1 Institutional Premises and Features

2.1.1 Three Institutional Premises, and Some Implications

We begin our survey of economic systems with what is both the dominant modern species—in terms of total product generated, share of world trade, and weight in the international political economy—and the point of departure for all modern system alternatives, whether actual or conceptual. At the beginning of the chapter we will deal with an idealized and abstract notion of the capitalist economic system, a model in which no modern industrial market economy may appear immediately recognizable, corresponding more closely to the economics textbook than to any actuality. Details and complications will emerge as the discussion proceeds, however.

In the previous chapter, we stated that economic systems could be identified and distinguished by the types of interactions regularly occurring among their elements. These interactions, which we also called institutions, include forms of ownership rights, modes of exchange, and methods of coordination of the division of labor. Our discussion of capitalism as an economic system begins by identifying a set of three economic institutions as its essential and distinguishing premises.

First, private rights in the use, consumption, disposition, and fruits of land, minerals, machines, buildings and other structures, human labor, and goods, are recognized and protected by law and the state. These rights, which are part of what we call ownership, include the right of the person holding them to lease or rent the items in question to another party on any of a variety of contractual terms, such as a fixed rental payment per unit of time or of resource flow, profit sharing or sharecropping, and so on. That person is also free to consume or put to further use the income thus obtained.

Second, when to the rights just listed is added the right to transfer all of these rights to the resource in question either by sale, or by bequest, we have the full institution of ownership. In the economic system we call capitalism, ownership rights exist with respect to most kinds of useful resources and goods. It is also central to the institutional structure of capitalism, however, that the status of labor is exceptional in this regard. While the ability to provide labor services can be viewed as a kind of asset or property 'owned' by the worker, and while the same rights of use and disposition listed in the previous paragraph also pertain to this form of property, transfers of labor ownership are prohibited under the law in capitalist economies. Work capacity can be leased or hired out, but not sold, purchased, or inherited (in contrast with the situation in feudal and slave-holding societies).

Third and last, the prices and terms on which leases and sales take place are unregulated except by the free negotiation of the parties involved, that is, the owner and the purchaser or lessee. By price, we mean simply the quantity of goods, services, or currency[1] given in exchange for transfer of ownership, or for temporary use, of the resource in question. The terms of exchange will also, in some cases, be stipulated as a share of output, of input costs, and so on, and in some transactions, one party becomes the sole claimant to the net cash flow generated by an activity after other parties have received their stipulated shares; in other words, that party receives the 'profit'. Wages and interest rates are also among the terms of exchange covered by the principle of unregulated agreement.

These three institutional premises—the existence of largely unrestricted ownership rights in things, the protection of 'self-ownership' rights in persons, and the unregulated nature of exchange—are both necessary and sufficient, we propose, to define an economic system as capitalist. Although they are features of a pure economic system type and fail to match exactly the observed rules of any particular modern economy, the adjective 'capitalist' will be applicable to real-world economies in so far as they embody or approximate these features to a greater or lesser degree.

While we hold the stated institutional premises to be sufficient for defining an economy as capitalist, they provide only a starting point for a description of capitalist economies. If we are correct about their sufficiency, however, the descriptive features of capitalism should emerge as implications of these basic institutions.

One major implication of the listed institutions is that the economic process is unplanned and uncentralized, in the sense that the aggregate outcome of production and exchange activities depends upon the choices and actions of a myriad of individual workers, investors, managers, and consumers, and is not guided by any authority or body at the level of the society as a whole. The system differs, in this respect, from both feudal societies and early empires, including the vertically stratified states of ancient Egypt, China, and Peru; in these, monarchs and emperors regulated a great deal of economic activity, with priests, or ethical canons and traditions, sometimes also circumscribing the kinds of transactions that could take place. It differs still more clearly from modern, centrally planned systems of the type existing in the Soviet Union since the late 1920s.

A second important implication concerns the determination of incomes. In a pure, free market capitalist economy, people's incomes are determined by their individual ownerships of productive resources (including their own skills and laboring powers), by their level of contribution of those resources to productive activities (or to the direct service of other individuals), by the prices which such resource contributions command, by the value of any residual or windfall income that might fall to them, and lastly (determining the purchasing power or exchange value of the resulting income) by the prices at which goods and services can be acquired for consumption. Since there are no prescribed limits to inequality in the distribution of initial resources, and since market pricing, reflecting scarcity, will lead to low returns to factors that are in abundant supply, there is no mechanism to guarantee that some individuals or households will not earn too little to secure their basic necessities, no limit to the amount of wealth that may be amassed by others, and no group in the community empowered to redistribute the outcomes of the market process if they do not accord with social standards of fairness. This can be contrasted with the distributive institutions of societies in which incomes are viewed as shares of a communal livelihood, the distribution of which is governed by social, ethical, or traditional principles.

In African tribal societies, for example, there were traditional rules, interpreted by elders, governing access to land and ownership of herds. Not only were these means of production subject to redistribution by the clan or tribe, but so also were their fruits, especially in times of hardship or when other members were in need. In Mao Zedong's China during the 1960s and 1970s, rural families belonged to farm production teams that guaranteed them a basic ration of grain, regardless of their ability to contribute to the productive effort. And the political scientist James Scott (1976) has argued that landowners in pre-colonial Vietnam regularly adjusted their rent collections, in recognition of the hardship suffered by tenant farmers in bad crop years, demonstrating the operation of a peasant 'moral economy'. To be sure, it has been argued—for example, in the theory of marginal productivity factor pricing—that ethical standards are built into the market mechanism, so that mediating social mechanisms are not required to assure an appropriate or just distribution of income. However, the ethical status of market distributive outcomes remains a subject of controversy in capitalist societies, and political interventions to modify those outcomes are common.

While not flowing as obviously from capitalism's institutional premises or system of codified property rights, other observed features of capitalist systems merit equal attention in an empirical characterization. First, capitalism spawns individualism and the prominence of the nuclear family, and under it, the individual and household become highly autonomous units in the spheres of consumer expenditure and factor supplies. This feature may be associated with the fact that ownership, under capitalism, is generally by individuals, rather than extended families, communities, or clans.

Second, by permitting the vigorous growth of commerce and the extension of markets, in connection with its principle of voluntary exchange, capitalism not only permits and coordinates, but also *fosters* a complex division of labor, both among industries, and within enterprises.[2] Third, coupled with the technological aspects of modern industry, the progress of which has been intertwined historically with that of capitalism, the system tends to produce enterprises of characteristically hierarchical structure. Within these enterprises, management and control, along with residual (profit) claims, reside directly or indirectly with the owners of capital assets. Laborers, accordingly, become subordinates within an authority relation in the work process, and agree to assert only fixed claims to income (that is, they disclaim any right to share in profits).

2.1.2 Why Capitalism Succeeds: A Preliminary View

The fact that capitalism is associated with a vigorous and complex division of labor means that it faces a coordination problem of the kind discussed in Chapter 1; yet a principal feature of the system is the absence of general planning. How capitalism can claim to avoid chaos in economic outcomes is therefore a question of great interest.

According to the well-known theory of competition or of the harmonization of interests, capitalism is blessed with a tendency to channel self-interested behavior into the service of broader social welfare. It accomplishes this by virtue of (1) its system of property rights, which return the rewards of allocative decisions to the factor owners who make them, and (2) its principles of non-regulation of transaction terms, which permit buyers to exert their influence upon what is produced and how, by their decisions about what and how much to buy at what prices. Any disproportion between aggregate demand for and supply of a commodity or service, under these arrangements, should lead its price either to fall or to rise; and such price changes should signal to self-interested factor-owners that greater profits could be earned by moving their resources out of or into production or supply of the commodity or service in question. If the balance of supply and demand across all commodities is ever at rest, this can only signify (under ideal conditions, at least) that consumers are receiving the best possible mix of goods relative to their incomes and preferences and, since profitability of resources would be further augmentable if it were not the case, that resources are being used with maximum technical and allocative efficiency to produce that set of outputs.

To take a fairly trivial example, suppose that consumers want more carrots and fewer tomatoes. They will increase their demand for the first and reduce that for the second product. At the original prices and with the original quantities supplied, there will not be enough carrots to go around, and there will be too many tomatoes. Sellers of carrots will find that they can raise their prices and still clear their stocks, while sellers of tomatoes will be forced to compete with one another in selling at lower prices in order to clear theirs. But at the new prices, returns from farming carrots will be higher than average, those from farming tomatoes lower; and since farmers will seek to maximize the earnings from their land and labor, they will grow more carrots and fewer tomatoes. The desires of consumers will thus translate into appropriate decisions by producers. (The fact that a carrot field cannot be converted into a field of tomatoes instantaneously presents a complicating factor to be considered later on.)

For an example illustrating the convergence of price with production cost, consider the case of producers of pocket calculators. Each firm tries to recover at least as much as its full cost of production, including average profit on its investment, and leaves the industry if it cannot do so over the long term. Suppose, then, that the industry is in equilibrium, temporarily, with all producers using the same technology and selling calculators of a common type at prices just covering their full costs of production. Any firm that discovers a way to combine labor services, machine time, and materials more cheaply to produce calculators, can continue to sell at the original price, earning a higher profit. In such a situation the firm also has an incentive to expand its market share, by producing more and selling at a slightly lower price. To compete, other firms are at pains to discover equally effective ways of lowering costs, but as they do so, prices will fall further. When the market is in equilibrium, given the new methods, prices will have fallen to the new, lower costs of production, or else additional firms, seeing the unusually high profits in the calculator industry, will divert resources into calculator production, adding to market supply and thus driving down the price. In the end, competition assures consumers that they will pay no more than the opportunity or resource costs of the products they buy, and competition also gives firms incentives to discover ways of further lowering those costs.

One question not yet considered here is that of the way in which production is organized. We know that not all resource allocation takes place as the immediate result of exchange; many decisions on resource use are made by large organizations that, in the limit (for example, General Motors or IBM), manage more resources than are available in many whole countries. The formation and existence of firms may be fit into the story by stating that where efficiency and cost minimization are thereby served, factor owners will tend to supply their services to production units that manage those resources, internally, in an organized, planned, and on-going manner. So while no central bureaucracy engages in resource management for the capitalist economy as a whole, a managerial function will arise at the dispersed centers of enterprise where and when this enhances the efficiency of resource use. Otherwise independent production or spot exchanges between factor owners, being more profitable to them, would replace organized production units (firms, enterprises) in the activities in question.

But what of the human costs: the transformation of the worker into an employee, into a subordinate in a hierarchy, or, nearer to the top, into an 'organization man'? The case for capitalism would say that even the worker is in an optimal position under the capitalist system, since he or she is free to seek whatever employment yields the best combination of income, job satisfaction, and work hours, from his or her own standpoint. With unregulated wages and assuming no coordination of labor supply among laborers, there should be full employment at a wage that just clears the labor market. At such an equilibrium employers must be competing for workers by offering them packages of wages, working conditions, and work hours that are sufficiently attractive to lure them from alternative options. If observed jobs are characterized by tedium or by rigid supervision, then this should in principle indicate that such disutilities are outweighed, for the individuals who freely choose to endure them, by attractive work hours, relative lack of physical strain, high remuneration, or other positive attributes.

2.2 Capitalism and the Evaluative Criteria: The Ideal Case

2.2.1 Material Needs and Equity

The arguments reviewed in section 2.1.2 state the case for capitalism assuming ideal conditions. These conditions amount to saying that the economy is marked by perfect competition among numerous agents, that each producer is a profit-maximizer and each consumer a utility-maximizer, and that information flows rapidly and is processed quickly by all economic agents. Since, on the one hand, we did not mention a government, but on the other, we assumed that producers responded efficiently to consumers' demands, we must also have been assuming that no desired goods have the property of 'publicness', to which we will turn a little later. Finally, we did not consider the possibility of externalities, such as the emission of pollutants as a by-product of production. In the present section, we will review the case for a positive evaluation of capitalism more systematically, considering in turn each of the five criteria introduced in Chapter 1. To allow the system to 'put its best foot forward', in this initial evaluation, we will maintain these ideal assumptions of perfect competition, no public goods, and no externalities. Our more realistic assessment, later in the chapter, will require that these assumptions be dropped.

To begin with the question of satisfying material needs, the argument for competitive capitalism here is that material require-ments can be satisfied by an economy that, given sufficient resources and adequate techniques of production, maximizes the productivity of resources and produces what is demanded by consumers. Consumers are 'sovereign', under capitalism, by virtue of the link between demand and profitability, and, the argument goes, they will spend their earnings to satisfy their basic needs (if the concept has any meaning) for food, clothing, and shelter before demanding other goods. Taking a more dynamic attitude, it can also be argued that capitalism provides incentives to discover both new resources and new technologies, and that it fosters productivity-increasing capital accumulation by raising surpluses through its complex division of labor, and by allowing those in possession of surplus funds to bid unrestrictedly for and earn maximum returns on those funds.

In Chapter 1 and above, we noted that competition might not guarantee each individual or household the purchasing power with which to command his or her necessities in the market. Modern economics provides no standard response to this dilemma, and its practitioners often support arguments for government interventions to address it, which means departing from the framework of the free market economy in the narrower sense. The eighteenth- and nineteenth-century economists, on the other hand, did offer a response to these distributional issues within a *laissez-faire* setting. This response emphasized the similarity or approximate equality of persons. Capitalism, the classical economists argued, tended to eliminate the hereditary privileges of class, and to permit individuals to compete as equals in labor and other markets. Although a small segment of the community, in their role as capital owners, would be positioned to control a disproportionate share of society's wealth, this fact would be rendered benign by competition, which would not only ensure that capital was applied efficiently in production, but would also prevent individual capitalists from consuming much beyond the levels of ordinary individuals, by forcing them constantly to reinvest their profits into productive ventures. Capitalists would thus be made to serve essentially as functionaries in the decentralized process of social capital accumulation. Landlords, however, could pose a problem, since population, pressing upon resources, might drive rents up at the expense of both wages and profits. But in general, at least a subsistence wage could be assumed to be assured to the worker, meaning that basic material needs would be met.

The position of classical economics on equity is implicit in these remarks on material needs. The breakdown of feudal privileges and the action of competition would ensure a fair link between contributions and rewards. Assuming competition, there is no ethical problem with capitalists' incomes, for capital owners will tend to be frugal in consumption, and to fulfill their roles with regard to the accumulation of capital for society more-or-less automatically. Only landlords' rights to rents were fundamentally challenged by certain aspects of classical economic thought.

Modern economists have produced an argument for the fairness of distribution under capitalism that is more complex and more elegant than that of their predecessors. In the theory of marginal product factor returns, it is shown that with perfect competition in input and product markets, each factor owner must, in equilibrium, receive the value of the marginal product of his or her contribution, which can be understood as the difference between the total value of social output *with* this contribution, and what that value would be *without* it. To some analysts,[3] this has seemed to be a good standard of fairness. We will consider some doubts about that in section 2.3.

2.2.2 Capitalism and Efficiency

A student of economic systems may be forgiven for wondering whether economists did not design their definition of efficiency precisely so as to fit the theoretical properties they see in a competitive private enterprise economy. Historically, western economics has developed its concepts of efficiency in the process of studying the theoretical attributes of perfectly competitive capitalism, so it may not be surprising that this criterion is found to be fully satisfied by that system under ideal assumptions. In view of the subtlety of the technical definition of efficiency in economics, and the manner in which economists have elaborated their proofs of the efficiency of competitive markets, it is worthwhile to devote attention, here, to each of the aspects of efficiency discussed in Chapter 1. (Those already familiar with the theory of general equilibrium in a market economy, or who are not interested in such technical matters, may skip to section 2.2.3.)

Efficiency in production is expected to be achieved under competitive capitalism because, as part of the process of maximizing their profits, firms will search for least cost methods of generating output, while input prices will come to reflect input scarcities relative to production potential and to final demand for the products into which they enter. In Chapter 1 we noted that efficiency in production is formally displayed by a situation in which production takes place at a tangency of *isoquants* (the curves or contour lines indicating input combinations yielding given output levels) in the Edgeworth box. According to economic theory, producers will attain technical efficiency, because knowledge of the best current technology is assumed to be freely available to them, and because profit can be increased as long as it remains possible to produce more from given inputs using that knowledge. Allocative efficiency in production, however, requires that each producer also chooses the appropriate mix of inputs.

Suppose, then, that producers of two goods, say television sets and toasters, use the same two inputs, say 'machines' and 'labor', in possibly varying combinations. The efficiency condition of tangency of isoquants means that they should each choose a combination of machines and labor such that the rate at which labor can be substituted for machines without reducing output—called the 'marginal rate of technical substitution' (MRTS)—is the same. Now, in a perfectly competitive market, the price of a homogeneous input will be the same for all buyers, and will reflect both the marginal productivity of the input, and the opportunity cost of diverting it from other uses. Economic theory says that a firm minimizes its production costs by selecting a factor mix such that the relative price of the inputs, which is the slope of its *isocost lines* (which show sets of input combinations that can be purchased for a given total expenditure), equals the marginal rate of technical substitution, which is the slope of its isoquants. Since the slope of the isocost line for labor and machines is the same to both television and toaster manufacturers (owing to their facing the same input prices), and since cost minimization implies that each will choose a factor combination at which its MRTS equals that slope, producers in the

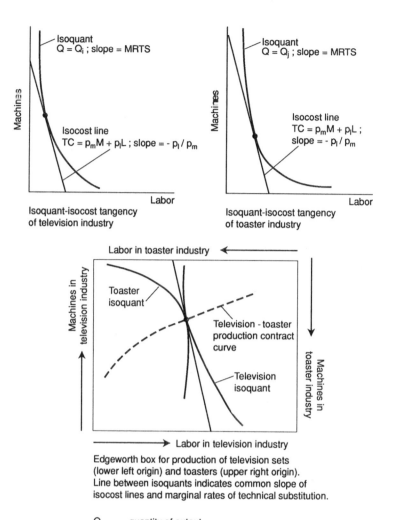

Fig. 2.1.

Efficiency in production under competitive capitalism

Cost minimization by television and toaster makers leads to efficient allocation of machines and labor among the two industries, so it is impossible to produce more toasters without sacrificing television sets.

two industries must select the same MRTS; this means that in the Edgeworth box, their isoquants will be tangent (see Figure 2.1). Profit maximizing responses to market-determined factor prices therefore lead to efficient resource allocation for production, which implies that it is impossible to produce more toasters without producing fewer television sets, and so on for all other industries and products. These arguments are summarized in the top portion of Table 1.

Consider, next, efficiency in the distribution for goods between individuals, which implies that no way of redistributing the available set of goods could make anyone better off without hurting someone else. Intuitively, this form of efficiency follows directly, under capitalism, from the fact that individuals are free to exchange goods with one another. Formally, distributive efficiency requires attaining a position on the *contract curve* of the Edgeworth box for distribution, where the *indifference curves* (the curves or contour lines each of which represents a set of consumption bundles that yield a constant level of satisfaction) of consumers are tangent. When any two consumers find their personal shares of televisions and toasters, or of tomatoes and carrots, to be such that they could mutually benefit through trade, it is to be expected that the trade will take place. Only when each consumer could only improve his or her position by taking from the other without compensation, will the possibilities for trade be exhausted, but then efficiency in distribution will have been attained.

Of course, real market economies are clearly too complex to imagine that swaps of tomatoes for carrots between Suzy and Bob are the main way that people obtain what they consume. Most people first obtain money income, then spend the money on goods offered by various firms.[4] The reason why the model of a competitive economy predicts efficiency under these arrangements parallels the explanation of productive efficiency in the choice of inputs. Consumers are on the contract curve when they have identical marginal rates of substitution (MRS), which are the slopes of their indifference curves. Now, in a perfectly competitive economy, each good will come to have a certain price reflecting demand and supply, and all consumers will therefore face the same absolute and relative prices for television sets, toasters, tomatoes, carrots, etc. But the theory of the consumer says that each consumer maximizes his or her own utility by choosing to consume any two goods in a propor-

Table 1
Summary of efficiency conditions and reasons for attainment in ideal perfectly competitive capitalist economy

Property	Verbal Statement	Formal requirement	Reason for attainment
Efficiency in production	It is not possible to increase the output of any good without reducing that of at least one other good.	$(MRTS_{i,j})_x = (MRTS_{i,j})_y$, where MRTS means marginal rate of technical substitution, i and j are any two factor inputs, and x and y are any two products.	$(MRTS_{i,j})_x \equiv$ slope of isoquant in any industry $x = -P_i/P_j \equiv$ input price ratio $\equiv$ slope of isocost lines, assuming cost-minimization by producers. Since P_i/P_j is identical to all industries, $MRTS_{i,j}$ must also be identical, so the requirement is fulfilled.
Efficiency in distribution	No alternative distribution of goods can increase any person's level of satisfaction without reducing that of at least one other person.	$(MRS_{x,y})_a = (MRS_{x,y})_b$, where MRS means marginal rate of (indifferent) substitution (in consumption), x and y are any two goods, and a and b are any two individuals.	$(MRS_{x,y})_a \equiv -MU_x/MU_y \equiv$ slope of indifference curve of $a = -P_x/P_y \equiv$ product price ratio $\equiv$ slope of budget line of each individual, which is the condition for utility-maximization by consumers. Since P_x/P_y is identical for all individuals, the requirement is fulfilled.

Table 1 (cont.)

Property	Verbal Statement	Formal requirement	Reason for attainment
Efficiency in the output mix	No feasible alternative set of outputs can increase any person's level of satisfaction without reducing that of at least one other person.	$RPT_{x,y} = (MRS_{x,y})_c$, where RPT is the rate of product transformation, x and y are any two goods, and c stands for the community.	$RPT_{x,y} \equiv$ slope of production possibility frontier between any two goods x and $y \equiv -MC_x/MC_y \equiv$ ratio of the marginal costs of producing x and $y = -P_x/P_y \equiv$ product price ratio, because $P_x = Mc_x$ and $P_y = MC_y$ are conditions for profit maximization by producers, and $MRS_{x,y} \equiv -MU_x/MU_y \equiv$ slope of indifference curve of any individual $= -P_x/P_y \equiv$ product price ratio $\equiv$ slope of budget line of each individual, is the condition for utility-maximization by consumers. Since both MRS and RPT equal the common product price ratio, they are equal to each other, so the requirement is fulfilled.

tion such that the ratio of their *marginal utilities* (the increase in well-being or satisfaction derived from consuming one more unit of a good) or their MRS, equals the ratio of their prices, which is the slope of their *budget line* (the set of consumption bundles implying a given total cost under prevailing prices). Since all consumers have the same MRS, their indifference curves are tangent in the set-up of the Edgeworth box, so efficiency in distribution holds, even without direct trades between Suzy and Bob (see Figure 2.2). These arguments are summarized in the second portion of the table.

Finally, consider efficiency in the mix of goods produced by society, which requires that the available resources could not be used to produce a different set of goods, thereby making at least one person better off and nobody else worse off. Economists intuitively expect that this kind of efficiency will be achieved, since any welfare improvement obtainable through alteration of the product mix would be communicated to producers via relative product prices and attendant profit possibilities. An equilibrium, in which profits are equalized across industries, thus presupposes attainment of the optimal product mix.

More formally, efficiency in product mix requires that the *production possibility frontier* (PPF, the set of output combinations (x, y) such that the quantity of x is a maximum for each y, given available resources and production technology) should be tangent to 'society's indifference curve' or, more meaningfully, that it should have the same slope, at equilibrium, as the indifference curve of each individual in society.[5] Now the slope of the PPF (known as the *rate of product transformation*) is the rate at which one product can be transformed into another by reallocating inputs across industries, and this is equivalent to the ratio of the *marginal costs* (the cost of producing one more unit) of the goods; and the slope of an indifference curve is the MRS, which equals the ratio of the marginal utilities of the goods. But in perfect competition, each producer will produce until the price he can get in the market equals the marginal cost of production, and if each price equals each marginal cost, then the ratio of marginal costs (which is the slope of the PPF) equals the ratio of the goods' prices. And on the other hand, the theory of the consumer tells us that each consumer maximizes utility by consuming goods in proportions such that their MRS equals the price ratio. Thus, through profit-maximization by producers and utility-maximization by consumers, the price ratio

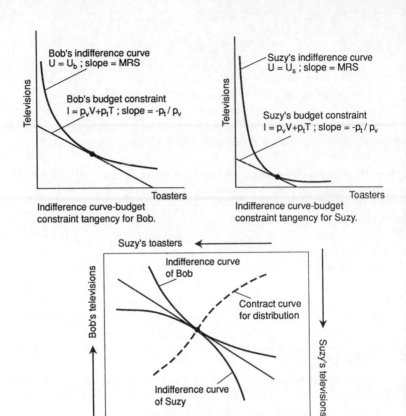

Indifference curve-budget constraint tangency for Bob.

Indifference curve-budget constraint tangency for Suzy.

Edgeworth box for distribution of television sets and toasters to Bob (lower left origin) and Suzy (upper right origin). Line between indifference curves indicates common slope of budget lines and marginal rates of substitution.

U	level of utility
U_b	a constant utility level for Bob
U_s	a constant utility level for Suzy
I	income
p_t	price of toasters
p_v	price of televisions
T	number of toasters
V	number of televisions
MRS	marginal rate of substitution

FIG. 2.2.

Efficiency in distribution under competitive capitalism

Utility maximization by consumers Bob and Suzy leads to efficient allocation of television sets (v) and toasters (t) among them, so that it is impossible to make Suzy better off without making Bob worse off.

will be equated to both the slope of the PPF, and the slopes of consumers' indifference curves (see Figure 2.3). Efficiency in the mix of goods must therefore have been obtained once market equilibrium is established in the economy as a whole. These arguments are summarized in the final section of Table 1, which also provides brief, formal statements of all three efficiency conditions.

2.2.3 Social Dimensions, Stewardship, and Bequest

Although economists' analyses of capitalism do not often devote much attention to the impact of economic arrangements on the satisfaction of social and nonmaterial needs, this does not indicate the absence of relevant arguments. The one most commonly put forward is that by dispensing with centralized authority over the economic management of society, capitalism is consistent with a high degree of personal liberty, including but not limited to freedoms of economic choice. Economic competition and pluralism are also said to be uniquely consistent with the free competition of ideas in the arts and sciences, and in politics, capitalist free enterprise is linked by some proponents with political democracy.[6]

According to some arguments, individual liberty also supports optimal feasible attainment of a wide variety of personal values. As stated previously, workers need accept unpleasant or dangerous working conditions or social relations in the production process only if they find that their best possible overall arrangement includes these features. A capitalist system leaves workers in principle free to be self-employed or to join, or link up to form, a workers' cooperative, a participatory firm, or an egalitarian enterprise, according to their tastes. Relations of hierarchy and subordination are entered into only when accepted by free choice, since no socially prescribed system of caste or class status exists under capitalism. Freedom of ideas, religion, education, and cultural expression also provide nurturing conditions for personal growth in intellectual, spiritual, and aesthetic dimensions, as well as for personal advancement through investment in 'human capital'.

Resource husbandry may not appear to all readers to be the strong suit of the capitalist economy. Yet proponents of capitalism argue that exclusive property rights over resources provides incentives to use them optimally, whereas common ownership or the absence of individual ownership rights leads people to abuse their

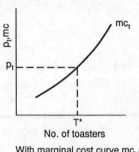

With marginal cost curve mc_t and market price p_t, profit-maximizing toaster maker chooses output T^*.

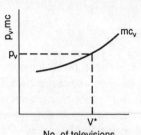

With marginal cost curve mc_v and market price p_v, profit-maximizing television maker chooses output V^*.

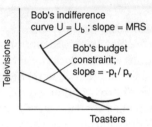

Indifference curve-budget constraint tangency for Bob

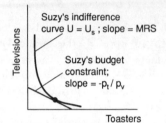

Indifference curve-budget constraint tangency for Suzy

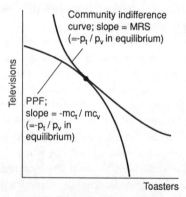

Tangency of production possibility frontier for televisions and toasters with highest attainable community indifference curve

U	level of utility
U_b	a constant utility level for Bob
U_s	a constant utility level for Suzy
I	income
p_t	price of toasters
p_v	price of televisions
T	number of toasters
V	number of televisions
MRS	marginal rate of substitution
mc	marginal cost
mc_t	marginal cost of toasters
mc_v	marginal cost of televisions
PPF	production possibility frontier

Fig. 2.3.

Efficiency in product mix under competitive capitalism

Profit maximization by television and toaster makers and utility maximization by consumers lead to efficiency in the mix of goods produced, meaning that no other combination of televisions and toasters could make one consumer better off while leaving others no worse off.

freedom of access to a resource. The classic example is of grazing pasture, which will ideally be managed by any one cattleman who owns it in such a way as to maximize its sustainable return. If many cattle herders each had access to the pasture without any one owning it, they would tend to overgraze it, since the damage to the pasture is shared by all of them, while the benefit of a little extra grazing seems (mistakenly, in a sense) capable of being captured exclusively by each individual cattle owner. Although the private owner of a pasture or similar resource is mortal, and might therefore become shortsighted regarding the care of his resource as he grows older, this shortsightedness can be overcome, in principle, because ownership rights include the ability to bequeath it to his heirs, or to capitalize its value by selling it. The sale price will reflect the value of the resource in future use, and will therefore motivate him to care for it properly right up to the day of sale.

Capitalism's ability to generate savings and capital accumulation rates sufficient to bring about sustained economic growth is often adduced on the basis of historical evidence from the Industrial Revolution in Europe and countries of European settlement, more recently joined by Japan and other high-growth Asian economies. While classical economics simplified matters by assuming all saving to be efficiently in the hands of frugal capitalists, contemporary economics presents a less socially-delineated theory of savings and investment choices, wherein a society's aggregate investment rate depends on individuals' preferences for present versus future consumption, on their decisions about the 'smoothing' of consumption (given an uneven income stream and varying family needs) over the life cycle, and on desires to leave personal bequests, on the supply side, and on the expected returns from available investment opportunities, on the side of demand. From a micro-economic perspective, one may both argue that adequate savings tend in practice to be generated by these forces, and that no optimal saving rate can in any case be defined independently of the preferences of the existing population. (Some macro-economists have worried, however, about the consistency of autonomous savings decisions with stable growth of output and population—the famous 'knife-edge' problem of Harrod.[7])

Finally, having in our discussion of static efficiency considered capitalism's effectiveness at converting resources into products according to known techniques, we must now consider the system's ability to improve the 'terms of trade' between inputs and outputs, over time, by generating new, more productive, technologies. Here, the claims put forward by pure economic theory have been far more modest than the folklore and popular wisdom of capitalism. Whereas that wisdom has it that capitalist competition is a powerful engine of technological progress, economic theorists have most often viewed technology as an engineering datum exogenous to the economic process. It is not difficult to suggest reasons why the folk view might be correct, however, and some have already been sketched out in the previous section, where we noted that the producer who succeeds in reducing costs by improving production methods can capture profits until his competitors acquire similar capabilities. Similarly, a producer who learns to make a product of better quality than his competitor may earn an extra measure of profit if some consumers are willing to pay more for the additional satisfaction they derive from it. Moreover, invention as a productive activity appears to be stimulated by capitalist property rights, which allow the inventor (by taking out a patent) to monopolize new methods or products for a period of time, earning monopoly rents as a reward for successful inventive effort. The historical record of technological dynamism under capitalism is broadly supportive of these expectations, and gives advocates a basis for asserting that technological progress is in fact endogenous to the economic arrangements of capitalism.

2.3 Counter-arguments and Problems, Assuming Perfect Competition

While reading the previous section, the critical reader will have thought of many ways in which the ideal case for capitalism would be weakened if the assumptions of perfect competition, free information, no public goods, and no externalities, were dropped. Before considering the problems that would then be raised, in the next section, it is appropriate to consider the fact that even in the ideal world thus far assumed, the capitalist organization of economic life is open to certain criticisms. Such criticisms are taken up in the present section.

The reader will forgive us for restating that the technical assumptions of perfect competition provide no assurance that incomes will exceed or even reach subsistence levels in market equilibrium. This observation could be viewed as one of the analytical advances of neoclassical economics over the classical writers, who, as noted, assumed wages equal to subsistence, sometimes even in the presence of unemployment. Of course, those whose incomes fall below their subsistence requirements in a perfectly competitive and *laissez-faire* society might be counted on simply to perish, or at least to emigrate, making the subsistence argument true *ex post*; but a system that allows starvation as part of its equilibrium adjustment mechanisms can be rated poorly with respect to basic needs provision.

Even when incomes reach the level at which basic necessities can in principle be obtained, critics who would give priority to the needs of the poor might argue that the market leaves something to be desired as a mechanism for providing those necessities, if it tends to generate income inequality and if there exist economies of scale in the production and distribution of goods. Suppose that basic types of food, clothing, and shelter can be provided most cheaply in very large quantities, but that only 20 per cent of the population are poor and demand these goods. Then resources will flow into production of the kinds of goods demanded by those with higher incomes, and the production and distribution of the more basic varieties of goods will take place on a smaller scale, as a result of which the poor will have to pay more for them, and will be poorer in real terms. In a sense, this criticism amounts to blaming the market for treating the demands of the poor like all other demands—equally, in so far as they are backed by purchasing power—and making no distinction between critical needs and discretionary wants or desires.

In the previous section, we intimated that the claim that distribution according to the value of the marginal product of each factor supplied in production is fair, is subject to challenge. What are the arguments involved? In the first place, in order to justify distributing income according to people's contributions of the resources that they command, one must be prepared to defend the existing distribution of (ownership claims on) those resources. This must include the defense of inheritence—a defense that could be based on the idea that the right to make bequests is a source of the bestower's incentives to produce and invest, and one that would have to contend with the counter-argument that the resulting inequalities among members of the inheritor's generation are unfair. Included in such a defense, too, there might have to be a justification of any present inequalities that have resulted from past plunder,

feudal privileges, slave-holding, and the like. Also to be justified
would be the maintenance of wealth inequalities that derive from
blind luck, in both the remote and the most recent past.

Assuming that the distribution of asset holdings is acceptable, one
must also explain why permitting one's land or funds to be used
gives rise to the same right to be remunerated, according to the
value of the marginal product of the asset, as arises from devoting
one's time and energy, and possibly risking one's health, in
production. To accept the view of neoclassical economics that each
productive factor contributes to output (and by extension, to the
value of output) according to its technical characteristics and the
way in which it is combined with other inputs, as opposed to Marx's
view that only labor creates value,[8] does not in itself suffice, for one
cannot reward the plot of land or the machine, and the 'factor
return' in question will go to its *owner*, who does nothing but make
his or her resources available. A partial justification can be built
around the need to motivate the owner to direct this resource into its
most productive use, but those who question the equivalence of
labor and property claims to the returns from production, may view
such arguments as unacceptable, and may ask whether effective
alternative institutions for allocating inanimate means of production
cannot be devised. Even those willing to accept the incentive
argument for cases in which it appears applicable might reject it for
the many situations in which a property owner earns a monopoly or
scarcity rent on property that would have been made available even
at a lower level of compensation.[9]

Differences in income that are attributable to variations in the
quantity and quality of labor will also be challenged, by some, on
the grounds that it is effort, not innate skill, strength, or a good
childhood environment, that deserves to be rewarded. Some of the
rewards for scarce skills, like those of a talented athlete, can be
considered rents which, by definition, are not really needed as
incentives. The problem, however, is that differences in labor
productivity due to effort cannot always be separated from those due
to ability, and differences in ability due to genes or the advantages of
upbringing cannot be distinguished from those due to education.
But, it is argued, society needs to maintain incentives to work hard,
and to invest in skills and education, and it also needs to provide
motivation to parents to raise their children in a socially appropriate
way. Once again, then, inequalities of return, including those that

might be excluded as unfair or unnecessary, if only it were possible to distinguish them, are justified by their defenders on pragmatic grounds. This may or may not convince ethical critics.

Efficiency, Social Effects, and Dynamics   The main point to be made with respect to the claim that capitalist economic arrangements are efficient is that while that claim is unassailable under the assumption of perfect competition, claims that efficiency in production, distribution, and output mean that consumer satisfaction is 'maximized' can be misleading, because the aggregation of preferences in perfect competition is always weighted by purchasing power. If there is something to the concept of consumer sovereignty, then, it is that it is demand backed by purchasing power, not consumer preference in the abstract, that is sovereign.

Many bookshelves could probably be filled with the attacks on capitalism made by those who view it as a destroyer of social values and of the quality of life. Alienation, over-specialization in the factory, the breeding of competitiveness and acquisitiveness, and the undermining of community solidarity, have all been attributed to the system, and these charges would be heard even if markets were perfectly competitive. Among the more important critiques are those that argue the endogeneity of values and preferences to the system of social and economic organization.

While neoclassical economics takes preferences as given, a strong case can be made that people's preferences, values, character, etc., are affected by their social environments, including the nature of economic arrangements. If this is so, then questions may be raised as to the kinds of personal, ethical, aesthetic, and other traits cultivated by capitalism. As Frank Knight put it, competitive enterprise is a game the playing of which places primacy upon certain skills and attitudes, while penalizing others.[10] If it is true, as many argue, that capitalism encourages acquisitive individualism, and that its behavioral premises stand in uneasy contradiction to the civic and community virtues promoted by the modern nation-state and by most religions, then an alternative economic system that encouraged such virtues more consistently could conceivably be preferred to it on these grounds, whether or not also on others.

With regard to the stewardship of nonrenewable resources, not all critics would accept the view that private ownership rights provide the best possible incentives for careful exploitation merely because the capitalized future value of a preserved resource is captured by the owner. For example, some critics feel that competition to extract the world's limited supply of fossil fuels does not adequately consider future energy needs. But defenders can argue that if energy were expected to be scarce in the future, owners of known reserves would have an incentive to delay exploiting them, since their value can be expected to rise over time. As long as we assume perfect competition and efficient markets, the argument then comes down to whether private individuals have less accurate forecasting capacities than the critics or members of public commissions; the latter, it could be said, are themselves in a position to make significant profits under capitalist arrangements if they are in fact better forecasters. (Other familiar arguments about resources and the environment involve externalities, and are therefore left to the next section.)

A well-known challenge to capitalism's properties with regard to the generation of savings centers on the idea that future members of society are not represented in the savings decisions of a decentralized market system. Late-developing countries, including Germany, Russia, and Japan, used state interventions to raise capital accumulation rates in support of economic growth. Contemporary underdeveloped nations may judge spontaneous savings to be inadequate, given the long time frame of European industrialization, the low savings rates in contemporary economies such as the United States, and the higher investment rates of socialist states and of capitalist nations (such as Japan and Norway) that intervene in their economies on behalf of investment. Defenders of *laissez-faire*, however, assert that private investors do consider posterity in their investment choices, and that there is no reason to assume that a public body can better speak for those not yet born, or that it would be motivated to do so, since the latter are not at present voters or participants in the political process. Also, one can take the position that growth is not a good in its own right, and that the present generation should be free to consume the fruits of its labor, or to invest them in the future, as its members may individually prefer.

2.4 Counter-arguments and Problems, Relaxing Perfect Competition

We step closer to reality by allowing that some industries may contain a few dominant firms; that some firms may have price-setting discretion; that workers, farmers, or entrepreneurs may collaborate both economically and politically; that there may be external effects of production and consumption activities; that there may be public goods which cannot be produced profitably by private enterprises; and that consumers, factor suppliers, and business managers may lack perfect information and perfect, costless capabilities of collecting and weighing information.

To begin with, alongside doubts already aired about capitalism's adequacy in the provision of material needs, we must consider certain flaws in the frictionless depiction of competition in a world of perfect information and full mobility of resources. Our tomato and carrot example serves well enough here. If too many tomatoes and too few carrots are brought to market, it may not be possible to grow more of the latter and less of the former until next year arrives. This year's planting decisions were simply based on erroneous expectations, so tomato growers will have to take losses, carrot growers will enjoy extra profits, and consumers will have to be satisfied with a less than ideal mix of produce in the market. This divergence between decisions based on expectations, and actual realizations, is repeated over and over again in every branch of a competitive economy, producing financially pinched investors and unemployed workers, happy windfall recipients and wasted resources, even as it creates signals for future resource allocation and rewards for superior forecasting. With imperfect human knowledge and forecasting abilities, the competitive process is neither completely without friction nor fully even-handed in the outcomes dished out to equally well-informed economic agents. Among the issues raised at the micro-level are the risks borne by workers whose skills could become obsolete, and for whom retraining may be costly or infeasible, especially at a more mature age (note the illustration of vulnerability due to division of labor). Also arising here are the costs of job seeking and relocation that fall on workers and their families. The macro-economic counterparts of these problems are the adversities facing members of the community because of the failure of a real-world capitalist system to guarantee full employment, and the suffering that may result from the alternation of growth with recession or depression, and from the consequent uncertainties affecting large segments of the population.

Other questions about the equity of income distribution in a capitalist economy arise when the assumption of perfect competition is dropped. Monopoly in product markets means that income is redistributed (as compared to a competitive situation) from consumers to producers, while monopsony among employers of labor (for example, the largest employer in a 'company town') means that income shifts from workers to the companies that hire them. Organized farmers may achieve price guarantees that shift income from consumers of their products, and any industry obtaining protection from foreign competition takes a bite from the income of buyers, who are denied both the option of buying lower-cost imports and the beneficial effects of foreign competition on the prices charged by domestic producers. Successfully organized workers may also boost their wages, which could ultimately affect consumers, including those with jobs not benefiting from unionization. Under imperfectly competitive conditions, women and members of minority groups may suffer discrimination in selection for good jobs, and may be paid less for doing the same job than are males and members of the majority.

Information problems also create trade-offs between incentives and maximum productivity, in the case of invention and technology change. The right to monopolize new technical knowledge, granted by patents, is simultaneously an incentive to invention, by virtue of the prospects of reward which it creates, and an obstacle to the rapid dissemination of knowledge, which if more widely diffused could more quickly lower production costs or raise product quality, with direct benefit to the consumer. Proponents of socialism have sometimes depicted this dilemma as an illustration of the social inefficiency of capitalism, but it is unclear how the trade-off can be avoided entirely, unless fully as many equally able inventors can be inspired to the same degree by medals, or by intrinsic satisfaction.

Imperfect competition also reduces efficiency. When producers have monopoly power, they will produce less than the efficient amount, in the sense that they could turn out additional units for less (that is, at lower marginal cost) than what those units are worth to consumers (the price that consumers are willing to pay). When employers of labor have monopsony power, they will hire fewer workers, causing labor to be misallocated to industries in which it has a lower marginal product, assuming that it finds employment at all; general monopsony power by employers, or monopoly power by organized workers, or both, could lead to some workers not being employed at all.

The existence of externalities means that the unregulated market, without government intervention, is inefficient. If production emits pollutants or spoils the beauty of a landscape, the profit-seeking producer will not take into account these costs of production, which are borne by society but don't show up as expenditures affecting the production decision. The good is likely to end up being produced in excessive quantities, in the sense that its true marginal cost, including the portion borne by the public, exceeds its marginal benefit, reflected in the price consumers are willing to pay. Or the good may be produced by a socially inefficient method, if less destructive methods are available but are rejected because of their higher private cost.

Consumers may also desire a certain supply of goods, such as the services of air traffic controllers and coast guard patrols, which it is not feasible to provide on a for-profit basis, since beneficiaries will not voluntarily contract to pay for the benefits that they will receive in any case. These are what we call public goods. Without collective organization to provide these goods using revenue collected by some form of tax, they will not be supplied or will be supplied in inefficiently small quantities; this means that resources are being used to produce a non-optimal mix of products that includes too many units of private goods and too few units of public goods.

Social and Intertemporal Problems Debate over the social costs and benefits of capitalism often centers on whether freedom of choice is sufficient when choice is restricted for many individuals by their initial factor endowments. Marx asserted that the freedom of labor in a capitalist society is double-edged: workers are free to enter into a labor contract with the capitalist of their choice, but are forced to do so with *some* capitalist because they do not own any means of production, and are therefore dependent upon capital owners who offer them the only available way to earn a living from their labor. Other radical critiques counterpose liberties and rights, asserting that rights to basic material and social needs (including education, health care, and employment) which *could* be guaranteed by societies at a certain level of prosperity, are not so guaranteed under capitalism.

Political and social participation, equality, and dignity are also said to be abridged within capitalist systems. In the workplace, the hierarchical nature of production and of claims on its fruits are said to cause alienation. Going further, it is argued that while the

assumption that people prefer leisure to labor and will work only if
financially compensated is a safe one to make under capitalist
conditions, this is a result of those conditions, not of human nature;
in an ideal society, labor is an end in itself, the ultimate form of
human self-expression and self-realization. The fact that workers
freely choose to take jobs within alienating organizational structures
does not prove the ideal character of those employment arrangements, these critics argue, because the economic reality includes
widespread unemployment and imperfect access to funds with
which workers might establish alternative enterprises. In addition,
the liberty to offer one's labor in a sale that entails forfeiting any say
in decision-making or profit sharing, is viewed as the abridgment of
a different right—that of participation in the workplace, which
would be embraced as fundamental and inalienable in an ideal
social system, according to these critics.

As already mentioned under efficiency, once the possibility of
externalities is admitted, capitalist enterprises' inherent lack of
interest in the environmental damage which might be caused by
their activities can be added to the list of the system's potential
shortcomings. The externality problem may also exist with respect
to savings and investment, in the sense that decisions on these
matters taken by individuals in isolation from one another may
produce a less than optimal outcome compared with choices made
collectively.[11] Public coordination and intervention may be justified
on these grounds.

2.5 Modified Capitalisms

We have already intimated that pure capitalism, in which private
ownership and unregulated exchange relations exist in the complete
absence of economic intervention or planning by society, is more a
theoretical construct than an observable reality. In this section, we
turn to the major modifications of pure capitalism found in actual
capitalist societies. The discussion is organized around general
classes of interventions, arranged from least to most fundamental in
their alteration of pure capitalist institutions, according to our
theoretical sense of that system's core characteristics. A few general
comments will be offered at each stage regarding the importance of
these modifications to the system's nature and evaluation.

Before considering government interventions in the economy in the sense in which that term is understood by economists, it may be helpful to recall the 'baseline' role of government and/or of the legal system that we have assumed to be present even in the perfectly competitive, *laissez-faire* capitalism with which we have dealt, thus far: protection of private property rights and enforcement of contracts. Without a collective or public institution performing these roles, it would be difficult to explain why, if people are as thoroughly self-interested as most economic analysis assumes, their pursuit of wealth and ease stops short of stealing goods from one another and ignoring contractual undertakings.[12] The government may also be presumed to stand behind the currency that circulates as the legally endorsed means of exchange so basic to the capitalist economy. Although both of these functions of government could be included under the provision of public goods, to be discussed in the next subsection, they are so fundamental that they are not viewed by most economists as interventions at all.

2.5.1 *Correcting Market Failures*

From the standpoint of the model of perfect competition and the associated ideology of free market economics, the first type of intervention to be discussed is the least contradictory to the essence of capitalism. The interventions covered are only meant to treat blemishes in the real economy so as to make it more like the ideal one. In fact, despite the deeply rooted philosophical preference of western economics for *laissez-faire*, most economists take at least some of the 'corrective' measures grouped here so much for granted that they would tend to see them as part of basic capitalism, not a modification of it. In that case, some of the criticisms of the last section (we will see which ones) could be dismissed as attacks on a 'straw man'.

The measures which we have in mind here include public efforts to prevent the formation of monopolies and the adoption of monopolistic practices by colluding oligopolists (in some versions, the targets would also include unions); corrective taxes and other measures for countering externality problems; and provision of public goods. The first two types of measures, while aimed at correcting situations in which the pursuit of private interests damages public welfare, still rely on free enterprise, since once these measures are in place and enforced, profit maximization is expected to work towards the social interest, as it does ideally in a competitive world without externalities. The best example is the effluent tax, which turns the social cost of pollution into a private cost for the firm, thereby creating incentives either to cut back production or to find less-polluting ways of producing. Moreover, unlike a law banning pollution outright, the tax is expected to lead to 'optimal polluting', since the firm should invest in pollution abatement only up to the point at which the marginal cost of lowering the effluent level equals the marginal benefit to society, on which the tax level is based. (Spending more or forgoing more output to eliminate the pollution entirely would be economically irrational, given its assumed social cost.) Public surveillance and prohibitions on mergers deemed harmful to competition are another simple example of interventions which, once in effect, leave private firms to proceed to solve production and resource allocation problems in the usual decentralized fashion.

The third category of intervention, provision of public goods, requires a definite departure from the principle of voluntary exchange, for it is recognized that individual citizens have no incentive to pay voluntarily for services the total level of which would be little affected by one more subscription.[13] The actual provision of the goods involved is itself often carried out by governmental agencies, but some are and others could be produced by profit-seeking firms that compete for government contracts.

The three new roles introduced in this section may imply a quite substantial government presence in the economy. Anti-trust activity involves costly monitoring and documentation. Judgments must be made with regard to possible trade-offs between competitive industry structure and cost efficiency, which can sometimes be promoted by large scale and by wide command of resources for research and development gained through the exercise of market power. Also, some interventions against monopoly might accept an economies-of-scale rationale for having a single supplier, and proceed by direct regulation (as with public utilities) rather than promotion of competition. Controls over externality problems may require monitoring, taxation, and regulation in the spheres of noise, air, and water pollution in which transportation, agriculture, power generation, and a great many other industries figure. Public goods provision may mean that the government directly undertakes or contracts for the construction of roads, railways, and harbors (often a major item in the total investment expenditure of a society), and that it provides for national defense (the largest chunk of public expenditure in several industrialized countries), and for posts, telecommunications, weather monitoring, coastal patrol and safety, and other functions. The state's role as a producer or purchaser of productive services in the public goods category alone implies that not insignificant shares of national income are claimed by the government through taxation.

2.5.2 The Political Economy of Corrective Interventions

In many cases, it is possible to identify responses to monopoly, externality, and public goods problems that will in principle restore complete economic efficiency. Fitting into this paradigm are: enforcement of appropriate anti-trust laws, determination of correct effluent taxes, and collection of tax revenues sufficient to finance the provision of the desired quantities of public goods, using taxes causing a minimum of disruption to work and investment incentives. One of the major roles of economics in market economies has been that of identifying such optimal policies. But simply to imagine a government manned by public servants who will follow these recommendations is to fail to apply the fundamental principle of economic analysis (which assumes that people act according to their self-interest) to those who man the government and those who involve themselves in political activity. The latter, after all, are also people.

Suppose, therefore, that our evaluation of capitalism as an economic system turns, in important ways, upon the presence of a government pursuing efficiency-inducing policies with regard to competition, externalities, and public goods. In order to reach any conclusions, it will be necessary for us to know something more about the institutions of government that will exist beside those of the capitalist economy, and to form an understanding of how those institutions are likely to behave.

A worst case, for example, might appear to result from assuming an autocratic government that stays in power through the use of force. If the government leaders and staffs take the same view of public life as economic agents are assumed to take of economic activity, then they may be expected to do whatever will increase their incomes and reduce their work-loads. They may fail to break up monopolies or prevent mergers, if they are paid off for the favor; they may permit pollution to continue in exchange for the payment of bribes of smaller amount than the optimal effluent tax (or they may set taxes higher than is optimal, if they can collect more for themselves in that way); and they may use tax revenues to line their pockets, or to aid their own social and ethnic groups, rather than to provide public goods for the society as a whole.

It is reasonable to suppose that the worst abuses could be controlled by making the government accountable to the people, which might be achieved by requiring that it be elected by a majority of them. There may or may not be strong reasons why capitalist countries tend to adopt democratic political institutions, but most of the more industrialized capitalist countries do have such institutions, so certainly capitalist economic forms and these forms of political democracy are not incompatible. The question remains, though, whether even in a democracy, government officials would be properly motivated to strive for the socially optimal response of the economics textbook, and not for divergent goals that suit their own interests. Bureaucracies, for example, may tend to grow in order to promote the interests of their staffs; officials may conspire with polluters, colluders, and sellers of goods (such as weapons systems) to the government because the latter can promise attractive jobs to those officials who leave public service with a record of which they approve; some public goods, the constituencies for which lack adequate power, may not be provided, while others, which benefit powerful interests, may be over-provided. Reasons why democracy may not benefit all of the people equally include inequalities of political power that may be related to unequal economic power; and imperfect monitoring of government by the public, who cannot gather and assess unlimited amounts of information without some cost, and whose members face a free-rider problem with respect to individual monitoring effort. The fact that democracy offers no political guarantees to the members of any group of up to 49.9 per cent of the population that consistently finds itself in the minority, is also worth noting (see the end of the next section).

2.5.3 *Redistribution*

Economists refer to the class of interventions just discussed as remedies for 'market failure'; their basic aim is to create or restore efficiency where the market fails to do so, though the measures that they advocate may also improve economic performance with respect to basic needs provision (of public goods) and (environmental) stewardship, among our evaluative criteria. The type of intervention to which we now turn goes beyond the aim of 'patching up' market failures. When effective political coalitions deem the existing distribution of property and/or the market's distribution of income to be unacceptable, the government may be called upon to transfer income or wealth from some segments of the population to others. Most often, the explicit aim is to help the poorest or neediest, especially those considered unable to help themselves, or in need of a hand to get back on their feet. This does not rule out the possibility of transfers that most help the present or future upper or middle classes—for example, some tuition subsidies for higher education.

In principle, redistribution is a most important modification of the capitalist system: the market and the capitalist production sector are deemed efficient at producing bundles of goods, but the particular bundles produced and the way in which they are distributed are judged socially unacceptable, either because income dispersions or gaps are viewed as too wide, or because the basic material needs of the poorest are going unmet.[14] Judging from the results in Sweden, Norway, other European states, and in some redistributionist states in the Third World, correction of perceived equity and needs-satisfaction defects of capitalism can go quite far towards altering outcomes, without changing the capitalist nature of ownership,[15] enterprise management, and economic coordination and exchange.

It is important to note, however, that a good many observers judge these programs to have had mixed success at redistributing wealth or income without hampering economic efficiency. Almost every practicable tax has effects on incentives or resource allocation; for example, progressive income taxes mean that those in the highest tax brackets have at least somewhat reduced incentives to be more productive, since only part of any extra earnings they generate will actually end up in their hands. Preventing individuals from taking unfair advantage of public benefits like sick pay may require tremendous monitoring expenditures, unless people voluntarily uphold high standards of ethical conduct. Generous unemployment benefits may reduce people's willingness to accept certain types of work, and can make it difficult for employers to discipline employees by the threat of firing them (a side effect that some might consider beneficial, since it may force the employer to find ways of increasing job satisfaction and of making work more intrinsically rewarding).

The extent to which redistribution can be carried out also depends upon political support. Such support may take into account the effects of redistribution on productivity, and the possible trade-offs between equity, efficiency, and other objectives. Which final distributions of income and wealth are politically favored are also, naturally, a function of who holds political power, and what their own objectives are. Altruism or the desire for justice cannot be ruled out as motives, nor should we forget the relevance of more selfish aims, such as the desire to remove the eyesore and annoyance of street people and beggars, or to defuse potentially explosive social conflicts. The conjunction of an economic system that permits wide disparities in wealth and income, with a political system giving formally equal rights to all citizens, may make some leveling through public intervention almost inevitable. However, the same conjunction of capitalism and democracy often allows the wealthy to exercise disproportionate influence, for example through contributions to election campaigns; and even when the influence of each citizen is equal, there are no guarantees that disadvantaged minorities can secure redistributive action favorable to them. This seems amply demonstrated by the fact that, with one in seven American citizens officially declared to be in poverty, neither major political party emphasized public assistance to the poor in its 1988 campaign for the American presidency; both campaigns chose to focus principally on swing constituencies in the middle not only of the ideological but also of the socio-economic spectrum.

2.5.4 Reactive Macro-economic Interventions

Fluctuations in the level of economic activity have been features of capitalist economies since they began to emerge in the trading centers of late medieval Europe. Beginning with the Great Depression of the 1930s, and perhaps partly as a result of the growing enfranchisement of common citizens in the industrial capitalist democracies, cyclical fluctuations of economic activity have been deemed by politically-decisive coalitions to impose unacceptable costs upon various members of society. Thus governments have been asked (or have expeditiously taken upon themselves) to intervene in their national economies to combat unemployment, business stagnation, or inflation, using adjustments in public taxation and spending, and in the rate of money creation and other monetary and financial controls.

With its appearance as a player on the field of macro-economic events, the government assumes a role qualitatively distinct from that which it took on as a corrector of market failures or as a redistributor of market outcomes. With either of these previously discussed classes of interventions, it remained possible to view the market as a self-governing coordinator of economic activity, and to believe in the basic self-sufficiency of the 'invisible hand'. In the case of standard market failures, the government merely ensured that competition was not prevented by collusion and monopoly, it attached a price in exceptional cases where the market had not done so (that is, to externalities), and it stepped in to supply a good that has the unusual properties of 'publicness'. In the case of redistribution, the market is still viewed as an ideal mechanism for allocating resources and producing goods and services; only its distributive results, which depend on initial endowments that are in part determined by accidents and historical processes for which the system itself is not to blame, are viewed as being in need of correction.

Government entry into the field of macro-economic policy, however, indicates that the self-regulating properties of the market economy are inadequate not only in specific instances, but also in the quite general sense that the pressure of disequilibrium forces upon prices is incapable of clearing labor markets, or of ensuring the full utilization of capital, within an acceptable time frame. The government is still not ready to take upon itself the role of coordinator of micro-economic decisions about what should be produced, and which inputs should be used. Atomistic and decentralized private profit and utility-seeking are still viewed as harmonious processes that will lead, on the micro-economic level, to an efficient allocation of resources, satisfying consumers' demands. What is needed, however, is an economic agent with an overview of the entire society, capable of correcting those aggregative imbalances to which the economy is prone from time to time. The government has in no sense entered the field of *planning* economic activity; but it has assumed responsibility for reacting to observed imbalances with what are deemed socially desirable corrective measures.

These statements can be clarified by considering the simplest Keynesian identity for national income,

$$Y = C + I + G,$$

where Y is national income, C is aggregate private consumption, I is aggregate private investment, and G is government spending. (Trade balances and other refinements are ignored.) If national income, as given by the variables on the right hand side, falls short of the level at which the full employment of labor and productive capacity can be sustained, then unemployment will result. If the 'invisible hand' works perfectly, a fully employed economy should generate demand for all of the goods that it produces, with the composition of those goods being determined by the composition of demand, including its division between consumption and investment goods. But for some reason, the mechanism does not work perfectly. Periods of high unemployment alternate with periods of 'overheating' of the economy, which help to produce inflation.

In the above equation, the level of C and I will be determined by the independent, self-interested decisions of a very large number of individual consumers and firms, who, even if they wanted to, would be hard-pressed consciously to coordinate their actions so as to achieve any particular desired effect on an aggregate level. On the other hand, if the government can be viewed as a bureaucratic entity under a single head, the aggregative variable G *can* be set in a conscious manner, to offset any observed imbalance in the sum $C + I + G$. If $C + I$ is low, G can be raised; if $C + I$ is high, G can be lowered.

Such actions by the government are a qualitative departure from the model of *laissez-faire* capitalism; there, consumers and producers were thought capable of bringing about desirable economic outcomes by individually pursuing their own separate interests, without regard for the common good. But now the system is seen to be in need of corrective action by one agent, the government, that compensates for imbalances in the aggregate decisions of the others by acting in conscious pursuit of the common interest, not merely as another self-seeking agent among the many. This analysis makes it clear that if the government really is needed in such a corrective capacity, the performance of the economy will hinge in part on whether it actually acts on behalf of the public, or whether it pursues some agenda of its own. In other words, the concerns of section 2.5.2 are once again relevant.

In so far as government succeeds in nudging the economy closer to full employment of labor and capital, or in calming inflation, these policies may have far-reaching effects on the economy and thereby on our evaluation of total system performance. Unemployment signals economic inefficiency because, even if the price system continues to steer employed resources towards appropriate uses in the right combinations, the idleness of some resources implies that social output remains inside the production possibility frontier, and that less utility is therefore realized by consumers. Successful macroeconomic policies thus contribute to efficient resource utilization, and, by raising output and allowing those otherwise unemployed to earn incomes, to the satisfaction of basic material needs. Macroeconomic stability may also promote savings and investment. Moreover, judging not only by political demands in the market economies but also by the value attached to these ends by workers under socialist economic systems, employment and income stability may be important social needs in their own right. Success in smoothing away economic cycles could be viewed as a major achievement, therefore, in the domain of nonmaterial satisfactions.

However, reactive macro-economic policies do not appear to have had an overwhelming record of success. Indeed, because of problems of timing and fine-tuning, some economists argue that such efforts may themselves contribute to the frequency, duration, or severity of business cycles. Moreover, in so far as capitalist economies exhibit a short-term trade-off between price stability and full employment, interventionist policies may become a political tool for favoring particular constituencies. In democratic countries, a 'political business cycle', wherein politicians fuel economic expansion before elections and fight inflation after them, may emerge as a direct by-product.

2.5.5 Indicative Planning and Industrial Policy

In each of the departures from *laissez-faire* capitalism that we have considered so far the government intervened in the economy in one way or another, but the basic principles of capitalism were maintained, and it continued to be safe to infer from them that no centrally positioned agent took responsibility for coordinating in detail the diverse activities in the economy. This was true even when the idea of self-interested behavior was modified by assuming a government reacting to perceived imbalances at an aggregative level, with the aim of promoting macro-economic equilibrium. The word 'reactive' was used in that discussion to emphasize that, rather than attempting to steer the economy in some desired direction, the fiscal and monetary policies in that modified form of capitalism simply reacted to problems as they occurred. Indicative planning and industrial policy, on the other hand, are attempts to provide direction to economic activities at the industry and even enterprise levels, with premeditation and specificity.

For the government to assume a planning function in the economy may appear at first glance to be overstepping the basic bounds of the capitalist system. Although the issue is essentially one of terminology, we prefer to consider the indicatively planned market systems (such as those found in Sweden, Norway, and France) and systems marked by government-led industrial policies (such as in postwar Japan) to be modified forms of capitalism, provided that they retain private ownership of productive resources, profit-seeking enterprises, and a central coordinating role for the price mechanism. But we agree that these modifications can be a major step away from the original model. Before further describing the institutions that are involved, and justifying retention of the term 'capitalist', we begin by considering the somewhat different sets of arguments that are made for indicative planning and corporative bargaining, on the one hand, and for industrial policy, on the other.

The basic argument for indicative planning starts with the view that the macro-economic problems of modern capitalism are results of institutional changes such as the emergence of concentrations of economic power in the hands of large business firms, labor unions, and other coalitions of economic agents. These changes mean that price-taking behavior is replaced by price-making and by non-atomistic competition for greater shares of output, causing wage and price volatility which monetary authorities find politically difficult to restrain. In the investment sphere, uncertainties over changes in demand, industry composition, and production technologies, become increasingly important because of the lumpiness and scale of major new investments by business enterprises. In forming expectations about business prospects, financiers and managers may give considerable weight to the investment decisions of other firms and to the overall 'business climate', but this means that there is significant interdependence of expectations (or guesses about the economy), and that rather than converging to reasonably accurate anticipations of the future, expectations may tend to rise and fall with the tides of group opinion, influenced by imperfect forecasting indicators, and thereby intensifying the cyclical nature of business activity.

When, for technological and institutional reasons, a return to a more atomistically competitive economy is deemed infeasible, this kind of analysis may lead to the conclusion that greater economic health can be brought about only by planned coordination of business decisions, and by the framing of cooperative agreements among interest groups so as to control counterproductive competition over the distribution of economic rewards. The economy remains capitalist in the sense that enterprises are privately owned and directed, workers are free to seek employment, and incomes are related to labor, capital, and other factor contributions valued at prices at least partly reflecting factor scarcities. However government, in this scenario, establishes planning bodies charged with promoting the overall coordination of economic decisions, and it may also attempt to bring together major labor and business organizations to hammer out agreements on wage, price, and profit constraints.

Although that institution may closely resemble indicative planning, the argument for industrial policy tends to focus on the dynamics of market conditions and technological change, rather than on institutional constraints to perfect competition. The argument may arise in the case of a less developed country looking for ways of catching up with more industrially advanced nations, and judging a *laissez-faire* approach to be a luxury that only the advanced can afford. (This idea will be discussed again in Chapter 5.) But given the rapid pace of technological change and the more intense competition among advanced industrial powers in at least three continents since the late 1970s, essentially the same argument has been put forth even for the most developed economies. The argument is that in order for countries to compete in the international marketplace, they must find ways to replace counter-productive competition among their own firms: they must have an organized strategy in which specific areas of technological advance, and specific industries, are targeted for development, with the support of governmental, financial, research, production, and trade sectors, and must make provisions for firms that would otherwise be competitors to play more complementary and cooperative roles in the process.

Types of Intervention   A spectrum of types of intervention is covered by the terms indicative planning and industrial policy. As has been convenient in other cases, we will describe them in the order of their degree of departure from *laissez-faire* capitalism.

The first aspect of indicative planning to be considered is one in which the government assumes the role of a collector and processor of information, but engages in no coercion or direction of enterprises; these continue to take their decisions quite independently, according to their own goals. In this kind of planning, an iterative planning procedure begins with enterprises communicating their production and input-use intentions to the planning authority, which then collates the individual enterprise plans and draws up an aggregated plan, sector by sector. Initial enterprise plans would have been based, in part, upon firms' anticipations of the behavior of other enterprises, for example, of the availability of their inputs from suppliers, of the actual demand (both final and intermediate) for their products, and of the shares of that demand which they may individually hope to fill. A chance to examine the collated national plan may therefore lead to adjustments in the decisions of the individual enterprises. Revised plans can be resubmitted to the planning authority, and through an iteration process they may converge to a set of mutually consistent decisions on the parts of the enterprises. The planning authority will have played the role only of an information broker, in this process.[16] Of the issues raised above, such planning is mostly aimed at the reduction of uncertainty associated with lumpy (that is, large and indivisible) investment decisions.

A small step towards more active involvement in the economy occurs if planners try to assist the convergence process by themselves checking for inconsistencies in the collated information, such as an imbalance between the planned output of the steel industry, and the steel requirements of other industries.[17] Through discussions with producers and users of such a commodity the planners may try to assist them in arriving at a more consistent set of decisions, thus avoiding overinvestment or production bottlenecks.

Here, the planners may again be doing no more than gathering and disseminating information, and the increased involvement only takes the form of a more active role in interpreting the data gathered, and in bringing relevant points to the attention of those concerned.

A major step further down the road of intervention occurs in both indicative planning and industrial policy when the planning body attempts to promote its own conceptions of which industries ought to expand, and which should be allowed to decline. These conceptions might be based on an analysis of the strategic options open to the nation's producers, or on social considerations, like the desire to promote development in particular regions of the country, to reduce urban concentration, to protect the environment, to diversify the economy, or to create more jobs of a skill-intensive nature. Whatever the origins of the planners' objectives, their promotion of these goals may be given teeth by selective tax and subsidy programs, and by controls over the allocation of building permits, of import and export licenses, and of access to credit. Such measures fall short of constituting commands directly dictating enterprise decisions; they do, however, alter the economic environment facing firms, and, by changing the relative profitability of alternative courses of action, they can provide decisive economic incentives. Thus, going beyond the first, more neutral, role of a facilitator of consistency in the capitalist economy, the state enters the business of steering the economy down particular paths chosen by political actors, perhaps in consultation with representatives of the business, finance, labor, or scientific sectors.

Finally, the corporative aspect of some versions of planning and industrial policy should be mentioned. The idea here, that of negotiating a framework for wage and price increases at the national level, arises rather naturally in countries such as Sweden, in which both the most important employers and the great majority of workers belong to associations and unions, and where the organizations on both sides are national in scope, or have a federated structure with an overall umbrella organization. Government may enter national negotiations between these organizations as an interested third party, or as a referee, or may simply establish rules to guide their negotiating process. The general point, as suggested earlier in this section, is that since employers and workers are both highly organized, and the model of perfectly competitive wage and price determination is of little relevance, inter-group competition to increase profits, on the one side, and real wages, on the other, can result in a spiral in which both prices and wages rise, without a clear victor. Antagonistic actions on the two sides also emphasize the 'zero sum game' dimension of their relationship, that is, the extent to which the gain of one must be the loss of the other. If cooperative understandings can be reached, on the other hand, both sides might focus on the 'positive sum' possibility of raising productivity, with the benefits to be shared out in the form of both higher wages and higher profits. And the government, in fostering such agreements, might succeed in controlling inflation without resorting to contractionary policies that would threaten to cause a recession.

Planning and Capitalism   Surely, once the planning body or group undertakes to steer economic activity in particular directions, and when wages and prices are substantially influenced by nationally negotiated agreements, the institutions of the economic system have moved some distance away from those by which we initially identified capitalism. The first institutional premise, that it is the owners of resources who alone determine their disposition or use, is at least modified by the presence of a central planning function. The third premise, that prices are determined by the free negotiation of the involved parties, might be said to be respected at a more overarching level; but the freedom to determine prices at the level of individual transactions, including specific employment contracts, may be constrained by the agreements reached nationally, even if it is true that those agreements are negotiated by agents formally representing the interests of the parties at the 'bottom'.

Compared, however, with centrally planned socialism, in which the government both owns and directs the use of the means of production, and in which prices play a relatively insignificant role in resource allocation, an economy such as Sweden's in which there are centralized efforts to steer economic activity, and general negotiations over wages and prices, remains fairly close to the original capitalist model. The great majority of the means of production are privately owned, and by far the larger part of production is by private enterprises, which determine what they will produce and what inputs they will hire primarily on the basis of profitability. To the extent that national planning influences an enterprise's decisions, it does so mainly by changing what it is profitable for it to do, in the same way as an effluent tax changes the incentives of a polluter. Wage and price agreements may reduce the flexibility of the price system, especially at the micro-level, but the extent to which they dictate specific prices should not be overstated, and the agreements themselves are still influenced by the basic market forces of scarcity and demand.

It is interesting to note that the motivation animating planning in a market economy can vary over a wide spectrum. On the one hand, the government may act primarily to assist the private sector, sometimes rather in the fashion of the promoter of a cartel. Production, profit, and technological advancement may be its basic aims; Japan in the 1950s and 1960s provides a possible example. On the other hand, the planners may have a social agenda that is quite distinct from the immediate interests of business, including regional, workplace, or distributive goals; a good example here might be Sweden. These differences in goals parallel differences in political base. Thus the indicatively planned capitalist economy may be principally a partnership between the state and private business (1960s France); or alternatively, when coupled with labor or populist political leadership, it might constitute an attempt to harness capitalism for a variety of social ends (Norway or Sweden).

2.6 The Performance of Modified Capitalism

In section 2.5, we found that the range of modifications of a strict free enterprise system, involving various degrees and kinds of public intervention, is quite broad. And we have already noted that any evaluation of capitalism under the assumption that unregulated private decision-makers, or 'the free market', are the sole allocators of resources, may amount to attacking a 'straw man'. Certainly, such unregulated forms of capitalism cannot be found in present-day industrial market economies. Thus our assessment of the strengths and weaknesses of an entirely unregulated capitalism may contain a warning to some who are still inclined to view such a system as desirable, but the more relevant questions in the final years of the twentieth century would appear to be how the various *modified* forms of capitalism compare as systems of economic organization, and which of them are more desirable.

We might begin by noting what these variants of capitalism are capable of doing, and what they cannot do. To begin on the 'can do' side: in so far as unbridled capitalism's defects include environmental degradation, inadequate provision of public goods, and monopolies, there are standard corrections for these 'market failures', which work if applied properly. If one's concern is with inequalities and with the fact that not everyone may be able to meet his or her basic material needs, redistributive programs are in principle capable of redressing this problem, too. If it is macroeconomic uncertainty and unemployment that is of concern, a set of policy 'patch-ups' seems to be available, once again. If inconsistency of investment plans or lack of coordination, in achieving national economic goals, or both, are considered a problem, indicative planning can be called upon. And if politically endorsed goals such as regional balance or achieving a higher rate of capital formation seem to be neglected by the unregulated market, economic levers can be built into the plan to induce individuals and enterprises to move towards those objectives. Thus, variants of capitalism offer hope of improving the system's performance with respect to every one of our evaluative standards, from basic needs and equity (redistribution), to efficiency (correcting 'market failure'), to meeting certain social needs, protecting natural resources, and promoting economic growth (environmental regulation and indicative planning).

The limitations of these tools, and of capitalist systems employing them, can be listed under two headings. First, we must consider problems with the effectiveness of each remedy, likely political constraints on their use, and trade-offs between desirable goals; then, we will ask whether there are drawbacks of capitalism that these remedies simply do not address. With regard to the provision of public goods, the correction of incentives in the case of externalities, and the thwarting of anti-competitive practices, political constraints have been discussed above (section 2.5.2). An instance of a trade-off between goals was mentioned in the case of anti-trust policy, where the efficiency benefits of greater competition might sometimes have to be balanced against the productivity and technological advantages of larger firms. Redistribution provides examples of all three issues: there may be problems with effective implementation, due to the difficulty of identifying the needy, possibilities of fraud, etc.; there are likely to be political limits to redistribution in capitalist democracies when those who have can defend their interests in the political arena, or when a majority votes selfishly with respect to redistribution towards a poor minority; and there are possible trade-offs between the extent to which the economy provides for the disadvantaged, and the productivity it elicits from its limited resources. (In so far as voters perceive such trade-offs, It Is the majority's judgments about the marginal benefit of more equity versus more efficiency—and not the views of the poor minority—that are most likely to pose decisive limits to redistribution.)

The effectiveness of macro-economic policies is a matter on which professional economists are further from consensus today than they were twenty years ago. There is radical disagreement not only about whether it is humanly possible to time their use so that they are applied when actually needed, but also about whether any of them in fact have predictable effects. Nevertheless, a student of old-style (Keynesian) postwar macro-economics might find evidence from recent decades that standard, theorized relationships hold (for example, a sharp recession in the United States in the early 1980s brought down the inflation rate) but might be concerned that different macro-economic goals, such as full employment and low inflation, are in conflict with each other, and that the cost of moving towards one by moving away from the other is getting greater with time. In this regard, one can raise questions about whether the costs of macro-economic stabilization, such as the one successfully carried out under President Reagan in the 1980s, are acceptable either by political standards (in that particular case, they did seem to pass this test), or when judged by independent criteria of welfare, including an accounting of their impact on the poor.

With regard to indicative planning, observation of the major planned capitalist economies in the early postwar decades shows relative success in smoothing out economic fluctuations, supporting the macro-economic theory behind such planning. Government tax and other policies have also succeeded in bringing about high rates of investment. Price and wage controls have been less successful, inflation being at least as serious as in unplanned capitalist economies, and economic growth rates have been approximately comparable to those of 'unplanned' economies. Although Japanese success in the global marketplace has led many to take a second look at strategic industrial policy planning, the usefulness of indicative planning *per se*, and the affordability of an extensive regulatory and welfare net have been called into question with increasing frequency, in recent years, in such countries as France, the Netherlands, and

Sweden. While environmentalists and critics on the left bemoan the
irrelevance or insufficiency of past policies in the social democratic
countries, business interests and conservatives point to the efficiency
costs of market interventions, including threats to investment and
work incentives and to the general dynamism of the market system.
Indeed, some economists have argued that it is under conditions of
imperfect information and less than 'textbook-perfect' competition
that the real advantages of the market process over attempts at
central planning are brought out. (These arguments will be
discussed in Chapter 3.) The resurgence of such viewpoints in recent
years is illustrated by the fact that, whereas a government planning
role seemed a real political prospect even in the free-enterprise
oriented United States of the 1970s, the 1980s have seen an anti-
intervention, pro-market backlash capture the political center stage
in the United States and Britain, and from there make headway
even in a nominally socialist France, most of Western Europe, and,
in philosophical influence at least, across the Communist world from
Poland to Vietnam.

There is a different type of limitation of the modified capitalisms
considered in this chapter, which we have not yet touched on. This
concerns aspects of the criticism of the basic capitalist system that
are simply not addressed, and probably not capable of being
addressed, by this set of system amendments. These problems are
related especially to the impact of the economic system on the social,
personal, and other nonmaterial dimensions of people's lives. A
prime example is the question of the impact of the system on
individual character, preferences, and values. If the view that
capitalism encourages acquisitiveness has any merit as a criticism,
the point seems to remain valid even if capitalism is rendered more
humane, from a certain point of view, by provision of adequate
social services and welfare guarantees to all citizens. The desirability
of capitalist organization from the standpoint of the quality of
working life is also not affected by any of the policies and
interventions discussed here. If people do not find their work
interesting or challenging, if they suffer psychological stress and a
diminution of self-respect owing to their subordination on the job or
their depersonalized treatment as a means of production, then there
is no reason to expect things to change simply because wealth is
more equally distributed, the government offers inducements to
reduce urban concentration, or recessions are less severe and shorter

in duration. (An exception, noted earlier, is that the elimination of unemployment or provision of generous benefits to the unemployed may lead to different strategies for managing labor.)

In the case of workplace characteristics, it would not be entirely unreasonable to view implementation of employee participation in management or quality-of-working-life programs, as being modifications of capitalism in the same sense as are income redistribution and indicative planning. These modifications might also be brought about through government inducements or legal requirements, which could perhaps be viewed as methods of correcting a market failure. Measures of this type have been enacted in several European economies, which we none the less continue to consider capitalistic.

It is largely for reasons of organization that we will not give more attention, in this chapter, to changes in the nature of work. Workers' participation in management will be the central feature distinguishing from other economic systems the arrangements to be treated in Chapter 4. For that reason, we will hold discussion of this theme for that part of the book.[18]

2.7 Summary and Conclusions

Capitalism is an economic system in which there is private ownership of resources, self-ownership and non-alienability of labor power, and freedom to engage in exchanges with other economic agents at uncontrolled, mutually agreed prices. There is planning and hierarchical coordination within production units, but no such planning of the overall economy, in which coordination is due to the operation of market forces. Incomes accrue to individuals as returns on labor and non-labor resources contributed to the production process, and reflect the scarcity of factors relative to demand, luck or success in entrepreneurship and arbitrage, and the distribution of initial factor endowments.

Markets provide coordination for the economy in the sense that investors and owners of firms seek to channel their resources into activities promising the highest return, and differences between the marginal valuation of products by consumers and the marginal cost of their production by firms are signalled to firms by the appearance of excess profits or losses in the activities concerned. Thus expansion and contraction of production in firms, and allocation of new capital across industries, tend toward an equilibrium in which the marginal return on capital is the same across activities. Competitive bidding for labor and other inputs leads to a similar result, and in combination, these tendencies imply that the total value of output is maximized after appropriate adjustments have taken place. Firms minimize production costs for chosen quantities of output by selecting factor combinations at which the marginal rates of technical substitution between inputs equal the ratios of the inputs prices, and the value of the marginal product of each input equals its price. Inputs are in turn priced by competition so that the value of the marginal product of each factor, equalized across activities, covers the marginal opportunity cost of its supply.

The existence of market power, externalities, or public goods, will cause the market process to be inefficient unless corrected by collective or public action. Monopoly in product markets causes firms to produce quantities at which marginal cost is less than price, which means inefficiency in the economy's mix of goods, since more resources should be devoted to the products of such industries. Monopsony leads to similar misallocation of inputs. There will be overproduction of goods with negative externalities, and underproduction of public goods, the benefit of which to the consumers cannot be effectively captured by the producer unless it has the power to mandate subscriptions (as governments do through taxation).

While a perfectly competitive economy (absent the problems just mentioned) should assure that resources are allocated efficiently and consumer demand is satisfied, whether or not the basic material needs of the population as a whole are satisfied depends upon the distribution of income, which in turn reflects initial resource endowments. For example, where the labor force is small compared to the stock of capital, the marginal product of labor will be high and workers' wages are likely to be adequate for purchasing basic consumption goods; whereas where the labor force is large and the capital stock (or cultivable land supply) meagre, the marginal product of labor is low and wages may be inadequate to command such goods. Consumers assert their sovereignty through the market, but it is demand, which reflects purchasing power rather than wants *per se*, to which profit-seekers respond.

The equitableness of the outcomes of the market process is a matter of considerable controversy. Market outcomes cannot be judged equitable by those who believe that income should be distributed according to need, or only according to labor contributions to production. Others accept the rights to returns on non-labor property as either just, or pragmatically desirable, although the latter judgments sometimes turn on the way in which property was initially acquired. Ethical interpretations of the marginal productivity theory of income distribution in competitive markets are sometimes advanced. Even if such interpretations are accepted, it would have to be noted that market failures such as the existence of monopsony cause the principle of distribution according to value of marginal product to fail to hold.

Market failure due to market power, externalities, or public goods can be corrected by appropriate government interventions, but while economists may be able to identify which interventions appear to be needed, economic theory implies that officials will follow their own perceived interests, which may not always lead them to act so as to increase efficiency. The existence of large inequalities of wealth and income, and the inability of some households to satisfy basic material requirements, may also elicit government interventions, such as entitlement programs to assure basic levels of welfare, progressive income taxation, public provision of education, and taxes on inheritances. The extent of such interventions can be expected to be determined by political processes, in the course of which the initial distribution of wealth and income itself may play a part.

In industrial market economies, perhaps because of the pervasive ability of large-scale units or organized groups of economic actors to influence prices and wages over long periods of time, market outcomes in which resources are fully employed do not seem to be assured.[19] Government fiscal and monetary policies are widely used to influence the level of aggregate economic activity, although it is usually difficult to pursue both full employment and price stability, at least in the short term. Many governments go beyond such reactions to macro-economic imbalances, and draw up sectorally specific plans for economic development. While not binding on individual firms, it is hoped that these indicative plans will provide information helpful in coordinating investment and other decisions. Also, a variety of economic levers and inducements may be used to encourage participation by major firms, so that while their decisions remain voluntary and profit-oriented, they are made in an environment that includes important plan-related incentives. Apart from intersectoral consistency, national plans may reflect political preferences for economic growth, for regional patterns of activity within countries, for expansion of industries requiring greater technical skills, and for pursuit of other social goals.

Capitalism modified by redistributive and welfare measures, antitrust and pollution controls, government provision of public goods, and planned guidance of the economy towards social objectives, is considerably different from the hypothetical capitalism of unregulated free markets. Many of the objections that have traditionally been raised against the latter system may be satisfactorily answered by it. However, critics on the left continue to decry the influence that holders of financial wealth exert over economic life and related political decisions. They argue that inefficiencies and social tensions become inevitable as more comprehensive welfare guarantees are provided to the population in an economy that remains capitalistic in productive organization. And they point to the lack of meaningful change in the relationship of workers to the production process, and the continuing promotion of materialistic and selfish values by the commerical media. Critics on the right, for their part, will also emphasize efficiency costs of market interventions, complain about the encroachment of government in the economy, view taxes and transfers as unfair appropriation of the fruits of enterprise and generators of dependency in their recipients, and argue that planning and high taxation of profits threaten the dynamism of the market system. Not only the final evaluation of capitalism, but also the long-term stability of the system and where its institutional equilibrium may lie, are difficult to judge with much certainty.

Notes

1. The special character of money is discussed briefly below.
2. It is incorrect, however, to imply that the great extension of markets observed in the capitalist countries over the centuries of that system's dominance took place without considerable government participation, especially in the development of transportation and communications infrastructures. To this extent, it is not to a pure capitalism as described above, but to a capitalism with a larger supportive role for government, that this feature should be ascribed.
3. The original proponent of this approach, John Bates Clark, was cited in Chapter 1.
4. Readers may notice that little attention has been given to what is in

some respects a uniquely important commodity—money. Some may wonder why its existence and role were not listed as fundamental economic institutions when defining the capitalist system. While certainly a facilitator of exchange and, in that sense, probably indispensible to the genesis of capitalism, money is not a phenomenon unique to that system, being found not only in all of the modern economic systems to be considered in this book, but also in economies pre-dating capitalism.

5. Technically, this condition is required in full only when each individual consumes some of each good; but we will not go further into such details.

6. This association may be more typical of modern conservatives such as economist Milton Friedman, 1962, and politician Ronald Reagan, than of classical liberals such as Mises and Spencer, who distrusted democracy (Polanyi 1970, p. 226., cited in Schweickart 1980, p. 133; see also Schweickart, p. 103). The current trend in economic theory, reflected in the economic analyses of voting and social choice, seems again to raise many more doubts than it affirms reasons for faith in democratic decision-making, or in political decision-processes quite generally.

7. Harrod 1948. Also see Domar 1957.

8. Note that it is only the extension to the domain of value that makes the two views contradictory, since Marx did not deny that non-labor inputs contribute to production in a technological sense.

9. The term 'rent' has the special technical meaning, in economics, of a payment to a factor of production over and above what is necessary to draw it into its most productive use. Consider, for example, a fertile plot of land used for growing grain. As population and demand for grain rise, less fertile and more remote plots will be drawn into production, at higher cost per unit of output, so grain prices will rise, and the rent on the choice parcel goes up. The income of the landowner thus rises more or less automatically, and it is not clear that the rent plays any incentive role. Differential rents might play a role, however, in signalling that the land should be shifted to another use. Also, the fairness issue may be raised against those who favor taxing away rents, in that the unanticipated imposition of such a tax could be said unfairly to punish those who invested in one specific type of asset, in the expectation that its value would appreciate, but not those who invested in securities or other assets with the same expectations.

10. On 'the human qualities developed by business activity and requisite to enjoyment of and successful participation in it', Knight quotes the following passage from Ruskin: 'In a community regulated by laws of demand and supply, but protected from open violence, the persons who become rich are, generally speaking, industrious, resolute, proud,

covetous, prompt, methodical, sensible, unimaginative, insensitive, and ignorant. The persons who remain poor are the entirely foolish, the entirely wise, the idle, the reckless, the humble, the thoughtful, the dull, the imaginative, the sensitive, the well-informed, the improvident, the irregularly and impulsively wicked, the clumsy knave, the open thief, the entirely merciful, just, and godly person.' Knight 1935, p. 66.

11. Individuals, that is, might be willing to reduce their current consumption for the sake of future generations as part of an overall program of social saving, but only if there is a mechanism for reaching and enforcing a general agreement on the matter (to avoid 'free-rider' behavior). A formal argument is made by Amartya Sen 1967.

12. It is undoubtedly simplistic to say that property rights are respected only because of legal sanctions, but this opens up a set of questions about behavior and social norms that are better left for examination elsewhere.

13. For example, if a national park exists, then even if I favor its existence and benefit from it, I prefer to spend my last dollar on private consumption goods or financial claims, rather than voluntarily offering it to the government, even if I am given the assurance that an extra square foot of park land will be purchased. On the other hand, if the park does not now exist, I also consider contributing a dollar to be a poor use of the money, since my one contribution will have little effect on whether the park is established. Even if there is a general agreement to establish the park with contributions of one dollar from each citizen, I am tempted to renege on my share, which will have little impact on the overall outcome. What is actually done, then, is that we collectively agree (through our political institutions) to create and maintain the park, and then assign government the role of coercing each of us to pay our share by collecting from us taxes which we do not have the choice of withholding. (In practice, though, good citizenship probably plays a big part in securing tax payments, which would be extremely costly to collect in its absence.)

14. Some commentators have argued that the principal reasons for redistribution in democratic societies manifesting wealth and income inequalities may be (1) self-interest of those who support redistribution toward themselves, and (2) envy or spite by those who support redistribution away from better off groups and towards third parties. This hypothesis highlights the need to exercise caution before attributing redistribution to a decision by 'society', in some more general sense.

15. Of course, the capitalist nature of ownership *is* altered if one takes the extreme position that redistributive taxation of wealth, income, or bequests represent thefts of property.

16. One may wonder why the government, rather than a private consulting firm, is needed for these tasks. A possible answer is that while the

consultant could conceivably make a profit by selling the information to some firms, not all firms might feel it worthwhile to pay for it, so its impact would be more limited. Also, firms would need some inducement to supply information, whereas the government could legally require that it be supplied, and it might also have some powers of moral suasion that induce firms to supply it.

17. For convenience, this part of the discussion overlooks international trade.

18. These remarks gloss over the question of how much change in work organization capitalism can successfully incorporate. From a substantive standpoint, many would consider too much attenuation of financier control rights to be incompatible with a workable capitalist economy; some discussions include Alchian and Demsetz 1972, Marglin 1974, Pejovich (ed.) 1978, and Bowles 1985. From a semantic standpoint, one could ask: when does capitalism cease to be capitalism and begin to be workers' self-management? If there is in fact a continuum of intermediate forms between the two pure system types, the answer would seem to be both rather arbitrary and rather unimportant.

19. Economic theorists Carl Shapiro and Joseph Stiglitz (1984), in an argument that bears some resemblance to one put forward by Marx in the nineteenth century, have demonstrated that unemployment may be a normal feature of equilibrium in the market economy, because without it, the threat of dismissal would not be sufficient to induce workers to exert themselves on the job. In the Shapiro–Stiglitz theory, wages are too high to clear the labor market, but this reflects an employer strategy to raise the cost of dismissal and hence elicit more effort on the job; it does not stem from the power of organized labor.

Suggested Readings

Childs, Marquis, 1961, *Sweden: The Middle Way*, New Haven: Yale University Press.

Childs, Marquis, 1980, *Sweden: The Middle Way on Trial*, New Haven: Yale University Press.

Cohen, Stephen S., 1977, *Modern Capitalist Planning: The French Model*, Berkeley: University of California Press.

Edwards, Richard C., Reich, Michael, and Weisskopf, Thomas E., 1986, *The Capitalist System: A Radical Analysis of American Society* (3rd edn), Englewood Cliffs, NJ: Prentice-Hall.

Estrin, Saul and Holmes, Peter, 1983, *French Planning in Theory and Practice*, New York: Allen and Unwin.

Johnson, Chalmers, 1982, *MITI and the Japanese Miracle*, Stanford: Stanford University Press.

Kohler, Heinz, 1986, *Intermediate Microeconomics: Theory and Applications* (2nd edn), Glenview, Ill.: Scott, Foresman and Co.

Lindblom, Charles E., 1977, *Politics and Markets: The World's Political Economic Systems*, New York: Basic Books.

Nicholson, Walter, 1987, *Intermediate Microeconomics and its Application* (4th edn), Chicago: Dryden Press.

Rosovsky, Henry and Patrick, Hugh, (eds), 1976, *Asia's New Giant: How the Japanese Economy Works*, Washington DC: Brookings Institution.

Vogel, Ezra, 1979, *Japan as Number One*, Cambridge: Harvard University Press.

3.
Centrally Planned Socialism

3.1 Institutional Premises and Features

The system to be considered in this chapter appears as the antithesis of the first in many of its governing principles. Such a relationship to capitalism is not surprising, given that centrally planned socialism styles itself that system's historical successor and logical antithesis. Since 1917, and especially since 1945, there has also existed a strategic and political antithesis between groups of nations practicing variants of these two systems. This conflict between the capitalist and socialist camps, which has been the dominant cleavage in the postwar world, is one major source of interest in the subject matter of this book.

As with capitalism, our discussion of centrally planned socialism as an economic system begins by identifying a set of economic institutions, or types of economic interaction, that will serve as its distinguishing features. Once again, the principles to be identified initially serve to characterize the system in an ideal and abstract form, and more realistic details are then added as the discussion progresses. We find this system to be identified by four principal features: state ownership of the means of production; guaranteed state employment, with wages as the exclusive factor return, and 'distribution according to work' as the dominant principle behind incomes; quantitative central planning of production and inter-enterprise transactions; and state determination of wages and prices, with consumer discretion over final purchases.

To expand upon the first point: the important means of production, apart from labor, belong to the state. To put this another way, the private ownership of productive resources that characterizes capitalism is abolished, and all powers over the disposition of such resources are reserved to itself by the government in the name of society as a whole or, perhaps, of its workers or 'progressive classes'.

The second feature is that people are guaranteed employment by the state, and are correspondingly expected to work as a matter of social obligation. The principle of remuneration is 'to each according to his labor', and since there are essentially no earnings from property ownership,[1] incomes are thus to be labor-determined, with the possible exception of certain transfer payments.

The third feature is that what is produced, how much is produced, and in what manner, are determined by a state authority, which we may call 'the planning commission' or simply 'planners'. Planners set quantitative targets for all outputs, and they determine how intermediate goods will flow to using enterprises from producing ones. Independent contracts between subordinate economic agents in the hierarchical economy are therefore at most a minor phenomenon in the system, as ideally conceived.

The last feature is that the composition of output and the distribution of income are determined by planners, who set wage scales and prices administratively. However, consumers have some freedom to purchase available products according to their own preferences, and within their budget constraints. The fact that prices and wages are set by the state deserves emphasis since, along with the principle of quantitative planning, it sharply distinguishes centrally planned socialism from the free exchange by which capitalism was characterized.

Overall, the most obvious economic difference between centrally planned socialism and capitalism is that rather than being subject to the interactions of the choices of a large number of separate economic agents, the centrally planned economy is in principle directed by a single administrative hierarchy. Although the planners may have among their goals the maximization of the rate of economic growth, it no longer makes sense to picture them as acting on the basis of a profit motive *per se*. The economic decisions taken by them are therefore more administrative than commercial in nature; they flow from the objectives of the planners or their superiors, and are shaped by the confrontation of those objectives, not with market data, but with society's inventory of physical resources, its stock of techniques for transforming them into desired outputs, and only indirectly, with the wants and needs of individual members of the society.

In characterizing capitalism we added to its identifying institutional premises mention of some key implications, and of commonly observed accompanying characteristics. In the case of centrally planned socialism, a few points ought also to be added to the principles by which we have identified the system. First, it might be pointed out that state ownership of the means of production does not mean elimination of privately owned consumer goods or savings accounts. Second, to varying degrees in the actual socialist countries (for example, the Soviet Union more than China) there exists a labor market, in the sense that workers are free to choose jobs that they prefer, and the wage and benefit package can be seen to adjust with the need to attract workers into unfilled jobs. Third, it should be recognized that even the country most approximating the centrally planned economy as an ideal type (the Soviet Union), has tolerated significant departures from the principles of state ownership and non-market resource allocation in the form of small-scale private enterprises (especially private farm plots), rural free markets, and collective enterprises (again, especially in agriculture). In this and in other respects, the model of the pure centrally planned socialist economy is at least as hypothetical in nature as is that of perfectly competitive capitalism, perhaps more so.

The universal fact of single party rule in all countries practicing some form of this system, and that party's self-identification as 'Marxist-Leninist', raises a special difficulty for this chapter. Our evaluation of centrally planned economic systems is likely to turn upon who controls the state, and in what ways, if any, they are accountable to the public. Some social theorists have argued that centralization of economic power and concentration of political power go hand in hand. This may or may not be true of necessity, yet there is little, if any, historical evidence with which to refute it.

For most of this chapter, we adopt an agnostic position regarding the character of the state, giving full consideration to the hypothetical possibility that the socialist state might somehow act on behalf of its citizens, and paying only limited attention to the realities of repression which have been so common under Communist regimes. This approach can be faulted for lack of political realism, but it allows us to focus on the purely economic case for, and problems of, centrally planned socialism, leaving to other inquiries the question of whether the system could exist in contexts other than those that have marked the nations coming closest to implementing it to date.

3.2 Marxian Thought and the Rationale for Centralized Socialism

Karl Marx, who inspired the centrally planned socialist economy, wrote little about it, but much about capitalism and earlier forms of economic organization. A useful framework for comprehending centralized socialism as an antithesis of capitalism can be drawn from the latter writings. A starting point is Marx's distinction between the 'use value' and 'exchange value' of commodities.

Marx emphasized that specialization and market exchange under capitalism meant that goods were overwhelmingly produced for sale to others, and not for the use of the producer. Their value to the producer, therefore, lay in their value in exchange, rather than that in use. Indeed, Marx's theory of equilibrium price determination asserted that use value is a necessary but unquantifiable characteristic of commodities, while goods exchange, under ideal conditions, at ratios proportionate to the amount of labor directly and indirectly needed to produce them. Marx's ideas were in this respect similar to those of Adam Smith and other classical economists, but very different from those of the neoclassical economists who wrote after him. For the latter, prices were determined by the interaction of both supply and demand,[2] and while supply could be traced to cost considerations, demand reflected marginal utility to the consumer. Supply and demand accordingly cause value in exchange and value in use to be closely linked in later economic theory, while for Marx, there was no such intimate connection.

Marx's critique of capitalism can be seen as centering upon the idea that that system deploys resources irrationally because producers are guided by the desire to produce goods of high exchange value, and have no immediate concern for use value. But in light of the views of the non-Marxian economists, just stated, and their concept of 'consumer sovereignty', according to which the pursuit of profits guides the producer to supply precisely what the consumer wants, what sense can possibly be made of Marx's criticism?

One approach is to consider Marx's view of markets. Rather than seeing them as ideal coordinating devices, he characterized unplanned interactions of buyers and sellers as 'anarchic'. Marx did recognize that markets could regulate the allocation of resources among industries roughly in proportion to quantities demanded, but he observed that such regulation was in a sense accidental—that is, that supply and demand would be equalized only by a fortuitous combination of unorganized responses to perceived opportunities. One can expect production to expand when profits are high, and to contract when they are low, but in any given period, production will exactly satisfy demand with normal profits only by chance. Our example of decisions to produce carrots versus tomatoes, in Chapter 2, illustrates this problem.

Marx thought that man's mastery over his environment through rationality and science was the essence of human progress. Accordingly, he assumed that replacement of the anarchic market by social planning would be a powerful step forward in human development. Moreover, a central authority could in principle determine how society's resources are to be employed with a view to the value in use of the products, rather than their value in exchange. A self-sufficient household deploys its resources according to what it needs for its own use. By bringing the various specialized units of production under the control of a single decision-making body, the entire economy could be treated as a household, and the complex division of labor could be made compatible with production for use, rather than exchange, without forfeiting the benefits of specialization and complexity. Socialism, for Marx, means the transcendance of the alienation and irrationality of a complex social division of labor under commodity exchange, and the consequent achievement of a high productivity, specialized, and interdependent economy under conditions of social solidarity and economic rationality. This achievement would be based upon the coordination provided not by markets, but by planned social resource allocation.

Criticism of Capitalism: Modern Interpretation

It is also possible to employ many of the criticisms of capitalism discussed in the previous chapter in an explanation of why production for exchange and production for use were viewed by Marx as being fundamentally different. For example, the set of activities in which resources are used in the market system may not match those that would best fulfill the needs and wants of the people in the society because of problems of monopoly, externalities, and public goods. And although the influence of demand upon production for profit was recognized by Marx, demand may be said to be a poor indicator of value in use, because the influence of use value on demand is distorted by an unequal distribution of purchasing power. Whereas 'use value' could be defined in terms of objective wants, demand reflects subjective preferences, and less 'objectively' important desires command greater attention than 'basic needs', in the market, if they are supported by the ability to pay. Relatedly, while the democratic state could in theory be called upon to redistribute property or income so that demand could be based on an equitable distribution of income, existing inequalities breed unequal political power, and in any case the role of unequal income distribution as an incentive in capitalism may make all but the poorest reluctant to tamper with the distributive mechanisms of the system.[3]

The market system can also be said to be inefficient because it fails to guarantee the full employment of available resources. In fact, argued Marx, the capitalist economy requires the existence of unemployment as a condition for extracting effort from workers who have sacrificed claims on their products and self-determination in the workplace in order to obtain employment. Unemployment cannot be eliminated by government action, in a capitalist system, without undermining the very basis of productivity under that system's institutions.[4]

Finally, Marx criticized the market for being myopic, in the sense that there is no one in the system with an interest in identifying social goals, including a desirable rate of economic growth, and no one holding the power to coordinate action aimed at achieving those goals, if they were to be identified.

It is worth pausing to note that the administrative and centralizing implications of planning can be viewed as being somewhat at odds with Marx's humanistic concerns with alienation and human self-fulfillment. Marx seemed to condemn capitalist hierarchy when he identified 'anarchy in the social division of labor and despotism in that of the workshop'[5] as a contradiction in capitalism—when he saw a tension, that is, between the fact that the division of labor takes a planned and hierarchical form within the enterprise, but an unplanned and spontaneous form in the market. But it seems that his thrust was in favor of planning and hierarchy, at the societal level, more than it was against centralization in enterprises. To understand why Marx the humanist gravitated towards an apparently more, rather than less, centralized society, we may look to his ideas about exploitation and social class, and also to his view of technological progress and social change.

Although Marx may have found the labor process under industrial capitalism distasteful, he was certainly by mid-life a confirmed enthusiast of scientific and industrial progress. To associate alienation with division of labor *per se*, and thus to embrace anti-specialization models that might involve restoration of handicrafts and 'a return to simpler ways of life', was ruled out. Marx instead defined alienation and exploitation more or less exclusively in terms of denial to the producer of access to means of production, and of control over the production process and its products. Exploitation was of the essence in capitalism, because profits were none other than that portion of the product of labor that is wrested from the working class by the private monopolizers of society's tools of production.

Capitalism failed to serve workers' needs because wages tended to be low, work hours long, and working conditions abysmal, owing to the employers' monopsony power and to the existence of unemployed or reserve labor. Moreover, as stated above, production for exchange failed to direct society's resources towards the properly ranked needs of its members, in Marx's view. Finally, capitalism bred economic instability and waves of technological unemployment against which workers were powerless. The alienation of the producer from his product and tools was not to be resolved by restoring self-sufficient production, however. Rather, the dynamic technological element of capitalism would be turned to the benefit of society as a whole; the reuniting of workers with their products and tools would take place at a societal or collective level. By controlling the production process in concert, in other words, as a class, workers would eliminate the source of their alienation, and the exploitative appropriation of the product of their surplus labor by the capitalist. Not only this, they would also eliminate unemployment, through planning of labor's deployment in conformity with the existing and growing stock of means of production. In addition, they would direct all productive activity towards real social and individual needs, and would achieve stability of prices and of the growth rate of output.

While Marx saw a hierarchical society as the predictable successor to capitalism, he did not view such a society as the resolution of all human conflicts and struggles. Socialism, in which economic activity would be regulated by planning and individuals would earn incomes depending upon their labor contributions, would itself be succeeded by a communist society, in which the centralized state would wither away, and in which the principle of work and distribution would be 'from each according to his abilities, to each according to his needs'. Since Marx wrote even less about this communist society than about socialism, and since it has never been approximated in a sustained way except by small communities, we will have little to say about such an economic system until our final chapter.

3.3 Centralized Socialism and the Evaluative Criteria: The Ideal Case

Our consideration of centralized socialism's performance, like that of capitalism, will move from an ideal model to the introduction of realistic difficulties, and finally to discussion of modified versions of the system. Ideal conditions for capitalism were the absence of market power, externalities, and public goods, and the rapid and complete flow of information, conditions under which that system is expected to perform with complete efficiency. An equally ideal set of conditions for centrally planned socialism should be in some sense equally favorable to that system. What we will assume, in particular, is that planners have access to perfect information about resources, capabilities, technologies, and needs, and that they are capable of processing that information without administrative or computational difficulties. In this section, we also adopt two assumptions about the behavior of the economic agents in the system, which could be viewed as creating optimal conditions in terms of human motivation. We assume that the interests of the state are perfectly aligned with those of the people as a whole, and that all agents are motivated to fulfill the plan to the best of their abilities.[6]

While the assumption about information is roughly parallel to that made for capitalism, and while the assumption concerning administrative and management abilities—that is, absence of 'bounded rationality'[7]—is also commonly made in neoclassical theoretical models of the business system, these unrealistic assumptions are often thought to be more favorable to centrally planned socialism than to capitalism. The motivational assumptions, moreover, were not seen as necessary for the ideal performance of capitalism, and are clearly very strong ones. On the other hand, the conditions invoked here are weaker than those assumed for capitalism in that the existence of public goods and externalities can be assumed from the start, without harm. As before, our procedure is to first imagine these ideal and unrealistic conditions to hold, then to drop them, in order to illuminate both the ideal case for the system and the nature of its problems in practice.

3.3.1 Basic Needs and Equity

As the above discussion has already indicated, arguments for centralized socialism emphasize that it directs society's resources toward the production of 'use values', whereas capitalism does not. Assuming that the state embraces this goal as a result of its political unity with the people, and that it is capable of coordinating the economy effectively (whether it will do so with full efficiency will be considered shortly), success in this regard is a reasonable expectation.

However, it must be noted that the central distributive principle of socialism does not guarantee universal needs satisfaction. Although abolition of property incomes lays the groundwork for a more equal distribution of income than that of capitalist economies, the socialist principle 'to each according to his work' still permits inequalities, since (to quote from Marx) 'one man is superior to another physically or mentally and so supplies more labor in the same time, or can labor for a longer time' so that '[t]his equal right is an unequal right for unequal labor' which 'tacitly recognizes unequal individual endowment and thus productive capacity as natural privileges'.[8] Socialist systems in fact supplement the 'according to work' principle with commitments to guarantee basic welfare levels, but again, how much can be provided depends upon the society's wealth-producing capabilities. Marx appears to recognize that application of welfare principles threatens to undercut the incentive function of the rule.

Intertemporal distribution choices may also threaten short-term needs satisfaction, for the ability to satisfy material needs is related to growth and accumulation of capital in a two-edged fashion. On the one hand, society's future needs-satisfying capacity is enhanced by accumulating appropriate forms of capital today; but on the other hand, to the extent that the constraint of scarcity binds tightly, deferred consumption today also means less current needs satisfaction.

With regard to equity, the classical socialist position[9] appears to be that the concept is to be viewed as socially relative, rather than absolute. This suggests that until the arrival of the day in which full

communism is feasible, socialism's income distribution will be
equitable in effect by definition, since it will adhere to its own
particular 'justice' of distribution according to work, provision of
whatever public welfare services are socially feasible, and no
property incomes. Such a distribution of outcomes will of course
measure differently against alternative conceptions of equity. For
example, socialist distribution may appear excessively egalitarian to
liberals prepared to countenance returns on private property (and to
justify that on much the same kind of incentive grounds as socialists
use to justify unequal incomes for unequal work); or it may be highly
inegalitarian (or unjust), viewed from the standpoint of believers in
rewards according to 'effort' or 'merit', distinguished from inherited
strength and intelligence. Be that as it may, the defender of
centralized socialism can argue in the system's favor that, unlike in a
capitalist society, the socialist state can use its vast control over
resources, without concern for the countervailing interests of private
businessmen, to achieve distributive goals. Leaders of many socialist
countries can indeed boast that their least advantaged citizens enjoy
access to health and other public services and to income guarantees
not shared by the bottom 20 per cent or more of citizens in many
non-socialist countries with equal or greater *average* incomes.[10]

3.3.2 Centralized Socialism and Efficiency

Although Marx may have viewed planning as a straightforward
administrative problem of allocating resources in appropriate
quantities to achieve social objectives, economists have, since the
late nineteenth century, debated whether a planning body would
really be able to accomplish resource allocation efficiently, without
reference to the scarcity- and demand-reflecting price signals that
are generated by markets under capitalism. Much of this debate
concerns problems of collecting information, computing an optimal
plan, and motivating plan fulfillment. Under the highly favorable
assumptions of the present section, these difficulties do not arise.
The only question, therefore, is whether an efficient solution to the
problem of allocating society's resources can in principle be found
by central planners having in hand a complete objective function (or
a ranking of all possible sets of products), full information about the
production technologies by which inputs can be transformed into
outputs, and knowledge of the levels of the available resources, in all

of their variety and specificity. The answer of pure economic theory is that such a solution can in principle be found, using mathematical programming techniques. The solution would indicate the quantities of each resource to be used in each production activity, and the associated level of output. Scarcity prices of the productive resources would not be needed by the planners as raw data. However, an implicit set of prices, with the same interpretation as the scarcity-reflecting equilibrium prices of a perfectly competitive market economy, would be generated as by-products of the problem's solution.[11]

Were such theoretical techniques to be usable in practice, the ideal case for planned socialism would be greatly strengthened. In the first place, the idea of 'production for use' rather than 'production for exchange' would be directly reflected in the planning procedure, which would make use of the planners' social objective function, without reference to exchange value data, in determining what was to be produced, using which inputs. Second, the planners could in principle deal with industries exhibiting increasing returns to scale (which might give rise to monopolies in a market setting), with production externalities, and with public goods, in a single comprehensive process of optimal planning, rather than as special interventions required in the face of market failures. Third, planners' objectives regarding the provision of basic consumption goods, and those concerning the division of social output between consumption and production goods, could be directly incorporated in the plan.

It must be stated here that, with regard to efficiency in distribution and in the mix of goods, it is the planners' preferences, primarily, that receive weight. If the outcome of planning is one in which some members of society could have been made better off without hurting any others, including the planners, then the plan must be regarded as having been inefficient. Is efficiency impossible for planned socialism even under ideal conditions, then? Not if, as in our listing of the system's principles, we assume that consumers make final decisions about purchases of goods. If individuals as consumers are in the end free to use their incomes as they like in the purchase of the provided consumption goods sold at prices which they will take as given, then there is nothing to block efficiency in distribution, even though planners control the distribution of purchasing power. Efficiency does not require that consumers' welfare be maximized except in so far as it remains possible to do so within the context of meeting the planners' objectives, which may include consumer welfare only as one of several different goals.

3.3.3 Social Dimensions, Stewardship, and Bequest

The ability of centralized socialism to satisfy the social and nonmaterial needs of society's members is, like equity, implied by definition in the system's conception. Whether this claimed ability is plausible turns on the system's political theory, wherein the working people are assumed to exert control over economic and social decision-making through their collective control of the state. If, as we assume in this section, there is an identity of interest between the workers and the state, then centralized socialism may be taken to have ideal properties because it eliminates labor alienation and gives people control over society's resources and, hence, over their personal destinies. The standard criticism that centralized control of economic life violates individual liberty cannot arise here, since the individual would not wish to do anything other than his or her part in the plan. All of this might be taken, however, as underscoring the artificiality of the present assumptions.

With respect to care of the natural environment and resources, and savings and growth, the evaluation under present assumptions turns on whether 'the people' whose interest the state shares are taken to include future generations, or, alternatively, whether the present generation values growth and resource husbandry. If either of these conditions holds, centralized socialism can be expected to attain a high standard of performance. With regard to the environment, superiority over the market system can be claimed because none of the effects of production would be viewed as an 'externality' from the standpoint of the all-embracing state. In so far as the state acts on behalf of the community as a whole, the value placed on the husbanding of resources is at least no less than that sanctioned by that community; it is never replaced by a sectional interest, such as that of a firm which may earn a profit from some resource-degrading activity without considering that degradation as a cost to itself.[12] The argument for private ownership of resources discussed in Chapter 2, which focused on individual appropriation of the capitalized value of the resources in question, need not hold any less true of state ownership under the assumption of the present section.[13] The 'tragedy of the commons' fails to occur here as yet because the people, acting in unison under state coordination, are immune to 'free-rider' problems.

The socialist argument about savings is that whereas capitalist investors make their savings decisions with only self-interest and wealth-maximization in mind, the socialist state can explicitly place some notion of the claims of the society's future on their decision scales. Also, while a portion of labor's output must be withheld from worker consumption in both types of society, the socialist state ensures that this goes entirely to replacing and expanding the capital stock, whereas in capitalism there is some leakage of this 'surplus output' into luxury consumption by capitalists and resource owners.

3.4 Problems of Centralized Socialism, I: Relaxing the People–State Identity

It is difficult to find drawbacks to the planned socialist economic system under the assumptions of the previous section, but easy to fault those assumptions for lack of realism. In the present section and in the one that follows it, we will consider how drawbacks can arise from two sets of factors: 'less than ideal' motivational conditions, and 'less than perfect' human capabilities. The first concerns heterogeneity of objectives, and lack of identity between the state and 'the people', whose collective interest may now be difficult to identify. The second concerns limits to the ability to gather and to process information.

If we relax the assumption of a state–people (or working-class) identity, but maintain those assumptions that permit the state to be viewed as efficiently carrying out its own program, various problems or potential problems immediately arise.

With regard to providing for the material needs and wants of the populace, the state can be counted upon only in so far as this is in its own interest. Sacrifice of popular needs for other, conflicting ends, is thus a danger. Another concern is that the state might classify specific groups as 'enemies of the people' and use its monopoly over resources to deprive them of their material requirements, when it so wishes.

Even assuming that a 'distribution according to work' can be objectively defined, we have already seen that the outcome of centralized socialism will fail to satisfy some conceptions of equity.

To that, we should also add the recognition that 'distribution according to work' is in practice an imprecise idea, which, especially under conditions of heterogeneity of interests, opens the door to state sanctioning of forms of inequality that help to perpetuate its own preferred social order (for example, by favoring government and Communist Party personnel). Inequalities that might be regarded as unjust by many citizens could thus exist, even without positing the existence of corruption and of illicit economic activities of the type that imperfect human capabilities are likely to give rise to in the centrally planned economy.

Since for the moment we continue to assume that the latter capabilities are unlimited, it should be possible for resources to be used efficiently in fulfillment of the state's objectives. The main point to be made here is that such an efficiency may have little to do with the economic valuations or preferences of the population at large, given monopolization of economic power by a state that could choose to disregard these.

In the realm of social dimensions, the abolition of alienation, which is hypothesized under ideal conditions, is especially vulnerable to the relaxing of the assumption of state–people identity. Given state direction of the economy along lines of planners' preference, and the possibly low wage rates and consumption levels chosen, for example, in the name of capital accumulation and/or defense, there is no reason to expect ordinary citizens to experience high levels of personal satisfaction. Indeed, monopsony on the employer's side in the labor market, and outlawing of independent labor unions, may mean that jobs are absolutely dispreferred to those found under capitalism, not only in terms of wages and work hours but also with respect to working conditions and the social relations in the context of which work takes place. Constraints on political expression, and on other individual rights such as those of personal mobility, may be invoked for the sake of efficient implementation of state plans. Such constraints are rendered more easily enforceable by the concentration of both economic and police powers in the hands of the state.

Here, it should be underscored that, in defining centrally planned socialism, we focused on economic dimensions and were largely agnostic with respect to political ones. Conceptually, as we suggest below, state control over resource allocation need not rule out popular control over the state. If, however, centralized economic management is in practice incompatible with basic political and civil liberties,[14] then this single finding might suffice to make centrally planned socialism unacceptable. The atrocities committed in the name of 'building' and/or 'defending socialism', from Stalin to Pol Pot to the recent 'democracy spring' in China, suffice to explain the lack of attraction that the model holds in so many quarters.[15]

The ideals of the internalization of externalities and of the representation of all generations also break down when the state–people identity assumption is dropped. The state may be perfectly prepared to see resources depleted and environments despoiled, and to inflict health damage upon the population, if this serves short-term objectives such as increasing the output of producers' and military goods, and achieving high rates of growth. The state's monopoly over the sources of information may help it to contain the unpopular effects of such policies. It may be difficult, for example, to launch an environmental movement when all communications media and means of gathering information are controlled by the government. Even under ideal conditions, it is unclear how anyone, however well motivated, would fairly arbitrate between the interests of generations when determining the division of output between consumer and producer goods. With the motivations of the government now open to question, it becomes relevant to consider the possibility that a socialist state accumulates capital rapidly only because the ordinary members of its living population have no say in the savings decision.

3.5 Problems of Centralized Socialism, II: Imperfect Information and Bounded Rationality

When, in addition to dropping the identification or equation of state and people, we further relax the assumptions that ensure efficiency of economic management—namely, that planners have perfect knowledge of relevant parameters and perfect computational capabilities, and that the incentives of agents in subordinate units of the economic structure can somehow be made compatible with the announced plans—then a set of economic management problems well known to students of centralized socialist economies is likely to arise. Although their effects spill over into each of our evaluative dimensions, the chief impact of these difficulties may be discussed under the heading of efficiency.

The basic issues may be comprehended in terms of an ongoing struggle between higher and lower units of a hierarchy, whose objectives are fundamentally opposed. This struggle is in many ways similar to that which can occur within the workplace in a capitalist economy, where it is in the short-term interest of employees (who receive the same pay regardless of their productivity) to minimize effort, maximize income and promotion possibilities, and avoid taking risks with respect to job tenure, and where those interests are often directly counterposed to the employer's goals of maximizing output and profit, and minimizing the outlay on labor for a given amount of effort. As a number of writers on the economics of management and the internal organization of firms have argued, this opposition of interests may well prevent not only the fullest direction of energies toward organizational goals, but also the organizationally useful flow of information from operatives to decision-makers. In the present case, the crucial employees, subordinates, or agents, are managerial personnel in state enterprises; the analogue of the employer is the state and, in particular, its central management or planning departments; and the enterprise or organization is the economy as a whole—or at least, that part of it with which the state is able to maintain formal connections. The goals of the planners have already been discussed under two alternative assumptions: that they somehow represent the population as a whole, and that they do not. The goals of the subordinates (here: managers), on the other hand, are similar to those of the employees in the analogous example of a firm: that is, minimizing effort and risk, and maximizing income, job tenure, and promotion possibilities. Here, also, the struggle between organizational (the center's) and individual (enterprise managers') goals is fought through the medium of information; that is, it revolves around the central agent's inability to observe precisely what the individual subordinate is doing, or under exactly what constraints he or she operates. The enormous geographic dispersion of the organization, in the case of the centrally planned economy, adds significantly to the problems posed.

In brief, the center requires of its enterprise managers information about resource stocks, capabilities, and technologies, which are basic data to its planning problem; and it also requires of managers compliance in carrying out plans, once formulated. In so far as managers are motivated by self-interest, the requirement of compliance will prompt the state to devise reward schedules that stimulate plan fulfillment. Thus, salaries, bonuses, job security, promotions, etc., will be tied to the degree of plan fulfillment. But this gives rise to a difficulty for the achievement of the first requirement (that of information provision): if a manager can understate the capacities of his unit, he may receive more plentiful inputs, or a more easily fulfilled target, and hence may more readily secure his own objectives. This means that the center's dual requirements of (1) information to be used in the planning process, and (2) compliance to plans once formulated, may be in conflict.

Out of their concern with maximizing output from available resources, planners can already be expected to devise plans that leave few if any unutilized resources as a backup for dealing with unforeseen production bottlenecks. The fact that managers have incentives to understate their production capacities may contribute in its own right to this 'tautness' of plans, because planners have an incentive to try to squeeze as much as possible from known resources if they are aware that there exists a tendency towards understatement by managers. But this produces a vicious circle: managers, knowing that the planned flow of resources may leave them vulnerable to bottlenecks that can prevent them from fulfilling planned targets, then have a still stronger incentive to understate their real capacities, and to acquire additional stocks of inputs without the knowledge of planners. The tautness of plans and danger of bottlenecks, leading to general unreliability of the planned supply of intermediate products to using enterprises, also generates an incentive to integrate input-producing activities into those enterprises; machine building, for example, may end up being carried out inefficiently (in terms of economies of scale and of specialization) within a large number of dispersed enterprises, rather than in the specialized machine-building sector. Finally, unreliability of supply from official sources leads to development of informal supply channels in which contacts, influence, and bribery may provide the grease.[16]

Apart from these problems on the capacity side, the devising of reward systems that promote systemic objectives may be subject to its own difficulties, commonly referred to as the 'problem of success indicators'.[17] This refers to the difficulty of defining target criteria according to which enterprises are to be rewarded or penalized. So long as enterprises maintain some discretion over assortment, weight, or other attributes of their products, target specifications may lead to systemically perverse responses. For example, targets stated in number of units promote production of large quantities of small, low-quality output with inadequate attention to product mix or spare parts; targets framed in terms of weight may, on the other hand, lead to wastefulness in materials use through irrational design; and so on. Because the producer is under no pressure to find customers for its output, which is to be transferred to another state organ, it is difficult to make even planners' preferences serve as an adequate demand constraint. Similarly, it is difficult to build rewards for technical innovation and cost-saving measures into a system that rewards the steady flow of output, and therefore tends to penalize the disruption that must be risked for experimentation and change. Technological lethargy has, in fact, become perhaps the most troubling shortcoming of centralized socialism in an era of ferocious technological competition and dynamism in the capitalist world. Finally, the fact that targets are to be met by particular dates—such as, at the end of a month—coupled with the high pressure, growth-oriented aspects of the system, give rise to cycles of activity: 'target storming' as target dates approach, followed by low-output lulls of recuperation, a pattern that may not match the most rational rhythm of production.

The above discussion has emphasized difficulties attributable to the non-conformability of enterprise managers' and planners' interests, but thus far, our view of managers' interests has centered on their desires most easily to obtain the rewards offered to them by the system as formally constituted. Yet, in discussing informal, semi-legal, and extra-legal methods used by managers to satisfy superior organs, it will have become apparent that the state's monopolistic control over social resources is itself incomplete, and that enterprise managers, and perhaps other participants in the complex state economic apparatus, can acquire substantial control over resources outside of state knowledge and plans. This being the case, it may be possible for them to use those resources not only to secure rewards from the state, but also directly to acquire or produce benefits in the form of perquisites, illegally earned incomes, etc. Evidence from centralized socialist economies suggests that substantial fractions of total output are generated and distributed outside of and often in direct conflict with state plans, in the sense that output expansion in the 'second economy' in which these extra-plan activities take place means that fewer resources are left for the official one. Incomes so earned accrue both to private individuals and to corrupt officials. The implications of this are that the achievement of state objectives is undercut, costs of official production are increased, and there is a redistribution of income towards those who control resources *de facto* but not *de jure*. This can mean that the attainment of relative equality and general satisfaction of material needs is partly offset by luxury consumption achieved by well-placed or unscrupulous individuals through illegal means.

A final problem requiring mention is that of plan construction itself. While we have already alluded to the difficulties engendered in this realm by obstacles to the flow of information between enterprise managers and planners, it should also be pointed out that even when planners possess the kinds of information required for plan construction, the methodology of planning tends in practice to fall far short of the sophisticated and theoretically optimal techniques assumed available in our earlier discussion. What actually occurs under the rubric of planning is a piece by piece fitting together of an economic puzzle, with emphasis on a few key sectors and growth targets, rather than the solution of a problem of simultaneous interrelations through either input-output or mathematical programming techniques. This means not only that there are possibilities of imbalances, but also that the opportunity costs of alternative strategies, and the relative valuations of resources, cannot be systematically considered in the planning process. Since enterprises are not choosing among alternative production techniques (and the associated sets of factor proportion's) so as to minimize costs in terms of scarcity-reflecting input prices, use of *ad hoc* administrative methods for allocating resources can achieve efficiency in production (diagramatically represented by attainment of a point on the contract curve in the relevant Edgeworth box), only by the most extraordinary of accidents.

Planners, lack the ability (and often, also, the desire) to take advantage of mathematical techniques for achieving efficient resource allocation. This too induces them to focus on a few important areas in the economy, and to emphasize the growth of production of those industrial products that they view as prime indicators of modernization. The irony of this is that whereas central planning sets out to better capitalism by producing 'use' rather than 'exchange values', it often ends up in practice taking quantitative indices of particular *intermediate* products as an end in itself, so that, according to a potent quip, bread becomes a mere input to the production of steel. From an economic standpoint, much of the problem is to be attributed not so much to Marxian value theory or Stalinist formulas for building socialism—although these have certainly played their parts in blocking progress towards use of more sophisticated and rational planning methods—as to the simple boundedness of human calculating abilities, and the extraordinary complexity of the problem of planning a modern industrial economy.

3.6 Modifications and Reforms

Two approaches to the adjustment of existing centralized socialist economic systems with the aim of countering the problems just surveyed, can be distilled out of discussions on the topic occurring both inside and outside the countries concerned. The first approach affirms the desirability of a highly centralized planning model, and the attainability of an identity of interests between the state and the people at large. The second seeks improved economic performance through at least partial decentralization of economic power. It may also be coupled with a socio-political theory that questions whether state goals and popular interests can coincide when decisions are taken at levels of a hierarchy necessarily remote from the great mass of ordinary persons. The three sections that follow discuss the centralizing and decentralizing approaches to socialist economic reform, with the middle section devoted to the question of democratic control over centralized socialism.

3.6.1 Strengthening the Central Planning System

Centralizers affirm the basic arguments for social planning that were summarized earlier in this chapter, and attribute problems in economic management and performance to correctable imperfections in the planning system. They point out that sophisticated mathematical planning techniques were developed only after central planning was initiated; that in their first trials, planners were forced to use crude methods; and that the practical use of mathematical planning depends on the development of large-capacity, high-speed computers that are only now approaching adequate levels of sophistication. The perfection of planning techniques is thus seen as a current prospect, and past imperfections as no proof of impossibility.

Where eliciting of enterprise support for state efforts is treated as a separate problem by centralizers, various alternative approaches are taken. One is to hope that more sophisticated techniques of plan formulation go hand in hand with sophisticated solutions to the apparent conflict between information supply and plan fulfillment incentives. Such solutions may take the form of bonus schemes that are free of conflicts between inducements to report on capabilities and incentives to fulfill plans. An alternative solution is based on raising system capabilities for monitoring and surveillance. Better discipline of functionaries might also be sought via improved training and selection procedures.

Perhaps more fundamental solutions of center–enterprise conflicts can also be sought in the political-ideological sphere. Rather than accepting that members of the economic hierarchy will always look out for personal rather than state and social interests when these conflict, centralizers may hold out hopes for advances in political consciousness. Improvement of planning methods coupled with the widespread will to further social aims as crystalized in plans might go a long way towards solving the problems canvassed. Thus Charles Bettelheim, for example, has argued that the causes of failures in Soviet-type economies should be sought not simply in the area of administrative mechanisms and economic incentives, but also in that of social structure and attitudes. He argues that socialist revolutions have given birth to new class systems that foster alienation instead of solidarity, but that such results are not inevitable.[18]

3.6.2 Democratization

Many of the existing objections to centrally planned socialism arise because Marxist beliefs in working-class solidarity and popular or class control of the state are at odds with experience in the Soviet Union and other socialist countries. Marx provided no explanation of how the popular masses would control government decision-making. Lenin's invention of the vanguard party seems only to have compounded the difficulties, and many Marxist-Leninists have expressed contempt for Western-style political democracy. Where, despite Marxist expectations, the accountability of the state to the population which it is supposed to serve has broken down—which is, arguably, in *all* historical Marxist–Leninist states—the concentration of both economic and political power in the hands of the government can become a most unattractive feature of the system. Among other things, it leads to much that is unappealing in the domain of social and nonmaterial well-being, such as the restraint of basic human rights and political freedoms, use of coercion and intimidation, and even the use of incarceration, forced labor, and official violence by authorities protected from accountability by control over information and the communications media. Surely, such authoritarian manifestations of state socialism must be weighed against assertions of the system's superiority based upon basic needs provision or equity considerations (which are themselves areas of ambiguity, judging by the empirical record). Merely boosting the efficiency with which the state achieves its objectives, along the lines given in section 3.6.1, does not address this problem.

Although the idea receives relatively little attention in most discussions of socialist economic reform, the possibility of combining centralized socialism with political democracy is of conceptual interest, and thus ought not to be overlooked. Assume, for the moment, that democracy means the effective control, by the population, of state policy-making. Then, with planner accountability to the public, an efficient centrally planned socialism might hope to achieve the ideal goal of letting the people directly determine how their society's resources are to be used in meeting their needs, as the people collectively assess them. Production for use rather than production for profit would be given meaning, because the political decision-making process would be able simultaneously to take into account questions such as those of savings versus consumption, of environmental protection versus short-run expansion of output, and so on, and to circumvent the need to trade off the benefits of large scale against the costs of monopoly, as occurs in a market economy where some industries are characterized by increasing returns to scale.

Apart from the difficulties involved in perfecting the planning system as such, however, this sort of democratically accountable central planning would face some special problems of its own. In the first place, it is obvious that it would be impossible for citizens to vote on the level of output, much less the input combinations to be used, for each of tens of thousands of different products, and to do so without violating the society's budget conditions (the overall set of outputs must lie within society's production possibility frontier). A possible response is to suggest that voting could be limited to a few basic decisions, such as that determining the allocation of resources between the producer and consumer goods industries, while planners could determine the optimal mix of goods by monitoring consumer purchases and/or conducting consumer surveys, and could use programming techniques to determine optimal production methods. Voting on whether to retain in office the present government or group of planners would ratify success and punish failure.

Other problems revolve around 'the paradox of voting', which is that the majority will may not obey the logical regularities expected of individual rationality. A rational individual's rank ordering of alternative proposals should always obey the principle that if A is preferred to B and B to C, then A must be preferred to C, and not the other way around; but that principle does not rule out majority preference of C over A, because the set of voters constituting the majority can be different in each case, and individuals' rankings of the three options may differ. This means that while there should be a unique most-preferred use of society's resources, from the standpoint of any one person, 'society's preferences' may be cyclical, with no highest preference.[19] This should not be construed as implying that the economic consequences of voting are always 'perverse'. Preferences among the alternatives might be 'single-peaked'. That is, each person may have a most preferred level of, say, pollution abatement, and may rank other levels by order of proximity to it. Then if we arranged all individuals along a line by order of the level each preferred most, a majority vote would in theory tend to settle on the level most preferred by the individual in the middle, the so-called 'median voter'. This will have a tendency at least to roughly maximize overall satisfaction, and minimize disappointment, with the outcome.

Finally, there is the question of rights raised by the fact that for every winning majority of voters in a democracy, there is a losing minority (excluding cases of unanimity). Assuming that the plan for social resource allocation will reflect the will of the majority, this leads to a comparison of market and democratic planning systems that does not clearly favor either one. In the former type of system, as noted in the last chapter, some needs receive higher priority than

others, because they are backed by purchasing power; needs without
ability to pay have no voice. In the latter system, each person would
in principle have an equal voice; yet members of a losing coalition
would carry no weight at all in the final result. To assume that
democratic control of the allocation process gives more protection to
the poor than does the market is, therefore, to suppose that the
needy are always on the winning side; but on what basis? Advocates
of popular control of the economy as a means of assuring basic needs
provision may have to provide either a supplementary mechanism
for protecting potentially 'disenfranchised' minorities, or else
suggest a method other than 'one man, one vote' for determining
social priorities.[20]

3.6.3 Decentralization

While perhaps accepting Marxist orthodoxy in viewing working-
class control of the economy as a prerequisite to social and economic
progress, the advocates of decentralizing reforms of the centrally
planned economy tend to be sceptical about the possibility of
solidaristic class or social control of decisions through central
organs. They may be less optimistic about the technical perfectability
of central planning, and they tend to take managerial self-interest
and the resulting opposition between system and managerial
objectives as facts of life. They also lean towards views of economic
organization that may have more in common with the outlooks of
economists Friederich von Hayek, Ludwig von Mises, and Joseph
Schumpeter, than with that of Karl Marx.[21] Where Marx's theory of
capitalism focused on value determination in *equilibrium*, and where
Marx assumed fixed technical coefficients in production, and growth
principally through capital accumulation,[22] these other economists
emphasized the dispersed nature of economic information, and the
importance of creativity and dynamism, thus elevating flexibility
and spontaneity above attempts at all-embracing and inevitably
static rationality.

   To elaborate for a moment on the philosophical background, it
is worth noting that in the early part of this century economists
debated the feasibility of socialist central planning. The Austrian
economists Mises and Hayek argued that the task of optimally
allocating society's resources would overwhelm planners, and that
the market mechanism was the most efficient device for directing

dispersed information toward the solution of the global resource allocation problem. To some observers, theorists Oskar Lange and Abba Lerner[23] appeared to have won the debate by arguing that planners could simulate markets via a trial-and-error procedure.[24] Moreover Soviet industrialization made clear that central planning was not an impossibility. However, the Soviet case has not proven planning to be efficient, and the Lange–Lerner solution implies a far more decentralized system than that actually practiced by Soviet-type economies, has proven vulnerable to criticism on theoretical grounds, and has failed to provide a usable model for decentralizing reformers.[25] An important aspect of the Austrian arguments is their claim that, while imperfect information can be shown to pose problems for the ideal models of both capitalism (Chapter 2) and centrally planned socialism (this chapter), it is only when the reality of the costliness and dispersed nature of information is considered, that the relative advantage of the market process over centralized governance of an economy becomes truly apparent.[26] Indeed, for the Austrians, capitalism is nothing other than an extraordinarily effective device for making efficient use of dispersed information.

The model of socialist reform through decentralization is one in which the state retains ownership of the physical plants in medium- and large-scale industries, but gives enterprise managers relative autonomy in formulating their production plans and in arranging sales. Private and cooperative firms are permitted to exist, especially in small-scale activities, and some private employment of labor is allowed. Prices are to reflect market supply and demand, with government interventions being of the 'indicative plan' variety discussed in Chapter 2, sections 2.5 and 2.6. Managers are to be motivated by rights to retain profits after taxes, both for distribution to themselves and to workers as bonuses, and for reinvestment in their enterprises. Workers are to be motivated by a combination of managerial supervison and bonuses chosen by managers with an eye to raising productivity. In more daring variants, workers may also be goaded by the fear of being fired if found 'shirking', with the incentive here depending upon at least partial retraction of the state employment guarantee, and on incomplete unemployment com-pensation. Finally, efficient resource utilization is to be promoted by charging utilizing enterprises scarcity rents on socially-owned capital.

This system, if fully implemented, would share some properties both of a modified capitalism (for example, indicative planning, redistributive taxation, and other social interventions to moderate income inequalities and correct market failures), and of classical or centrally planned socialism (especially state ownership of the means of production). As in capitalism, market competition may be the principal method of economic coordination, and the mechanism relied upon to promote efficiency and assure that consumer needs are met. As in some modified capitalisms, government intervention may be relied upon to break up monopolies, correct externality problems, redress income 'maldistributions', and ensure provision of public goods. Unlike capitalism but like centralized socialism, incomes are to be determined primarily by work contributions and welfare provisions, and individual appropriation of the scarcity returns on capital and other means of production is present only in the small private sector, or in the case of disequilibrium profits that are captured by managers and workers in large firms.

This, at least, is the model of a fully decentralized socialism; but whether such a system can in fact be created is in some doubt, after several decades of efforts in that direction in Hungary and, more recently, China and the Soviet Union. The experiences in those countries have given rise to a now familiar complex of problems along the road to a decentralized socialist system from the starting point of a traditional centrally planned socialist economy. These problems can be related to the general political difficulty of more harshly exposing the population to the economic constraints facing the society in the aggregate, through the scarcity-regarding forces of the market mechanism. For although societies practicing centralized socialism have not been noted for efficient resource use or for a satisfactory mix of good quality products, they have scored successes in delivering on their promises of full employment, stable prices, and affordable basic goods. Movement towards more differentiated wage scales, towards 'disciplining' enterprises with the possibility of bankruptcy and workers with the possibility of dismissal, and towards freeing prices, to the possible detriment of workers' purchasing power, frequently engender worker resistance.

Efforts to make enterprises accountable for losses repeatedly run up against a bureaucratic inability to shake off the habit of shoring up units that fall into financial difficulties. Indeed, giving enterprises more decision-making powers and granting managers the right to reward themselves out of profits can give rise to serious dysfunction, when financial accountability is undermined through always-negotiable state support, and when still-administered product and input prices leave profitability useless as an indicator of efficiency. The Hungarian economist Janos Kornai has argued that socialist enterprises have an insatiable appetite for capital, because they expect government assistance if they are unable to cover their own costs. The enterprises are said by Kornai to have 'soft budget constraints'.[27] Once the door begins opening for prices to be determined by demand and supply, long years of resource allocation without reference to these forces more or less guarantee large price changes, but there seem to be far more pressures to increase than to reduce prices. Since many industries are dominated by a few large enterprises and there is no routinized mechanism for new firm creation, monopoly price-setting is also to be expected.

Workers' fears of the negative by-products of reform can be used to advantage by 'conservative' political leaders, bureaucrats, and ideologists. The road to reform will likely contain many bumps, including those of the more visible corruption that can be invited by a semi-market, semi-planned environment,[28] inflation, worker resistance to price increases, and accumulations of international debt. Unless reform can quickly provide palpable benefits to a large constituency there exists an ever-present possibility that these difficulties will strengthen the hand of reform opponents, set up political roadblocks to reform, and bring on at least some recentralization measures.[29] As if these economic problems were not enough, the fact that the old system went hand in hand with political repression, and that increasing freedom of economic choice invites calls for political freedom—in turn threatening the power of the entrenched Leninist political elites—also endangers economic reform in countries under Marxist–Leninist rule.

Supposing that 'market socialism' proved to be politically possible, many economists in both capitalist and socialist countries would still question whether the system could compare favorably with market capitalism in the area of efficiency. The main issue here is the way in which capital is allocated when no individuals possess ownership rights over it. The term 'market socialism' includes one variant in which the state retains powers to determine both the rate of capital formation and its allocation among sectors, and another in which intersectoral capital allocation is more decentralized, primarily reflecting enterprises' abilities to earn surpluses that can be channeled into investment. Regarding the former variant, questions are raised about the state's ability to make efficient allocation decisions and to discern the productivity of capital in alternative uses. Regarding the latter approach, there are major doubts about managers' incentives to invest retained earnings rather than distribute them as bonuses, and the care with which existing capital goods will be husbanded given that, except through its effect on productivity, their market value cannot be captured as income by managers and other enterprise personnel. In so far as at least some benefits of an enterprise's capital can accrue to its workers and managers in the form of higher earnings reflecting higher productivity (which presumably would be their motivation for making the investments in the first place), there is also the ideological problem that such earnings can be interpreted as overstepping the bounds of 'to each according to work' and of the 'social ownership' of non-labor resources. We will devote more detailed attention to some of these issues in the next chapter, where they arise again in connection with the practice of workers' self-management.

Finally, supposing that a full-fledged and relatively efficient decentralized or market socialism were achievable, it would no doubt have its critics on ideological and other grounds. To proponents of centralized socialism, 'market socialism' is clearly a retreat from the effort to perfect direct collective control over resource allocation in the name of 'production for use', and a restoration of the unplanned market as the chief allocator of resources. The distributional deficiencies of capitalism, as seen by socialists, may perhaps be adequately addressed by public ownership of non-labor means of production plus egalitarian provision of education, progressive income taxes, and the like; but there remain the standard market failures, to which socialists might add wasteful expenditures on advertising in the attempt to help form preferences profitable to firms; duplicative and uncoordinated expenditures on research and development; and other perceived irrationalities of competition. In the 'nonmaterial' realm, criticisms would be leveled at the tendency to reproduce and strengthen materialistic, selfish, and uncooperative behaviors, which could be seen as barriers to the society's transition towards a more perfect economic and social system: communism. By strengthening particular over common or general interests, and by failing to promote worker control of production either at the factory level or at that of society as a whole, it could be said that the capitalist system makes no headway against alienation, and holds no promise of improving the quality of working life or 'the social relations of production'.[30]

3.7 Summary and Conclusions

Centrally planned socialism is an economic system in which the state owns the major means of production, guarantees employment to workers, distributes income primarily in the form of wages, plans production and inter-enterprise product flows in physical quantities, and sets all major prices. The Marxian rationale for the system is that a complex social division of labor integrated only by market forces raises labor's productivity, but at the costs of alienating workers from their products, of maintaining suboptimal coordination of economic interdependence, and of causing production to be governed by profit or exchange value considerations, rather than by assessment of the ability of the products to meet people's needs. Marx's concept of socialism proposed to reunite workers with their tools and products, to give them control over production, and to establish planned allocation of resources guided by use value, through state ownership of the means of production, state control of the economy, and worker control of the state.

The success of this project depends on both the attainability of the imagined identity of interests between workers and the state, and the costliness of information and ability of state personnel to gather and process it. In a market economy, efficient resource allocation is at best achieved only in relation to the distribution of income and subject to the government's diligence in correcting market failures. In a planned economy in which planners have perfect information and calculating abilities, it is in principle possible to specify an optimal solution to the problem of resource allocation with reference only to preferences, technology, and resources, and thus without regard to prices influenced by a specific income distribution and pattern of demand. The phenomena giving rise to market failures in a competitive economy can be dealt with as part of the comprehensive planning process, rather than requiring a separate set of corrective measures. Not only will resources be used efficiently, by such planning, but collective concerns with basic needs provision, equity, savings, and resource stewardship can all be given optimal expression in the plan, subject to objective constraints. If Marxian class solidarity exists, then alienation is eliminated, liberty presents no problem (the plan is not at odds with anyone's desired activities), and the system is thus also ideal with respect to its social and nonmaterial dimensions.

This assessment begins to unravel, however, if, as appears to be the case with nearly all practical trials, the identity of interests between those controlling the state and the population at large, and the accountability of the former to the latter, is significantly flawed. (Among other reasons for such flaws, we have noted the possibility that the population itself is heterogeneous, and hence that 'the will of the people' is difficult to define.) In that case, widely shared notions of equity and desires for basic goods may be largely ignored, the environment may be spoiled for short-term ends, and alienation, low quality of working life, and suppression of personal liberties may appear. The economy might still run efficiently, relative to planners' goals, if they can use their imagined perfect information to enforce plan fulfillment through draconian threats. However, the distinction between planners' preferences and those of other people, including enterprise managers, suggests a new set of problems once we adopt more realistic assumptions regarding information and calculating abilities.

If it is costly for planners to confirm information about resources and capabilities from the dispersed sites of production, and if managers are not inherently motivated by a desire to fulfill the plan, then planners need to provide enterprise managers with incentives both to supply information and to fulfill plans. But the two aims tend to be contradictory, for by understating existing capacity, input requirements, and production possibilities, managers can obtain more easily fulfilled targets. Moreover, it is difficult to choose performance indicators on which to base bonuses without inadvertently eliciting dysfunctional managerial behavior, such as excessive emphasis on output quantity or weight, or neglect of cost-reduction opportunities. It is also notoriously difficult to generate and implement technological innovations. Finally, the complexity of the practical problem of computing an optimal plan dictates that the methods of plan construction will fall short of what is hypothetically possible, so that even if feasible and fulfilled to the letter, plans will tend to be inefficient owing to inadequate assessment of relevant substitution possibilities in production and consumption, and to imperfect representation of resource scarcities and preferences. Indeed, adopted plans may not even prove to be technically feasible or consistent, because planners, ever struggling against managers' information distortions and attempts to improve their own resource bases, often push out to the limits of supply constraints, leading to excessive tautness of supply. This, in turn, reinforces managers' incentives to hoard resources and to increase their autonomy through vertical integration. Apart from jeopardizing the efficiency of the system, these problems may undercut its ability to satisfy basic material needs, and may contribute to the growth of illegal and semi-legal economic activities, some of which will have deleterious impacts on the system's equity.

Existing socialist societies depart from the pure model of centrally planned socialism in that plans are usually incomplete, much of agriculture is organized in collective (as well as private) production units, and there are some private markets. The existence of the 'second economy' is another departure from the model, although not a sanctioned one. Attempts to rectify the problems of centrally planned socialism include some that would perfect the system through improved planning techniques and political change, either of a sort that seeks to restore revolutionary purity, or (perhaps more hypothetically) along lines of genuine democracy. Other approaches to reform, however, would modify centrally planned socialism at least as drastically as the indicatively planned, redistributionist democratic welfare state does capitalism. In the limit, in fact, the system would cease to be planned except in broad outline; it would give way to 'market socialism', in which large capital goods and factories remain state property, but managers are free to deploy them so as to maximize profits, most of which they can retain for bonus funds and enterprise expansion. Much of the justification of socialism as a way of transcending the fragmented division of labor characterizing capitalist market economies would clearly have to be dropped by the wayside, preventing the ideologically orthodox from signing on to such changes. A more practical problem is that the transition from centrally planned to market socialism begins to break down the framework of job security and price stability by which a classical socialist regime wins acceptance. State reluctance or political inability to expose workers to risks of real income declines and firms to risks of bankruptcy therefore prevents reform from being completed. Finally, there are both efficiency and equity (or ideological) issues raised by any attempt to combine markets with 'social ownership' of capital.

Notes

1. Interest on savings accounts is a minor exception. Another is that portion of earnings from farming private farm plots that can be viewed as a scarcity rent on land, rather than a return on labor.
2. Marx and the classical economists also recognized the impact of these forces upon short-run or market prices, but not on long-run equilibrium values.
3. To put matters in perspective, it is probably useful to note here that the democratic state as we understand it today was little in evidence in Marx's day, so some of the present argument follows the elaborations of later Marxists.
4. Compare note 19 of Chapter 2.
5. Marx 1967a, p. 356.
6. Such uniformity of interests might be understood to mean that there is a common social utility function shared by all economic agents. A similar assumption is adopted in the 'theory of teams' developed by Marschack and Radner 1972.
7. See Herbert Simon 1957.
8. Marx 1978, p. 530.
9. 'Right can never be higher than the economic structure of society and its cultural development conditioned thereby.' (Marx 1978.) See also Wood 1972, and Roemer 1982.
10. Statistical analysis of income and social indicators such as those published by the World Bank (see the *World Development Report*, annual from 1978) show that life expectancy, infant mortality, and similar indicators are often more favorable in socialist than in non-socialist countries of comparable per capita income, especially at the lower end of the income scale. In 1986, for example, China, which had only a slightly higher GNP per capita than India's $290, had a substantially higher life expectancy (at birth) of 69 as opposed to India's 57, and a similarly lower infant (age 0 to 1) mortality rate of 34 per thousand, compared to India's 86. Cuba, at slightly lower GNP per capita than Guatemala's $930 and Peru's $1,090, had considerably higher life expectancy of 75 years than Guatemala's 61 and Peru's 60, and considerably lower infant mortality rate, of 14 per thousand, than Guatemala's 61 and Peru's 90. However, low-income Sri Lanka (GNP per capita $400), which has had a mildly socialist but non-Marxist government, achieved figures comparable to China's (life expectancy of

70 years and infant mortality rate of 29 per thousand), and Costa Rica, a little richer than Peru at $1,480 per capita income, did much better on life expectancy (74 years) and infant mortality (18 per thousand), suggesting that central planning *per se* is not necessary to such achievements. (Data from 1988 report, with reference to 1986. No income estimate is provided for Cuba.)

11. See Dorfman 1953, Nemchinov (ed.) 1964, Hardt 1967, Seton 1977, and Cave 1980. For a simplified treatment of the use of mathematical programming in a centrally planned economy, see Kohler 1989, pp. 314–23. See also Kohler's discussion of input-output planning methods on pp. 88–102 of the same text.

12. This ignores the problem of how the 'interest of the community' can be defined, if the interests of individual members were not identical—a problem to be considered shortly.

13. That is to say that, if the community with which it identifies does the same, the state may internalize all long-term opportunity costs and benefits of the uses to which it assigns social resources. The practical problem of the absence of a market price to signal the resource's value does not arise, yet, because we are still assuming unbounded ability to process information.

14. See Friedman 1962, and Hayek 1973, 1976, 1979.

15. One can also note, with Steven Rosefield (1981, p. 16), that 'the superficial correspondence of some aspects of the Bolshevik system with the tenets of socialism cannot offset the fact that the real content of social, political, and economic life in the Soviet Union is fundamentally inimical to the values most socialists claim to affirm', whereupon it may legitimately be asked whether the Soviet system is socialist at all. This is largely, of course, a semantic question. In this book, I try to avoid unnecessarily tarring 'socialism' with the Soviet brush (assuming that to be the likeliest consequence of such an association) not only by adopting (as just explained) an agnostic position on the political correlates of the centralized model, but also by identifying not socialism in any broader sense, but *centrally planned* socialism, as the subject of this chapter.

16. For further discussion, see Levine 1959.

17. See Nove 1962.

18. Bettelheim 1975.

19. Consider what the majority prefers when there are three individuals, the first of whom prefers *A* over *B* over *C*, the second *B* over *C* over *A*, and the third *C* over *A* over *B*. A large technical literature on the 'paradox of voting' and related problems has been stimulated by the work of Kenneth Arrow. A good introduction to this field is Feldman 1980, chapter 10.

20. The troublesome character of democratic voting from the standpoint of
    income distribution and poverty is closely related to the problem of the
    'informational bases of alternative welfare approaches' discussed by
    Amartya Sen (1974). As Sen emphasizes, voting allows for a social
    accounting of individual rankings of alternatives, but no accounting of
    the intensity of preference, of the differences in well-being attributable
    to moving from a more to a less preferred alternative, or of the relative
    importance of such differences to different individuals.
21. See Hayek 1935 (ed.), 1945; Schumpeter 1949; and Mises 1951.
22. This must be said despite the fact that Marx himself was a pioneer in
    the incorporation of technological change, and macro-economic dis-
    equilibria, into economic analysis.
23. Lerner 1944; Lange 1964.
24. In brief, planners find prices at which markets clear, by lowering prices
    whenever inventories build up, and raising them when supply cannot
    meet demand. Socialist managers are instructed to operate their plants
    at the levels at which marginal cost equals the prices set through this
    procedure.
25. In Lange–Lerner socialism, unlike that of the Soviet system and of the
    ideal centrally planned socialist system discussed in this chapter,
    planners set prices, but not quantities. The main theoretical problem is
    that it is not clear how managers can be motivated to produce where
    marginal cost equals price, unless planners can verify that condition,
    which again raises the information problem. Giving managers a share of
    the profits could help, but only for industries producing non-public
    goods under increasing marginal costs of production and without
    externalities. In practice, decentralizing socialist economies such as
    Hungary have tended towards a model of market socialism in which
    prices are determined by markets, not by planners following a Lange–
    Lerner trial-and-error procedure. For further discussion, see Kohler
    1989, chapter 8.
26. Strictly speaking, since Austrian economic thought denies the relevance
    of neoclassical models of competition, which it regards as abstractions,
    its proponents might find the statement that 'imperfect information
    poses problems for the ideal model of capitalism' to be meaningless.
27. See Kornai 1980.
28. For example, officials charged with allocating scarce resources among
    competing, profit-seeking enterprises and businesses may appropriate
    the difference between official and scarcity prices as personal income by
    accepting bribes for allocations. The same may occur under full
    centralization, but the magnitude of the problem and the amounts of
    money involved can be increased by the opening up of profit
    opportunities, and the easing of restrictions on personal receipt of

profits by enterprise managers and private businessmen.
29. On the problems of reform in centrally planned economies, see Hewett 1981; Hare, Radice, and Swain (eds) 1981; and Reynolds (ed.) 1987.
30. These last criticisms have also been leveled against the Soviet type of centralized socialism, which makes liberal use of material incentives in an attempt to obtain managerial compliance with planned objectives. To holders of such views, market socialism is merely one more step in the wrong direction.

Suggested Readings

Abouchar, Alan (ed.), 1977, *The Socialist Price Mechanism*, Durham, NC: Duke University Press.

Arrow, Kenneth, 1963, *Social Choice and Individual Values*, New York: Wiley.

Bahro, Rudolph, 1981, *The Alternative in Eastern Europe*, London: New Left Books.

Bergson, Abram and Levine, Herbert (eds), 1983, *The Soviet Economy: Toward the Year 2000*, London: Allen and Unwin.

Bornstein, Morris (ed.), 1981, *The Soviet Economy: Continuity and Change*, Boulder, CO: Westview Press.

Brus, Wlodzimierz, 1975, *Socialist Ownership and Political Systems*, London: Routledge and Kegan Paul.

Nove, Alec, 1980, *The Soviet Economic System* (2nd edn), London: Allen and Unwin.

Powell, Raymond, 1977, 'Plan Execution and the Workability of Soviet Planning', *Journal of Comparative Economics* 1:1, 51–76.

Riskin, Carl, 1987, *China's Political Economy: The Quest for Development since 1949*, New York: Oxford University Press.

Sweezy, Paul M., 1968, *The Theory of Capitalist Development: Principles of Marxian Political Economy*, New York: Monthly Review Press.

4.
Workers' Self-management

4.1 Institutional Premises and Features

Compared with competitive capitalism and centrally planned socialism, the third and last economic system to be discussed at length in this book, self-management, is one on which there is less complete agreement on definition, and less historical experience to which to refer. While the central institutional premise by which workers' self-management is to be identified is relatively clear, which other features should be viewed as aspects of the ideal model of self-management, and which ones as modifications or variants, cannot be as easily pinned down. Perhaps self-management should be treated as a facet of an economic system, rather than a complete system in itself. But because the major principle in question sharply distinguishes self-management from at least the core variants of both the capitalist and the planned socialist systems, and because the desirability of embracing that principle in some form is one of the most discussed and most interesting issues in the domain of economic system studies today, we judge extended treatment to be warranted.

To make it possible to proceed on roughly parallel tracks to those followed in the previous two chapters, we therefore provide a picture of self-management as a complete economic system, making clear where the central focus lies and where, on the other hand, we are filling in details in a more debatable fashion. To preview the discussion, we treat the most basic feature of self-management as the principle that, in this economic system, producers jointly control the production process at the level of the production units or enterprises. With respect to coordination of the relations among enterprises and between enterprises and consumers, we assume that this role is largely performed by markets, but we also assume an array of interventions along the lines of the indicatively planned industrial capitalist economies (or market socialism). Finally, throughout the chapter, we leave open the question of whether capital ownership and financing follow a state and collective approach, or a private

149

one. Later discussions will make explicit what we consider the likely implications of this choice to be.

4.1.1 The Central Principle of Self-management

Capitalism and planned socialism, the dominant economic systems of the twentieth century, can be said to differ from one another, in terms of basic principles at least, in two fundamental respects. First, capitalism is based on private property in productive assets, while socialism makes the same class of assets 'social' property. Second, capitalism uses free interactions of agents in markets as its principal means of coordinating the division of labor among economic units, while socialism attempts to meet the coordination requirement through government planning. If we draw a two-by-two matrix of system features, placing ownership system on one axis and coordination system on the other (as in Figure 4.1), we find pure capitalism in one of the four resulting boxes, and classical centrally

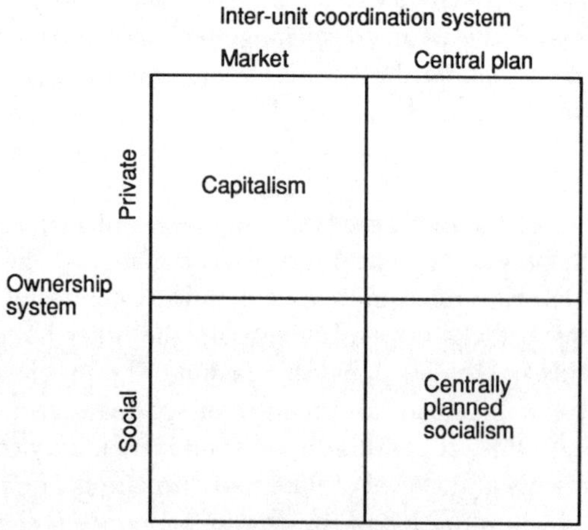

FIG. 4.1.
Classification scheme I: coordination and ownership
Workers' self-management cannot be identified with any position in this framework for characterizing capitalist and centrally planned socialist economies.

planned socialism in the diagonally opposite box, with two boxes remaining empty. However, rather than helping to fill one of the empty boxes, or fitting handily anywhere on such a diagram, the self-management alternative to capitalism and socialism, in its central principle, at least, falls altogether outside of this schema. (An alternative scheme that successfully locates all three systems on a similar grid will be introduced in Chapter 5.)

The basic principle of self-management concerns neither ownership of resources nor coordination among economic units, but rather the nature of the division of labor within units of production. In both capitalism and centralized socialism most production takes place within enterprises that are under the ultimate control of the owners of the capital—in capitalism, the private owners or equity holders; in socialism, the state. In both systems workers are hired by enterprises, are paid wages for their labor, and work at the instruction of supervisors ultimately responsible to management, which is responsible to the owners. The division of labor is hierarchical, in the sense that there exists a pyramid of authority, with managers, who are either owners or appointed by them, at the top, and with production workers at the bottom.[1]

In a self-managed economy, production takes place within enterprises that are under the ultimate control of those who work in them. Instead of being employees of the enterprise, they may be thought of as its cooperating members. Instead of being pyramidal, the structure of authority in the enterprise is horizontal (workers share authority equally) or circular (workers collectively delegate authority to leaders or managers, who direct them in their activities but are ultimately also responsible to them). The workers therefore determine the manner in which production is organized within the enterprise.

At its heart, then, self-management is concerned with the method of coordination of the division of labor within production units, and this leaves open the question of the method of coordinating the relations between units (such relations must exist unless those units are self-sufficient), as well as the question of property rights. It is for this reason that we began by stating that self-management may represent a system feature more than it does a complete system. To describe self-management as an economic system, in the proper sense, we must at least provisionally fill in some missing pieces.

4.1.2 Extra-firm Coordination under Self-management

Even if self-management's central principle looks to a different dimension from the set of variables that distinguish capitalism and planned socialism, the menu of choices for coordination of economic units, including inter-enterprise relationships, may be the same as that facing the other two systems. That is, coordination of the discrete units of the economy may have to be either by central plan, by markets, or by some mix of the two. Most economists believe that these are the exclusive choices for a complex economy, unless, that is, it is to be fragmented into a set of essentially independent local subsistence economies. For now, we will accept this assumption, and save for our final chapter discussion of whether there are or can be other alternatives to market and plan. The only question we will address here, then, is where the self-managed economy will station itself along the spectrum from unregulated market economy to centrally planned economy.

While certain anti-market advocates of self-management are in favor of maximum restrictions on markets, and would advocate implementation of social planning (perhaps by a representative decision-making process in which self-managed enterprises are the local units),[2] the argument identifying self-management with a significant degree of economic decentralization is more commonly made and at least arguably more compelling. If the conventional socialist theory that the economy can be popularly controlled by way of political mechanisms at the national level were credible, then there would be little reason to reject the centralized socialist model. Even in a planned economy, self-management might appear to represent an important change in the internal structure of the enterprise. Yet if quantitative plans are to be binding on enterprises, so that resource allocation for the whole society can be determined by 'use value' criteria, those plans must be detailed, therefore leaving little room for enterprise discretion. If workers would have little to control at the enterprise level, it is difficult to see how meaningful involvement in enterprise decision-making could develop.[3]

To assume that self-managed enterprises freely determine their levels of output, membership size, and input usage, is consistent with the large theoretical literature on such firms, and on economies composed of them, that has emerged in the past thirty years;[4] it also accords with the 'market socialism' direction to which Yugoslavia turned after embracing self-management in the early 1950s, and with the situation of individual worker-run firms found in many other countries. We will assume that the 'market' in this compound term means that at least a good many of the prices to which self-managed enterprises respond are determined by competitive forces, and not by administrative fiat.[5]

On the other hand, it seems possible to delimit the position of a self-managed economy on the plan–market spectrum still further by ruling out the extreme free market end of that spectrum. The reason is that while a high degree of maneuverability seems necessary in order to make micro-level self-management meaningful, the political and social philosophy underpinning a worker-managed economic system, with its emphasis on social equality, personal development, and satisfaction in the production process (see below), seems unlikely to be one that would put complete faith in competitive market forces as a means of directing economic activity. The interrelatedness of income distribution, demand, and industrial structure, the problems of public goods and intergenerational trade-offs, and other themes that have arisen as rationales for governmental interventions in the last two chapters, again present themselves here. While accepting the desirability of decentralized and competitive arrangements as a means of promoting both micro-level self-management and the efficiency and demand-responsiveness associated with market systems, then, the partisans of a self-managed economy are likely to lean towards a certain amount of state activism and intervention, perhaps in the form of indicative planning and of fiscal policies favoring the growth of particular lines of economic activity.[6]

4.1.3 Ownership and Self-management

A second conventional spectrum separating 'capitalism' and 'socialism' is that of property rights in non-labor means of production. In this case, there may be even less hope of identifying a consensus position, or an a priori argument, for stationing the self-managed economy at one spot instead of another. Yet what system of property rights, and the closely related matter of what methods of financing self-managed firms, are adopted, can be expected to have a crucial effect on the system's performance. Our approach will be to identify one strictly hypothetical and two more realistic alternatives, in the present section, and then to examine and evaluate the self-managed economy under each of these systems of property rights and finance.

We have already stated that the basis of workers' control rights in self-managed enterprises is their status as members of the enterprise work force, not as the enterprise's 'owners'. This leaves open the question of who, if anyone, owns the physical and financial capital and the material stocks with which the enterprise works, who finances their acquisition, and what rights to economic returns are associated with those roles. And in relation to this, we have not yet established whether under self-management there could be private ownership of, trading in, and income payments to capital and other scarce resources, or whether those resources and their returns are controlled exclusively by the state or collective entities.

The hypothetical ownership system alluded to just above is one of complete state ownership and rental of capital goods to firms. The two more realistic property rights systems to be considered later in the chapter are, first, one in which all rights in capital belong to the state and collectives, and second, one in which some of those rights belong to individuals.

Exclusive State Ownership: A Hypothetical Case Consider first the hypothetical case in which the state owns all capital goods and allocates them among self-managed enterprises according to a central investment plan. In the limit, enterprises pay no specific charge for use of such capital. A likely result would be that the enterprises would treat capital as a free good and petition the state for as much of it as possible. This would make it difficult for the state to acquire from enterprises the kinds of information needed to allocate the society's capital effectively. Suppose, on the contrary, that the state supplied capital and as payment, collected all net enterprise revenues above fixed earnings for the enterprises' workers. In that case, it is difficult to see what incentives for efficient production would be left to the workers, and it is unlikely that the state could allow workers much discretion in managing the firm. Finally, consider the somewhat different, but still hypothetical case of a system in which the state allocates capital to firms that rent it at competitive prices. This kind of system will be assumed as an ideal case in section 4.3. However, for reasons touched on later (in section 4.4), this case also does not appear to be fully realistic.

Mixed State–Collective Ownership: A First Realistic Model   Imagine, now, that when the state supplies some capital to worker-run firms, workers' earnings are not strictly fixed in advance. With discretion over the disposal of residual income, another source of enterprise capital comes into being: workers' enterprises can add to their capital stocks by investment out of profits. This is one way of motivating our first realistic specification of property rights, which entails the existence of both state and collective ownership of capital. We say collective, because, in this scenario, workers are assumed to forfeit all personal claims upon the value of any assets created out of retained enterprise earnings. Although we say that these assets are collectively owned by the firm, it makes little difference if they are said to be owned by 'society' but used by the firm, whose workers will find their incomes to be augmented on account of it to the extent that it raises their productivity. The difference between state and collective capital, in this first realistic model, is only that the latter results from the retained earnings of firms.

Western economists have pointed out that since collective investment entails a reduction in members' current incomes for the sake of enhanced future earnings, their willingness to so invest would depend upon their individual expectations of remaining with the enterprise, and on the payback period of the capital goods purchased. With long-lived capital goods and short membership horizons, there would be a disincentive to collective investment, especially if workers had the alternative of paying themselves higher current incomes and placing some of these payments in savings accounts having returns competitive with those on physical assets.[7]

To add to collective investment by enterprises, the state could set mandatory profit retention levels, requiring that retained funds be invested within the enterprises that generated them. Enterprises could also be required to set aside funds for the replacement of their existing capital goods with new ones of equal value, though not necessarily of identical type or function. Another approach is for the state to gather finance directly by taxing enterprise profits, workers' incomes, and sales of final and intermediate goods. The funds thus obtained could then be provided to enterprises on loan or grant basis for the purchase of capital goods.

Individualized Ownership: A Second Realistic Model   In our second realistic model of ownership and self-management, individual ownership of capital goods and financial instruments, and receipt of earnings based upon them, are introduced. A large part of aggregate savings is assumed, in this model, to be by private individuals, in savings accounts and bonds, and by individuals or the state (on their behalf) in pension and insurance funds. These funds are made available to self-managed enterprises by banks and other financial intermediaries—themselves labor-managed—at interest rates that bring supply and demand into equilibrium. Workers' enterprises having in view investment projects with expected rates of return above this rate will seek and acquire these funds, so that all projects having anticipated productivity higher than the going rate, and only those projects, will be funded. An enterprise may also sell bonds directly to workers or other investors, and its own workers may hold claims to a share of its capital assets. The horizon disincentive to investing retained profits, and the planning information problem previously discussed, do not arise here.

While in the model just sketched out workers can own equity in their own firms, considerations of 'portfolio diversification' suggest that they would rarely prefer to do this to any great extent. Nevertheless, if capital markets are highly imperfect, which might, for example, be the case for most smaller firms, then substantial self-financing by an enterprise's own workers might be unavoidable. With individualized and redeemable claims in the form of equity shares, internal capital accounts,[8] or bonds, the horizon problem of collective investment from undistributed profits continues to be avoided. But still to be faced is the bearing of a large burden of risk by workers, whose returns to specific human capital as well as to financial wealth are both then tied to their enterprise's fortunes.

One point must be underscored with reference to the individualized ownership model: that even though both workers and outsiders may hold claims on an enterprise's assets, this in no way entitles them to a say in directing those assets' use. Nor would the decision-making powers of individual worker-managers be permitted to vary depending upon the number of shares each owned. In a system of pure workers' management, enterprise control rights derive from the status of worker-membership, not ownership. Of course, hybrid forms in which both asset ownership and worker status confer control rights might exist elsewhere—they will be discussed briefly in section 4.5, below—but they take us beyond the realm of self-management as a pure system type.

4.2 Sources of the Self-management Impulse

Whereas a dominant rationale for capitalism exists in the free
market ideology of classical liberalism, and a similarly conventional
rationale for centralized socialism exists in Marxism, no single motivation for the recently widespread interest in self-management,
and in 'participatory' and 'democratic' economic forms more
broadly, can easily claim such a dominant position. In this section,
four distinct rationales for self-management are discussed briefly.
They derive, respectively, from (1) the impulse to expand the
domains of liberty and democracy, from (2) radical aspirations to
empower workers and end alienation, from (3) the humanistic desire
to improve the quality of working life, and from (4) the organizational design concern with eliciting consummate performance from
all members of an enterprise's workforce.

4.2.1 Self-management, Liberty, and Democracy

Although conventional liberalism and libertarianism oppose the
institutionalization of self-management, which they see as a constraint on people's rights to enter voluntarily into mutually
beneficial contracts, an influential view of self-management is that it
represents an extension of the liberal and democratic revolutions.
From the standpoint of liberty, self-management extends the liberal
prohibition of slavery—the inalienability of the laborer as a
person—to include prohibition of the conventional wage contract,
which it sees as equivalent to rental in the short term of that which
the slavery prohibition renders illegal to purchase on a once and for
all basis. In the wage contract, workers trade the rights to their
products (or to the revenue for which they can be exchanged) and
rights to control their work process, in exchange for a specified
money wage. A fully self-managed economy outlaws such trades,
just as a capitalist economy outlaws voluntary agreements to enter
into slavery or indentured servitude.

   With regard to democracy, it has been argued[9] that meaningful
control by ordinary people over the social dimensions of their lives
requires the practice of democracy at levels on which the individual
can be immediately effective—the community and workplace—as a
school for participation at more remote levels such as the nation. In
addition, the democratic theory of governance, according to which

those who are directly affected by a decision have a right to a voice in making that decision, is said to apply to the workplace for the same reasons that it applies to ordinary government. In this case, the position of self-management advocates is that it is workers, by virtue of their presence in the workplace and their subjection to the authority relations that reign within it, who are entitled to such governance rights, rather than owners, who are frequently far from the scene and for whom the effect of enterpise decisions is a more 'indirect' one (that is, it has an impact on their wealth rather than on their persons). Another frequently put argument is that democracy, being about equality of power among persons, remains incomplete if not extended to the economic domain, where crucial aspects of personal welfare are determined.

The liberty and democracy arguments for self-management can be tied to the central standpoint of this book by observing that the problem of specialization and coordination within enterprises shares the features of the division of labor problem as described more generally in Chapter 1. Productivity seems to be enhanced in many spheres of production, at least up to a point, by expanding the scale of the enterprise and the extent of the division of labor within it. As individuals take on more specialized roles, some of the familiar problems of coordination arise: how will specialists sort themselves out in the right proportions, how will rationality of the total process be assured, and how will the benefits and costs of specialization (including the personal impacts of varying work roles) be distributed?

The conventional liberal answer to this problem, with regard to inter-unit interactions, is that coordination is achieved by the market. The market protects the anonymity and respects the juridical equality of all agents, who enter only into mutually beneficial interactions. The problem, as seen by a liberal proponent of self-management, is that enterprises emerge as rational spheres of planning within which specialization takes the form of organizational hierarchy. Also, for reasons of risk aversion, portfolio diversification, and unequal wealth, control of that hierarchy is generally held by non-workers, or by people who also are workers, but acting in their capacities as asset owners. Thus, the logic of the capitalist economy fails to reproduce, in the relations of production within the workplace, the freedom and equality of exchange observed in the market. The right to be free to control one's work and one's product, and to do so on a basis of equality with those with whom one jointly labors, must therefore be put forward as a separate and distinct principle.

4.2.2 'Factories to the Workers' and Alienation

Marxism and other radical ideologies reject welfare-minded social reforms that would achieve equity by redistributing products without changing the organizational dimension of the sphere of production. A central concern for Marx was alienation in the work process. He criticized economists' equation of work with drudgery on grounds that this equation, rather than being natural, is the product of specific social conditions, and that productive labor is actually at the heart of man's humanity and at the core of human self-realization.

Just as peasant movements have often demanded that land be given to its tillers, so radical labor movements have demanded that factories be turned over to their workers; this rhetoric was embraced, for example, by the Bolsheviks in the Russian Revolution of 1917. However, as the last chapter emphasized, the main thrust of Marxism has tended to be one in which the struggle between workers and owners of capital is viewed as taking place at national (if not international) levels, and in which socialism is seen as a system giving workers power over society's resources, and the ability to direct them toward the production of 'use values', at the level of the state, rather than the firm. As important a Marxist authority as Friedrich Engels wrote in 1872: 'Wanting to abolish authority in large-scale industry is tantamount to wanting to abolish industry itself, to destroy the power loom in order to return to the spinning wheel.'[10] And Marx's own disparaging remark on the tension between 'anarchy in the social division of labor and despotism in that of the workshop'[11] under capitalism appears, as we have seen, to be more a call for replacing markets with society-wide hierarchy than a call for democracy in the workplace.

The apparent contradiction between Marx's concern with alienation and his advocacy of central planning can be resolved either by supposing that he naïvely imagined worker democracy and central control of the economy to be compatible, or by understanding his conception of socialism to be one of stages, with the elimination of authority and alienation coming only after a preliminary period (or periods) of socialism had been completed.[12] In any case, even if it is not the dominant line of radical thought, the foundations of a radical case for self-management are easily constructed. This case would begin by abandoning the state socialist project of empowering workers and ending alienation through worker control of the state, because it is too indirect, too unrealistic about the problems of centralized economic management, and too utopian with regard to workers' abilities to act in concert and to identify with actions taken in their name at remote levels. It would then embrace self-management of enterprises as the most obvious vehicle for establishing meaningful control by workers over their economic destinies, and for eliminating alienation from the work process, the tools of production, and labor's fruits.[13]

4.2.3 Quality of Working Life

A third rationale for self-management centers not on rights, power, or alienation in the Marxian sense, but on the quality of people's working lives. This framework emphasizes the fact that work is not only a means of obtaining income, but also a direct source of utility or disutility, as an activity in which people spend a large, and often the most active, portion of their waking hours. Monotonous, unchallenging work performed simply to earn a wage and to avoid provoking penalities from watchful supervisors, may cause not only low satisfaction on the job, but also a lowered sense of self-esteem, and a general depression of creative faculties that can spill over into leisure time and relationships off the job. On the other hand, challenging, creative work motivated both by intrinsic and extrinsic rewards may not only provide job satisfaction, but also an opportunity for personal development, increased self-esteem, and more rewarding personal relationships and uses of leisure time. Playing a part in shaping one's work environment may both serve the instrumental function of facilitating the design of better job characteristics, and be a direct source of enhanced satisfaction and pride.

The main question to be asked of this approach, from the standpoint of free market economists, is why the institutionalization of self-management should be necessary to optimal working conditions. In a perfectly competitive market economy, employers must compete with one another to attract workers, by offering packages of job characteristics that include wages and payment arrangements (that is, whether earnings will take the form of piece rates, whether bonuses will be offered, etc.), promotion and lay-off prospects, working hours and intensity, and workplace organization and technical conditions of work. If workers value a non-hierarchical workplace with non-monotonous, challenging jobs, employers will offer these to them unless they can be provided only at a sacrifice in terms of wages, working hours, or other factors, to which workers assign still higher value. Even fully worker-run firms will appear in a market economy whenever the benefits they offer exceed their costs, as perceived by workers; there are no legal barriers to their formation.

Those who advocate the institutionalization of self-management respond to this argument in several ways. In the first place, the persistence of unemployment suggests that competition among firms for limited workers is the exception, and competition among workers for limited jobs the rule, in most market economies. Second, even if employers do compete for workers, the fact remains that if employers are unilaterally responsible for job design, and if willingness to accept and remain on a job is the only signal of workers' valuation of different aspects of the overall job package, workers' global preferences over all the relevant dimensions of jobs may fail to be communicated to employers.[14] Third, managers or capital owners may have an interest in maintaining their power within firms, both for its own sake and in order to protect their shares of the firms' earnings; such an interest may lead them to avoid certain organizational changes. At the same time, there may exist obstacles to the formation and survival of strictly worker-run firms (for example, such firms may have difficulty financing the acquisition of capital so long as investors have the option of buying equity that comes with voting control rights, which they prefer[15]). Finally, socialization to accept monotonous and vertically supervised jobs, and insufficiency of education to take on the challenges of running more democratic workplaces, may be pervasive in the capitalist society, so that endogenously formed preferences and abilities serve as a constraint on the development of potentially more fulfilling types of work organization.[16]

4.2.4 Participation and Productivity

The last approach to self-management, rather than advocating it as a nonmaterial good for which narrower economic ends should be sacrificed, views it as a means to achieving one of those ends: namely, maximum productivity. Among the arguments here is that if workers themselves are not the immediate beneficiaries of higher or better quality output, and of lower resource costs of production, they have incentives to minimize effort and to be indifferent to input wastage except in so far as their work is monitored; but monitoring is costly, and it remains imperfect at the point where the employer equalizes its marginal benefit with its marginal cost. Therefore the effort that employers succeed at eliciting is obtained at an unnecessarily high cost. With profit-sharing and worker control of production, on the other hand, each worker sees a link between productivity and earnings, and workers are motivated to monitor one another even while engaging in production, so that productivity is maximized subject to the opportunities for transforming subjectively costly effort into valued income. Other productivity arguments for self-management include the idea that people will more enthusiastically carry out decisions that they helped to make, and the possibility that workplace satisfaction engendered by self-management may be correlated with worker productivity.

The productivity arguments for self-management are difficult either to prove or to disprove on a priori grounds. Although some shirking may be unavoidable in conventional firms, members of profit-sharing, self-managed enterprises might also be inclined to shirk effort, because the individual's share of any added revenue may be small, while the benefit of reduced effort accrues to him directly. Self-managed teams may therefore also need to link individual reward to individual effort by monitoring the latter, and it is difficult to decide on theoretical grounds whether they will do so more cheaply or effectively than will firms where claims on residual earnings are less widely shared. The more psychological arguments linking participation with productivity clearly require empirical testing. There is accumulating evidence that participation and profit sharing in individual firms in market economies are frequently associated with higher productivity, but many free-market economists ask why such innovations are not more common, if they can in fact raise productivity. For their part, enthusiasts of self-management point to capital market or other problems, of the sort mentioned in the previous section, as possible answers.

4.3 Performance of the Self-managed Economy: The Ideal Case

When considering how capitalism and centralized socialism measure up against our evaluative standards of material needs provision, equity, efficiency, social effects, and stewardship and bequest, we began by assuming conditions ideal for the performance of each system. As a form of market economy, the ideal conditions for self-management may be similar to those for capitalism: namely, the conditions supporting perfect competition, including a large number of economic agents individually lacking market power, and perfect information, so that markets move quickly towards equilibrium. We will go a bit further and insist here that productive factors be highly mobile and that adjustments to equilibrium be rapid in an ideal self-managed economy, for reasons to be made clear shortly. Given the assumption, in the present case, of a government prepared to intervene to correct market failures, redistribute income, and otherwise steer the economy in desired directions, where these do not automatically result from the market process, the additional assumptions that there are no externalities or public goods may be unnecessary. In view of possible difficulties in the financing of self-managed enterprises, one extra assumption is added in this section: that firms can rent all capital goods they might wish to use in perfectly functioning rental markets, and that rental is no less efficient than would be the use of enterprise-owned capital goods. This leaves open the question of who in fact owns the capital goods (we may hypothetically assume it to be the government) or what motivates investment in them; but the assumption is not meant to be realistic, and it is abandoned in section 4.4.

4.3.1 Material Needs and Equity

In a highly competitive environment with fluid factor markets, it is possible that self-management will result in the same distribution of income as that generated by a capitalist market economy. If what is produced is entirely determined by market forces, then this would mean that such an economy would have the same advantages and limitations with respect to needs fulfillment as does perfectly competitive capitalism. On the other hand, even with factor mobility, it seems conceivable that the internal dynamics of self-management within firms might lead to more equal incomes, at least at the firm level. For example, a more equal, cooperation-engendering income distribution within a firm might lead to higher worker productivity, causing enterprises to opt for such patterns; or decision-making participation may lead to less hierarchical organizational styles involving a wider distribution of training opportunities, and thus less differentiation of workers' marginal products. If less inequality at firm levels carries over to the economy as a whole, then the market will support more production and broader consumption of goods satisfying basic needs.

The possibility of government intervention to steer the market towards social goals could also mean that production of basic goods, consumer and environmental protection, redistributive income taxation, etc., are promoted, with the result of a more complete satisfaction of basic material needs than either the perfectly competitive capitalist or the labor-managed economies tend to achieve in the absence of such interventions.

The standard of equity against which most proponents of self-management would have the system measured is one according to which workers are rewarded in proportion to the quality and intensity of their work effort, with equal contributions rewarded equally. If there is perfect competition, there will be no economic profits in equilibrium. Windfall profits and rents on scarce, fixed resources could be appropriated by the state (or other organizations) for further investment or social expenditures, or both. The society, to an extent consistent with its general level of development, would ensure that basic goods and services are provided to the infirm and elderly, and training to the unskilled.

The perfectly competitive labor-managed economy in long-run equilibrium satisfies the equity requirement of equal pay for equal work at least as well as does the perfectly competitive capitalist economy. In both cases, there remains the question of whether the scale of differentiation of pay established by market forces is itself ethically acceptable. Without an activist state, the requirement of equity, at least as construed by some, might not be met; but a redistributive remedy is consistent with our expectation of a mixed plan/market system.

4.3.2 Self-management and Efficiency

Imposition in this section, and abandonment in the next section, of the ideal assumptions listed above, helps to bring into focus some important efficiency problems identified by the theoretical literature on self-managed firms. Those problems fall into two groups: on the one hand, misallocation of labor and backward inclined or inelastic supply curves of products, and on the other hand, a tendency to underinvestment in capital goods, and the unwanted consequences of state interventions to offset that tendency. The first set of problems have so dominated the discussion of self-management by economists that it is helpful to introduce them at the outset, although we will see that they are ruled out by our provisional assumption of perfect competition and rapid adjustments to equilibrium. The second set of problems is avoided, for the time being, by our assumption of efficient rental of capital goods. In this case, discussion is deferred until section 4.4.

Product Supply and Membership   Economic theories of self-managed firms[17] generally assume that they are distinguished from entrepreneurial or profit-maximizing firms in that their objective is to maximize the per-period profit or net revenue per worker-member, rather than *total* profit per period. Whether this difference in objectives makes a difference to behavior depends upon a great many assumptions, but the simplest model of self-management suggests strongly that there could indeed be a difference.[18] If worker-managed firms can freely take on new members or dismiss present ones so as to adjust their membership size to the one that maximizes profit per worker, then the single product firm with labor as its only short-run variable input can be shown to respond 'perversely' to changes in product price. Instead of increasing output when the price rises and reducing it when the price falls, as would a profit-maximizing counterpart, the labor-run firm reduces its membership and, thus, output, when the price rises, and increases both when price falls. It is assumed that reducing membership when conditions are profitable has two effects: reducing the number of units on which profit can be earned, and reducing the number of workers among whom it will be shared. The second effect, which means an increase in per-worker profit, tends to be dominant over a range of outputs and number of workers. On the other hand, increasing member-

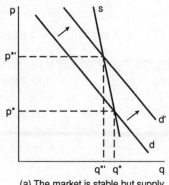 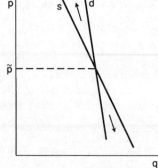

(a) The market is stable but supply responds perversely to demand.

(b) A stable equilibrium price does not exist. At p>p̃, there is excess demand, so price tends to rise. At p<p̃, there is excess supply, so price tends to fall.

p   price
p*   initial stable equilibrium price
p*' stable equilibrium price following increase in demand
p̃   price at which supply equals demand in the unstable case
q   quantity supplied and demanded
q*   initial stable equilibrium quantity transacted
q*' equilibrium quantity transacted following increase in demand
s   supply curve
d   demand curve
d'   demand curve following increase in demand

FIG. 4.2.

Aggregate demand and supply curves in a simple model of the self-managed economy

Stability of market equilibrium in a theoretical self-managed economy in which aggregate supply curves are backward bending depends on the relative steepness of the demand and supply curves.

ship when conditions are unprofitable spreads the losses. Hence, the quantity of product supplied varies inversely with price, and whether markets would function at all in an economy of self-managed firms depends on whether demand curves are more or less steeply sloped than the backward bending supply curves (see Figure 4.2).

Factors that might offset this hypothetical tendency are numerous. For example, if firms produce several products, or have several variable inputs, product supply curves will be either less negatively sloped, or positively sloped. The model described in the previous paragraph also ignores the fact that willingness of nonmembers to join the firm depends on what they expect it to pay them. An upward sloping supply of workers to the firm (in other words, a condition in which the higher the expected pay-out is per worker, the greater is the number of workers who want to join) may be enough to render its output supply curve positively sloped. Moreover, the assumption of free dismissal of workers who become 'redundant' when prices increase, made in the simple model, ignores the interests and rights of those dismissed. If workers vote on dismissals and if those who will be dismissed are chosen randomly, the perverse outcome will not occur, for voting workers will consider not only their higher earnings if they remained with the cooperative, but also their fates if they are discharged by it. If firms can charge a fee to new members, and if they set it at what the market will bear, this can also be shown to lead them to respond to demand changes in very much the same fashion as do conventional firms. Finally, if existing firms move in and out of product markets, or firms are formed and disbanded whenever returns from a given type of labor are unequal across industries, then a change in demand in any one industry will lead to reallocation of labor and capital among industries until these returns are again equalized, at which point factor allocation will be fully efficient. There is nothing 'perverse' about responses to demand changes once such factor mobility is assumed to obtain in a competitive self-managed economy, and so this section's assumptions of perfect competition and rapid movement to equilibrium suffice to eliminate misallocation of labor and product supply responses as problems for self-managed economies.

The tendency of worker-members to avoid reinvestment of earnings in their firms when capital becomes collective or 'social' property was mentioned earlier in the chapter. But with rental of all capital goods, underinvestment should not occur. In perfectly competitive markets, users would appropriately rent any capital goods the value of the marginal product of which exceeded their rental price, so capital goods would be efficiently allocated across firms and industries. Problems in the absence of perfectly efficient rental markets will be addressed in section 4.4.

Work Incentives and Managerial Efficiency In the previous section, we discussed the claim that worker-run firms can achieve higher factor productivity by providing better incentives to effort. Because

workers' earnings vary directly with enterprise performance in a
worker-run firm, workers may be more likely to cooperate with one
another to maximize output, and they may monitor one another's
performance, rather than ignore or even collude in shirking work.
Workers may also be more conscientious when implementing
decisions in which they have had a voice. The opposite position has
also been argued by some economists, however. These analysts
suggest that there is an incentive problem in teams in which the
effort of the individual member is difficult to observe and impossible
to infer directly from total team output. One variant of the argument
is that while any way of sharing the resulting income fails to prevent
'free riding' by individual team members, optimal effort might be
induced if an employer, contracting with the whole team, can cred-
ibly commit himself to paying each team member only if the total
output is consistent with *all* team members having provided their
contracted effort levels.[19] Such a procedure could in theory make
monitoring redundant, and would be difficult to replicate when net
income is automatically divided among members; however, it seems
remote from observed practice in conventional wage-paying firms.
A different variant of the argument says that the 'free-rider' problem
is best addressed by monitoring work performance, and asserts that
giving the monitor exclusive claim to the firm's profit provides the
best incentive to get that job done.[20] While intriguing, this argument
is not fully convincing, among other reasons because supervisors in
most capitalist firms are not the main profit recipients, because work
monitoring, and (evidently, then) the motivation to perform it, can
also be found in worker-run firms, and because more participatory
firms can often engender higher levels of worker productivity using
fewer supervisors, which means savings on supervisory costs.

Another set of problems relevant to the efficiency of self-
management are those relating to the decision-making process. The
potential inconsistency of democratic decision-making was discussed
in the previous chapter, and its relevance to democratic firms should
be obvious. Some economists have argued that because a larger
number of people are involved in decision-making in worker-run
firms, forcing more time to be spent on communication and
deliberations, and because those with the strongest leadership
abilities are not able to assume full decision-making powers and to
assign others to tasks according to their comparative strengths,

labor-managed firms will be less satisfactorily managed and less successful at grasping new opportunities and adapting to changing environments. However, it is not clear that more people need be involved in most decisions in a labor-managed firm, since management or leadership responsibilities can be delegated, and the number of *ultimate* decision-makers (the workers) will not necessarily be larger than is the number of their capitalist counterparts, the shareholders of a corporation. Worker-run firms may be able to balance the job enhancement and motivational advantages of participatory decision-making against the costs in time and in returns on expertise, thereby to arrive at optimal mixes of hierarchy and democracy in management. (Note that our definition of self-management did not say that all workers are equally involved in decision-making, or that there is no managerial hierarchy. Rather, it said that workers are the *ultimate* decision-makers, which means that a hierarchy that is accountable to workers is quite admissible.)

The similarity of the shareholder-manager relationship in corporate capitalism with the worker-manager relationship in workers' self-management suggests to some economists with an interest in financial markets yet another potential problem for self-managed firms. Under capitalism, they argue, the financial markets help keep managements on their toes, not only because investors' changing evaluations of enterprise performance translate into variations in the cost of capital to firms, but also because present or raiding shareholders can install new managers, and have an incentive to do so when they believe that they can manage a firm better and hence raise share values. Under pure self-management, only incumbent workers are in a position to oust inefficient managers, but their abilities to assess managerial competence may not match those of specialist financial analysts, nor might they have the incentives of a raider, who can individually capture much of the gains from better management.[21] On the other side of this question, the efficiency of corporate takeovers remains a much debated question. Workers' motivations to monitor managerial performance, and their abilities to do so, may be stronger than those of most shareholders, and there may be both efficiency and social benefits in having managers who are accountable to a working community, rather than to financiers to whom the needs of incumbent managers and workers are of no direct relevance.

4.3.3 Social Dimensions, Stewardship, and Growth

Enthusiasts of self-management argue that, given proper policies and institutional arrangements, a self-managed economy can be at least as efficient as any alternative. It is also asserted that a worker-run firm can become still more productive than any alternative because of better work incentives, a cooperative approach to problem solving, and more willing implementation of decisions by members of the enterprise team. Yet the principal argument for self-management may lie not in the area of efficiency or productivity, but instead in the sphere of nonmaterial attributes. In the previous section, the rationale of a self-managed economy was presented from the standpoint of grasping the advantages of a complex division of labor without engendering the alienation and subordination of the ordinary working man and woman. Needs for dignity, involvement, and a sense of equality in the productive community, if such needs can be shown to be real and to have significant weight when set against competing ones, must be considered in the social and nonmaterial satisfaction category of our evaluation scheme.

It seems relatively safe to suppose that, at least up to a point, some active engagement in shaping the work process generates intangible benefits to most people, in their capacities as workers; but it must also be asked: at what price? If participation can only be effected at the cost of reduced productivity of material and financial resources, as some economists believe, then the real question is: how much, if any, of their material returns from labor are workers willing to sacrifice for the sake of participation? These same economists, pointing to the fact that both participatory enterprises and less regimented production facilities are available to workers in market economies, argue that the voluntary selection of high-paying but hierarchical, unpleasant, and even alienating work, reveals workers' underlying preferences more directly than do any verbal expressions of dissatisfaction.

In conjunction with this last point, it should be recalled here that just as some would judge positively, from the standpoint of rights as a social good, an economy in which self-management rights are institutionalized, it is possible for others to take quite the opposite position. According to that view, a self-managed system is seen to have a serious deficiency in the domain of rights: namely, that in the self-managed economy, workers are not free to trade their rights to control their productive activity and products, for desired wages and other job attributes. This clash between two rights is in no sense unique; the same occurs when societies outlaw slavery, narcotics sales, or prostitution. Ultimately, social value judgments must be made as to whether the general right of 'liberty' should or should not take precedence over other proposed rights or social prohibitions.

Environmental concerns, resource husbandry, and savings are not often mentioned as important pros or cons of self-management. Nevertheless, some interesting arguments might arise here.[22] With respect to production externalities and the environment, it may be suggested that as a decentralized market system, self-management will tend to have the same myopic properties as capitalism, with environmental integrity scarcely counting as a 'good' on the profit ledgers of individual enterprises. However, a possible check on this tendency would come into play if workers resided in communities adjacent to their work facilities. In that case, workers and their families, friends, and neighbors would directly bear the costs that enterprises might inflict on their immediate environments. In addition to the concerns of would-be polluters for their own health and safety, social pressure could be expected to be brought to bear on any decisions they made that were known to affect the community's appearance, recreational resources, and sanitation. The systemic difference between capitalism and self-management, in this regard, arises because of a difference between capital and labor in market economies: the owner of capital need not be physically present in order for this factor to be used, whereas the laborer must be. Since capital is more 'mobile' than labor under both capitalism and self-management—in this instance, in the sense that the owner of capital and the resource can be at two places at the same time—workers' control of decision-making could lead to outcomes more favorable to the community than would control by capitalists. Of course, this factor may have no bearing when it comes to workers considering whether to dump toxic wastes into a river where most of the effects will be felt many miles downstream.

Savings and Growth   Turning to assessment of self-management's dynamic features, we have already disposed of the question of the efficiency of investment incentives by means of the ideal assumptions of this section. But even if self-managed firms respond efficiently to investment opportunities, the *rate* of investment need not be as high as that generated by a capitalist economy. The rate of new capital formation may be affected by such factors as the rate of technological change, the rate of growth of the demand for goods and leisure, and the distributions of income and wealth and of the associated propensities to save. Some or all of these factors may be system-specific. It is possible, for example, that in spite of perfectly efficient institutional mechanisms for investment, the proportion of output channeled into producers' goods will be smaller under self-management than under capitalism. This could be because of (1) a more equal income distribution coupled with lower savings propensities by those with smaller incomes;[23] (2) a slower rate of technological change, perhaps brought about by a smaller number of very large firms that can support substantial research and development activities; or (3) a slower growth rate of demand for goods, and greater demand for leisure, perhaps brought about by reduced advertising effort on the part of self-managed firms which are less preoccupied with expansion,[24] or even by a shift in values encouraged by the self-actualization perhaps associated with self-management. On the other hand, the macro-economic planning that might take place in a self-managed system could encourage a high level of investment, for example by taxing various incomes (and wealth, inheritances, etc.) to create a pool of investable funds. If the polity is highly democratic, the level of investment will reflect the evolving social consensus on this issue. (If the majority are relatively unwilling to sacrifice present for future consumption, that would presumably lead to a lower investment and growth rate.)

The interesting question is: what outcome should be considered a good one, from an evaluative standpoint? It can be argued that if the self-managed economy is efficient in the sense that individuals can allocate their disposable incomes according to their own time preferences, attitudes toward risk, and the existing investment opportunities, then any resulting level of investment is equally good (economically optimal). If this neoclassical criterion is augmented with an egalitarian one, moreover, it could be argued that a good investment level is one that reflects the preferences of the entire population weighted as equally as possible. In this case, the result of either voluntary savings under a more equal income distribution, or of a political decision regarding investment that is arrived at democratically, might be considered superior to the outcome of a market process with a highly skewed distribution of income. These remarks leave aside the question of the 'interests of future generations' that, as argued in Chapter 1, can itself be viewed as a matter of distribution or equity among generations. The problem, of course, is that the unborn literally cannot have a voice in either a market or a political decision process.

4.4 Self-management, with Relaxation of Ideal Conditions

A convincing assessment of the self-managed economy requires more realistic assumptions about underlying conditions. No economy is perfectly competitive, much less capable of making adjustments to long-run equilibrium without significant delays. And for reasons to be explained below, having firms rent all capital goods used is unlikely to be workable. We turn, then, to consider the worker-managed economy under imperfect competition, markets that adjust with moderate or longer time lags, and some collective or individually owned capital goods.

4.4.1 Employment, Efficiency, and Equity Issues

Mention has already been made, in the last section, of the efficiency problems confronting a self-managed economy when perfect competition and rapid reallocation of resources cannot be assumed. Those problems are relevant now that those ideal assumptions have been dropped. The only new point that needs to be added, here, is that when self-managed firms have market power, they may well be even more restrictive in employment and output than would corresponding capitalist monopolies, because the maximum profit per worker is likely to occur at a still smaller level of output than does the maximum total profit. This tendency will sometimes and to some degree contain its own antidote, though, since the relative smallness of self-managed oligopolists could allow more firms to enter an industry, increasing the degree of competition.

The essential point remains that labor may be misallocated in the short run, and that without rapid movement of firms into profitable industries and out of unprofitable ones, misallocation may persist. To illustrate, suppose that the demand for bicycles rose and that that for motorbikes fell. The simple model predicts that bicycle producers will expel some workers and cut back production, while motorbike makers will take on additional workers and increase output. Since the pay-out to labor will be higher for bicycle than for motorbike workers, individual workers would be happy to leave motorbike firms for bicycle firms. But they would not be accepted there, because more workers mean less profit for each of those already in the firm. Since the value of the marginal product of labor will be higher for bicycle than for motorbike workers, labor is not producing goods of as much value as possible in the economy;[25] but the misallocation will not be corrected unless motorbike firms can switch into producing bicycles, or their workers are able to leave their firms and start their own bicycle factories. If demand curves are steeper than the backward bending supply curves of the two industries, as in Figure 4.2(b), it is even possible that the market process could break down entirely: bicycle production could fall more rapidly than quantity demanded, producers would bid the price of scarce bicycles higher, and production would continue to *fall*, with the process moving towards an infinite price and zero output. With motorbike output increasing faster than quantity demanded, on the other hand, sellers would be forced to bid prices still lower, inducing ever more motorbike output, moving towards zero price and infinite quantity (see again Figure 4.2).

These extreme and unstable scenarios are unrealistic, however. Even without perfect competition and rapid entry of competitors, factors mentioned in section 4.3 would oppose the tendency of supply to respond to demand 'perversely': bicycle firm members will not readily vote to expel one another; motorbike firms may not be able to recruit additional workers at the low earnings they now offer; firms in both industries may also produce other products and use more than one variable input; labor adjustments can include changes in the number of hours worked, and not only in the size of firms' workforces. The realistic problem, from a supply standpoint, would be sluggishness of supply responses to demand changes, but not supply perversity.

Employment creation seems to be a more likely source of problems than are chaotic markets or unresponsive industries. Without perfect competition, and with barriers to the formation of new firms,[26] there could conceivably be a dearth of jobs. Assuming that unwanted members are rapidly expelled leads to the conclusion that self-managed firms reduce employment when demand improves. Assuming, more realistically, that democratic procedures, group solidarity, or social norms prevent easy dismissal of fellow workers, downward adjustments of a firm's workforce become difficult, but this in itself may cause firms to be conservative about expanding membership when short-run conditions suggest that they should. In either case, a tendency to restrain job creation may be a cause for concern.

Employment Security   Evidence of employment problems is often drawn from Yugoslavia, the only national economy embracing workers' self-management as an economic system principle, and an economy whose rates of unemployment have been high; yet that country's employment problem may be better explained by factors common to other countries at its level of development,[27] than by the self-management system. While theoretical considerations convince many students of self-management that worker-run firms are unlikely to be an unusually dynamic force for employment creation, some proposals for worker ownership or self-management none the less surfaced in connection with the desire to save jobs threatened by the industrial slump in Western nations during the late 1970s and early 1980s. That workers' management might be a means of achieving employment stability from the vantage point of a community, is suggested by the fact that workers and their families have roots which make their geographic mobility more costly than the transfer of financial capital from one state, region, or country, to another. Workers therefore have an incentive to stick with faltering enterprises and to seek out alternative economic bases for their communities, while 'capital' is indifferent between investments in any two localities, and will freely move with profit opportunities, despite the possibility that owners will inflict harm on communities left behind as an unweighed externality of their decisions.

Another way in which self-management may contribute to employment security is via its potential for greater wage (or earnings) flexibility than is exhibited by capitalist firms. Where relations between workers and capitalist employers are adversarial in character, wage adjustments tend to fall into a ratchet pattern in which workers push for large wage increases in good times, and resist wage cuts in bad times, even if this increases the probability of lay-offs. Members of worker-managed firms may be committed to avoiding the dismissal of fellow members if at all possible, and, being free of the suspicion that wage reductions will benefit management or owners, they may respond flexibly to changing conditions by implementing work sharing, wage reductions, etc., as seems appropriate.[28] (Where there is in fact no pre-fixed wage, or where full earnings consist of a wage plus a profit share, such flexibility may be more or less automatic.) Thus, job security may be an advantage of better-functioning forms of workers' self-management in meeting basic material (as well as social and psychological) needs. Some analysts also argue that with greater wage flexibility, a self-managed economy may have an advantage, rather than a disadvantage, relative to capitalist economies, with respect to the tendency to achieve full employment at the level of the macro-economy.

The 'labor market' problems (in some ways, this is a misnomer for the phenomena in question given the institutions of self-management) of a self-managed economy also have implications for equity outcomes. As an extreme example, consider an imperfectly competitive self-managed economy with rationed, collectively owned, capital—a reasonable description of Yugoslavia. There, workers possessing identical skills and being equally willing to work could receive very different incomes, depending on whether or not they succeed in gaining employment (enterprise membership) at all, and if so, whether their firm is in a more profitable sector of the economy, and how much capital it has to work with. Once again, unless there is vigorous entry of new firms to compete away profits, there is no tendency for labor to be invited to move from firms having lower marginal labor productivity to those having higher marginal product of labor. The failure of the marginal product of labor to converge when successful labor-managers earn the windfalls of strong product demand or large capital allocations can therefore be seen not only as a source of inefficiency, but also as an equity problem. Of course, the feasibility and effectiveness of counteracting forces, including new enterprise creation and factor mobility, must be known if we are to assess the seriousness of this problem.

4.4.2 Investment and Financing Issues

The other main issue requiring discussion in this section is the impact of dropping the assumption of perfect capital rental. That assumption is restrictive and probably unrealistic for several reasons. A firm that owns the capital goods it uses in production has an incentive to monitor their use, and it can do so at lower cost than an outside owner, since monitoring can be done jointly with productive activities.[29] Several writers on economic organization also stress dangers posed by opportunism when the owners of firms' capital goods are outside agents and capital goods are highly specialized to particular firms and locations. For example, the outside owner can renege on the existing contract and demand a larger fee, citing some changed circumstance, and thus 'hold up' the user when an alternative source is lacking.[30] These and other factors mean that capital rental and capital ownership by firms are often not equally low-cost alternatives. The problem therefore arises of how self-managed firms will finance the acquisition of capital goods.

Collective Financing and the Yugoslav Case Here, the difference between the two models of finance introduced earlier in this chapter comes to the fore. If labor-run firms own their capital collectively, or if their capital is considered to be *social* property, then a number of problems will arise. First of all, as we have seen, members will be less willing to see earnings reinvested in their firms than would be the case were they to retain individual control over some of the created asset value. This will especially be so if their expected tenures with the firm are shorter than the period over which the investment is paid back by enhanced productivity and higher revenue. The reason is that, unlike privately owned savings instruments, collective investments in enterprise assets are irreversible from the individual's standpoint, and cannot be recovered upon leaving the firm. Enterprises might finance the purchase of capital goods using bank loans, and if the banking system operates competitively and arrives at a market-clearing interest rate for the economy, then it can be expected that financial resources will be distributed efficiently, since firms will only seek loans for projects on which the expected rate of return is greater than or equal to the interest rate. However, to minimize the probability of default, bankers might insist that borrowing firms also commit some of their own capital resources, so complete external supply of finance may not be possible, or may, if imposed, entail hidden efficiency costs. 'Moral hazard' concerns of this sort may help to explain why most firms in market economies use a mix of debt and equity finance.

Yugoslavia illustrates some of the problems that might arise when self-management is instituted not only under collective ownership rules, but also in an only half-reformed centralized socialist economy. Such an economy can be expected to manifest the 'soft budget constraint' phenomenon of coddling by the state (so that firms do not fear bankruptcy), and a strong (sometimes local) governmental push for rapid growth and industrialization.[31] Workers' reluctance to reinvest theoretically distributable earnings is countered, in Yugoslavia, by a number of political interventions in the decision-making process, including pressure on enterprise directors to oppose the 'short-sighted' interests of workers, guidelines on investment levels, and constraints on distribution of earnings. Also, the government has allowed or encouraged the banking system to supply large amounts of credit at low or negative real interest rates, ensuring a high demand for bank-financed investment but preventing the rate of return from serving as an allocator of scarce capital among competing projects. The same process contributes to high rates of inflation by pumping money into the hands of demanders of investment goods, who compete with one another and with consumers to purchase a limited total supply of goods and services.

Going further, to make sure that workers do not simply 'consume' the society's capital by selling off enterprise assets and distributing the earnings among themselves, or by failing to replace assets as they depreciate, the Yugoslav government forces firms to maintain the book value of their fixed assets by replacing old capital goods with new ones of equal value. This 'capital maintenance requirement' reinforces the problems of non-ownership and short horizons, referred to above, since it means that the original or principal value of investments is never again available for distribution, even in the long run and to the successors of the present workforce. Finally, the 'soft budget constraint' reaches new heights in the Yugoslav economy, where an additional source of financially undisciplined credit creation appears: widespread inability to collect payments due from other firms means that an enormous amount of credit comes into existence in the form of outstanding debts of one firm to another, arising not from borrowing and lending in the usual sense, but simply from unpaid bills.

Government regulations, the pumping of money into the banking system, negative real interest rates on bank loans, laxness in the settling of business accounts, and enterprises' appetites for the extremely cheap capital thus available to them, have combined to ensure that Yugoslavia does not suffer from low rates of capital formation. Instead, inflation, inefficient allocation of capital among investment projects, immobility of capital across regions, and large differences in the value of capital's marginal product and in workers' wages, across firms, are observed.[32]

Individual Financing and the Mondragon Cooperatives What about the individualized alternative? Here, it is assumed that much enterprise investment is also financed with bank loans, but this time, they are made at scarcity-reflecting interest rates, in noninflationary amounts (the government runs a responsible monetary policy, and banks obey strict reserve requirements when making loans), and they allocate funds according to the rule of equal expected marginal return.[33] To the extent that enterprise self-financing out of retained earnings is required, workers hold individual titles to the capital value created, with the enterprise keeping an internal account of each worker's share of self-financed capital, crediting interest to it, and paying it out to the worker upon retirement or withdrawal from membership, perhaps also allowing earlier deductions or borrowing against these accounts. Retention of earnings may follow a collective decision of the workforce or a preset rule, or it may be left to the discretion of individual workers. Large enterprises might obtain additional financing by floating bonds, or otherwise borrowing from individual members of the community and financial intermediaries (such as insurance and pension funds) at fixed interest. Finally, some firms may sell non-voting equity shares paying dividends linked to net earnings before distribution (that is, to the level of 'profit per worker').

The best known illustration of the individualized financing approach, incorporating some (but not all) of the features just described, is the network of worker-managed enterprises in and around the town of Mondragon in the Basque province of Spain. In 1985 these included 111 production enterprises, a bank, and 17 housing cooperatives, with a total of 19,000 workers and an annual total sales value of US$806 million. Founded in 1956, the enterprises grew at an average annual rate of 10 per cent per year, in terms of output value, and 8 per cent per year, in terms of employment, in the two decades from 1965 to 1985.[34] Since the early 1970s they have been Spain's largest producer and exporter of consumer durables, such as stoves and refrigerators. The enterprises also include a range of industries, including casting and forging, machine tools, machinery; control equipment, components, materials; and packaging, construction, food and agriculture, and services.

Workers in each production enterprise elect its governing board, but the enterprise group as a whole selects the leaders of the 'second stage' cooperatives, such as the *Caja Laboral Popular*, the group's bank. Individual workers pay a membership fee upon joining, which serves to open their individual capital accounts; new increments to the accounts derive from each worker's share of their cooperative's net earnings in excess of pre-specified wages, and another portion of net revenue is used to add interest on to the existing individual capital accounts. In 1987 the *Caja Laboral Popular* had 180 branches accepting deposits from people throughout that region, with total deposits amounting to roughly US$1.13 billion, making it roughly the twenty-fifth largest bank in Spain. The bank's main purpose is to help finance the existing enterprises and launch new ones, and to that end it has a special division that engages in technical and marketing research; this unit estimates the returns on alternative investments and assists in every aspect of launching new enterprises.

Theoretically, the financial institutions of Mondragon fall short of perfect economic efficiency for several reasons. First, at least 30 per cent of investment out of retained earnings in the enterprises is not credited to the individual capital accounts, and therefore has the character of collectively-owned capital. Second, since the decision on the percentage of earnings to be reinvested is not taken freely by each individual, and since individuals do not have access to the value of their capital accounts before leaving their firm, investment decisions may not perfectly track individually preferred and in that sense optimal savings decisions. Third, while the existing entrance fees are not nominal, there is no real market for membership. Since workers cannot 'capitalize' the value of better-run enterprises through selling their memberships in such a market, their incentives to push for fully efficient management are arguably incomplete.[35] Finally, much of most workers' real private wealth portfolios are tied up with the fortunes of their individual firms or with that of the Mondragon network. Cautious workers might prefer, on the other hand, to diversify their risk by investing in mutual funds or in other financial instruments that would spread their wealth over a wider portfolio of investments.

It may be possible to come closer to fully efficient financial institutions while maintaining (as in the Mondragon cooperatives) the principle that enterprises are controlled by their workers (of all ranks) and by their workers alone, and without distinction by amount of capital contributed. Perhaps limitations exist in the Mondragon model, owing to the network's smallness, and to its embeddedness in capitalist surroundings. Yet such features as mandated capital contributions and collective ownership of some capital may reflect justified social steering (solving a collective choice problem, after the fashion of capitalist indicative planning at the national level) to support a high rate of savings and new job creation, and might be opted for even under the most ideal conditions. In any case, the relative success of the ownership and financial arrangements of Mondragon, such as it is, suggests that this dimension of a self-managed economic system need not be a limiting factor or a negative element in the system's overall evaluation. It suggests the possibility of linking control rights to the functional role of being a member of the enterprise workforce, rather than an owner of its capital. It does this without diminishing, in any discernable way, the incentive to invest or the efficiency of investment, and without the use of distorting and dysfunctional devices such as artificially cheapened external funding and injunctions to maintain capital stock in perpetuity.

To the extent that Mondragon's success turns out to be replicable, or capable of being improved upon elsewhere, the problems introduced with regard to investment by dropping the pure rental assumption of the previous section, can be judged to be quite manageable, and an explanation for many of the observed difficulties of Yugoslav firms and of cooperatives following other institutional principles will have been provided. On the other hand, to the extent that Mondragon's success turns out to result primarily from special circumstances, such as ethnic solidarity within the Basque community, charismatic leadership, and unusually favorable market opportunities, the question will remain open.[36]

4.5 Variants and Hybrids

As mentioned above, since the model of the self-managed economy is less clearly delineated than are those of competitive capitalism and centrally planned socialism, it is more difficult to distinguish variants. Alternative models of ownership and investment financing under self-management have already been discussed. Certain proposals to increase the efficiency of a self-managed economy might also be considered to give rise to variants to the standard model. For example, an economy in which worker-run firms charge market-clearing entrance fees, as suggested in the last section, would in theory eliminate the potential inefficiencies of self-management in the absence of such a market, yet might conflict with the aspiration of some self-management advocates to 'decommodify' labor. Another modified self-management would permit cooperatives to set a period of apprenticeship or candidacy before full membership rights are granted to their workers, so that two classes of workers could exist in such a firm.

The main topic to be addressed in this relatively brief section is the relevance of partial forms of self-management, or participation, in which control rights are not exclusively reserved to members of firms' workforces, but are shared with non-workers. Cases falling under this heading, interpreted broadly, range, in market economies, from essentially conventional owner-run firms soliciting workers' ideas and suggestions, to substantially worker-run firms in which control rights are unequally distributed in view of unequal owner-ship stakes, or where there are some hired non-member workers, or some non-worker owners who share control rights. In the middle of this spectrum is the 'co-determined' firm, in which representatives of both workers and shareholders hold positions on the board of directors and/or other policy-making bodies. Instances of factory democracy in the centrally planned economies have been widespread but of questionable influence; Chinese state factories and rural col-lective enterprises, and cooperative firms in Poland and elsewhere in Eastern Europe, have been viewed by some observers, however, as involving a meaningful admixture of workers' self-management with more traditional state socialist forms, and will therefore be briefly considered in the second part of the section.

Participation and Co-determination in Market Economies

Cooperative firms, in which most workers are members and most members workers, have existed in the western market economies for well over a century, but their numbers have been small (reaching a maximum, among industrial market economies, of about 20,000 co-ops providing 200,000 jobs, in Italy in the early 1980s). In recent years, a trend towards more participatory management approaches has appeared within many of the conventional firms of countries such as the United States, under such code names as 'quality circles' and 'quality of working life' (QWL) programs.[37] Legislatively-mandated co-determination has been instituted in many Western European countries. The increase in participation might be explained by reference to the potential productivity implications of self-management. The Japanese industrial model of secure ('lifetime') employment, more level pay scales and egalitarian company culture, and employee participation in product quality improvement efforts, has been especially influential in western management circles in view of its apparent achievements.[38] The motivation for co-determination puts more emphasis on workers' rights to a say in decisions influencing their lives, including those affecting job security and working conditions. While peripheral to self-management as defined in this chapter, the rising incidence of profit sharing and employee stock ownership in capitalist economies might also be viewed as related trends.

Participation and co-determination can be viewed as blends of capitalist and self-managed institutions, and thus as variants of both of those systems. From the starting point of capitalism, they may be looked upon as ways of increasing work incentives, of humanizing the workplace and improving the quality of working life, of increasing the upward flow of information to management, and of safeguarding worker dignity in the production process. If combined with greater flexibility over remuneration (whether through profit sharing, work sharing, or other means), they might also increase employment security and the tendency towards full employment at the macro-level. From the starting point of workers' self-management, they may be seen as means of strengthening the rights of capital owners so as to spur investment and improve the efficiency of capital allocation. They may also be viewed as ways of facilitating worker risk-sharing with financiers, and in general, of permitting Pareto-improving trades between these partners, even as they overstep the boundary of what is an inalienable right to the supporter of pure self-management. In view of its potential efficiency and its political and philosophical attractiveness, a system mixing elements of self-management and of capitalism at the enterprise level could well be an important real-world model of the future.

An area of controversy regarding co-determination is the question of system-wide adoption through constitutional or legislative means. While economic analysis offers no reason for concern about voluntary adoption of new organizational forms, some economists view the tendencies to legislate co-determination and to offer tax and other incentives towards participation and profit sharing as dangerous interventions in the free market.[39] If worker and shareholder welfare could be increased by sharing control rights, these economists argue, then co-determination would be adopted without legislative prods; if workers benefit while shareholders lose, the innovation would still be adopted if it was worth it to workers to pay shareholders for the privilege. It would be inefficient to adopt such changes otherwise.

Even if the argument that politically-mandated co-determination entails costs to economic efficiency is true, such programs need not be viewed as 'socially inefficient', if enough people favor the guarantee of the rights involved despite those costs. However, it is also possible that the failure of co-determination to emerge without legislation results from its having a 'public good' character, and thus from a market failure justifying state intervention. Some relevant arguments were reviewed, for the case of full self-management, in section 4.2.3, and need not be restated here.

Participation and Cooperatives in Centrally Planned Economies

During China's 'Cultural Revolution' (1966–76, but especially the earlier part of that period) radical leaders urged workers and other ordinary citizens to reject authority, and many factory managers were temporarily replaced by workers' committees. Despite official efforts to strengthen managerial authority in the post-Mao era, workers appeared to have gained enormous influence as a constituency in Chinese state-run enterprises in the 1980s. Like their counterparts in the large-scale industrial sector in Japan, these workers enjoy great job security, rely on their enterprises not only for wages but for other benefits, and work in an atmosphere of relative social and pay equality. Unlike Japan, weak or nonexistent profit motives and lack of pressures towards efficiency allow workers to influence managers in placing great weight on increasing workers' welfare as a primary enterprise objective.[40] In view of the prevailing distortions in prices, the 'soft budget constraint', and the importance of bargaining with the bureaucracy to the determination of profits, such worker influence is unlikely to have a very salutary effect on overall economic performance. Also, since that influence is exerted within the context of a paternalistic relationship with management, rather than through direct participation in it, most arguments for a positive productivity effect would not appear to be applicable.

Chinese rural collective industrial enterprises, run by village and township governments, also share some characteristics with worker-managed firms. In particular, local officials may place local economic growth and job creation at the top of their agendas, and workers may succeed in pressing for higher wages. Although not formally democratic in structure, the identification of managers with community needs, the relative immobility of capital accumulated in the community, and the ability of local opinion to influence decisions, mean that 'community entrepreneurship' in rural China may share some similarities with local or regional self-management sectors, such as the Mondragon complex in Spain.[41]

In some Eastern European countries, of which Poland is notable, workers' cooperative or collective firms exist side by side with state-owned factories.[42] While their status as either worker-run or employee-owned is doubtful, such firms do tend to exhibit a greater degree of financial accountability, and hence more cost-effectiveness in production, than their more capital-intensive state sector counterparts. With the growing interest in market-oriented reforms in Soviet-type economies, cooperative-like enterprises, though lacking the full autonomy of the self-managed prototype firms discussed earlier in this chapter, could attain increasing prominence in the socialist East, even as the forms of participation discussed earlier in this section gain importance in the capitalist West.

4.6 Summary and Conclusions

The basic principle of a self-managed economy is that people who cooperate in production in all ranks of an enterprise's labor force jointly control the enterprise. To complete a description of self-management as an economic system—it may otherwise be viewed only as a system element—we assumed the existence of decentralized pricing and free markets, modified by governmental interventions ranging from anti-trust and monopoly regulations through indicative planning. Two different institutional regimes were considered in the area of capital ownership: one in which capital is owned by the state and workers' collectives, another in which capital is owned by individuals. (Part of the discussion also proceeded under the strictly hypothetical assumption that all capital goods are rented from the state.) In all cases of full self-management, ownership of capital does not entail rights to control an enterprise using it. Workers in a firm may be among the owners of its capital, may own that capital exclusively, or may have no ownership stakes; in each case, control derives from having the status of workers, and is not linked to ownership.

Four arguments for self-management as an economic system were discussed. The first one says that workers should have inalienable rights to control their work process and its fruits, and sees this as an extension of the principles of liberty and democracy (although we pointed out that it is in conflict with a different freedom, the one that would allow people voluntarily to trade away these rights). The second rationale begins with the radical project of handing economic power to the working class. Arguing that worker control of the economy through control of the state is either unsatisfactory or unrealistic, this view sees worker control at the level of the firm as the most effective and direct way of giving workers power and ending their alienation from the production process and its results. The third argument gives central importance to the quality of working life, and asserts that no other way of organizing the economy promises equal attention to the welfare implications of the social and technical dimensions of work, while also satisfactorily providing for the production and distribution of goods and services. The fourth and last rationale argues that self-management provides an ideal basis for maximizing workers' productivity by giving them the incentives of masters of production and owners of its fruits. With all these views, self-management can be seen primarily as an attempt to solve perceived problems raised by the division of labor within enterprises. This solution at the firm level then makes use of an approach to the problem of division of labor between enterprises (that is, the market) that is shared both with capitalism and with market socialism.

Some economists have raised questions about the efficiency of self-managed firms from the standpoints of work monitoring, decision-making, and managerial shirking, but it is unclear whether purported deficiencies in these dimensions are real. Assuming that there are no special liabilities in internal organization or managerial dimensions, that there are rapid adjustments to long-run equilibria, and that capital goods are rentable, the competitive labor-managed economy should be efficient in production, distribution, and output mix.

A competitive labor-managed economy might generate a more equal distribution of income than would a capitalist counterpart, because of a tendency to engender a more equal distribution of skills, and because of possible productivity dividends from more level pay scales. However, with private wealth-holding and competitive markets for funds, income distribution in a competitive labor-managed economy could conceivably be much like that of a capitalist system. To the extent that concerns arise from the standpoints of equity and basic needs, these might be responded to by tax, transfer, training, and other programs.

A major advantage of self-management may appear in the nonmaterial domain, in the form of enhanced job satisfaction and opportunities for job enrichment. Institutionalized self-management rights are judged positively by some, negatively by others, as a 'social good'. With regard to resource 'stewardship', self-management may have 'community effects' mitigating negative environmental spillovers. It is not clear whether self-management would increase or reduce savings, but what savings level should be considered optimal is difficult to say.

In the absence of perfect competition, of rapid movements to long-run equilibrium, and of full capital rentability, a number of efficiency problems may arise. A firm able to adjust the size of its labor force and bent on maximizing per-worker earnings would respond negatively to higher prices, and the price mechanism could not function at all in an industry composed of such firms if the aggregate supply curve were less steep than the demand curve. However, because worker managers would tend to protect themselves against expulsion, because additional workers could not easily be obtained by unprofitable firms, because firms often produce multiple products and use several variable inputs, and because worker-run firms may more readily vary hours worked than membership size, relative inelasticity of supply curves and conservatism in recruiting new members are more likely problems than are perverse supply responses. Although job creation may be a weak point for the self-management system, its potential strength with respect to job preservation may arguably be set against this on the evaluative balance sheet. Labor-managed firms with monopoly power might be even more output-restricting than capitalist counterparts, although under some circumstances this would allow for more firms and, hence, more competition. In summary, economic analysis suggests that government measures to facilitate new firm creation and to assure competitive industry structures should receive special priority in a labor-managed market economy.

When labor-run firms need to acquire their own capital goods rather than rent them, problems appear likely if rights to the financial value of those goods, and to the income streams reflecting their value to users, cannot be vested in individuals. If capital goods are simply allocated by the state, a self-managed economy will exhibit the same inefficiencies in capital use as are shown by centrally planned socialist economies. If capital created from retained enterprise revenues becomes collective or 'social' property, workers will face a 'horizon' disincentive to such investment. Outside bank funds will be sought if the interest rate is below the expected rate of return on the investments for which they can be used, and a hypothetical system in which banks finance all enterprise investment at a market clearing interest rate would in principle be allocatively efficient. However, assuming that the combining of bank and debt financing with internal financing and/or equity—practices observed in market economies, including Yugoslavia—are efficient solutions to problems of risk bearing and moral hazard, then some internal financing will probably be needed; the horizon problem therefore remains relevant as long as ownership is collective. Yugoslavia appears to avoid observable underinvestment, but only by flooding its economy with underpriced loanable funds and by using other questionable tools, such as a capital maintenance requirement. The results of these policies include inflation, and both inefficient and inequitable capital allocation.

With individualized ownership of capital, the horizon problem need not arise. Much of workers' savings, pension, and insurance funds could be channeled through banks and other financial intermediaries and made available for productive investment on competitive terms. Reinvestment of retained earnings in self-managed firms could be done in a manner that gives each worker an individual stake without linking control rights over the enterprise to the size of these stakes. Large and successful worker-run firms might even issue bonds or non-voting stock. An example with some of these

features is the Mondragon complex, which appears to have
performed well with respect to capital formation and efficient capital
use, as well as in the areas of growth, job creation, and productive
efficiency.[45]

Notes

1. To be sure, this ignores the claim that workers are in control of the
   socialist firm by virtue of their collective control of the state. But to do
   so seems reasonable enough when it is hard to find a single disinterested
   observer who argues that such roundabout control is of much
   operational relevance.
2. Examples of the advocacy of self-management but not a market
   economy can be found in Knight and Roca 1975, and Network of
   Solidarity Organizations in Leading Factories (Poland) 1981.
3. This line of reasoning admittedly leans heavily on an idealized
   conception of central planning. If we think, instead, of the struggle
   between planners and enterprise managers and of the maneuverings of
   the managers described in Chapter 3, we may begin to imagine a
   worker-managed variant in which stratagems like capacity conceal-
   ment, target-storming, and so forth, are engaged in as team projects,
   with workers colluding to maximize shared advantages, rather than
   exploiting whatever power they may have to win concessions from
   managers who need cooperation in their battles against planners, as in
   the conventional variant of the centrally planned economy. But it seems
   unlikely that this picture corresponds to a system to which anyone
   would actively aspire.
4. See, for example, Vanek 1970; and for more recent surveys, Ireland and
   Law 1982, and Bonin and Putterman 1987.
5. Our approach here means that one final possibility for implementing
   the classical socialist dream of allocation by 'use value' must also be
   abandoned. That possibility is for central planners to solve the problem
   of allocating available resources among socially chosen objectives
   through mathematical programming techniques, but to 'decentralize'
   the solution by fixing the accompanying 'shadow prices', then letting
   each enterprise determine its production plans with reference to them.
   There is a philosophical problem of whether the enterprises in such a
   model would be any more free in fact than are those to which physical
   output targets are dictated. More operationally, though, the idea would
   be jettisoned for the foreseeable future, by most analysts, because of the
   practical difficulties of information gathering and computation discussed
   in Chapter 3.
6. Admittedly, this line of reasoning can also be criticized, and is not fully

symmetric with the approaches of the last two chapters, in that it takes a rather 'voluntaristic' view of an economic system as the product of intentional design. One might want to take the alternative approach of asking whether the constellation of interests created by arrangements of self-management at the enterprise level would make one or another set of macro-level institutions more likely to survive over a long period. What the approach taken here implies is that the self-managed economy would come into being as the product of a social or political movement rallying around a definite and coherent ideology. It would take us too far afield to consider the controversies that might be raised over this assumption. As a partial defense of the approach taken here, however, the author would venture the opinion that it is reasonable to view coherence of ideology as a condition for long-run viability of an economic system.

7. See Pejovich 1969 and Furubotn and Pejovich 1970.
8. See section 4.4.2.
9. See J.S. Mill 1936, Pateman 1970, Dahl 1985.
10. Engels 1978, p. 731.
11. Marx 1967*a*, cited earlier.
12. Pagano 1985, sees a tension between Marx's 'anti-firm communism' and his 'anti-market socialism'. He criticizes Marx for failing to notice the absence of a path by which the second would metamorphose into the first. For an argument that Marx—who once asserted that he himself could not live in such a world—foresaw a darker side to early socialism, see Avineri 1968.
13. Such a radical case has been constructed in Yugoslavia, which continued to profess allegiance to Marxism after its adoption of the self-management model.
14. The argument is made formally in Dreze 1976. A related argument can be made using Hirschman's (1970) distinction between 'exit' and 'voice'.
15. See Ben-Ner 1988, Putterman 1988.
16. See Gintis 1972, Bowles and Gintis 1977.
17. For an extended discussion and further references on the somewhat technical points compressed into these paragraphs, see Bonin and Putterman 1987, sections 1.1–1.7.
18. This model was initially presented by Ward (1958), and has had an enormous impact on the literature that followed it.
19. See Holmstrom 1982.
20. See Alchian and Demsetz 1972.
21. See Jensen and Meckling 1979. More generally, see Nalbantian (ed.) 1987. Also, Putterman 1984.
22. Many of these arguments will be found in Vanek 1970.

23. '[A]ccording to all recent studies, only the upper income groups save; the total savings of groups below the top decile are fairly close to zero'. Kuznets 1965, p. 263.
24. Neoclassical analysis suggests that profitable labor managed firms might be smaller than capitalist firms producing the same product for the same market with the same technology. For example, when returns to scale are constant and there are positive profits to be made, the capitalist firm facing a horizontal supply curve wants to expand indefinitely to increase its total profit, whereas there would be no similar inducement for a worker-run firm, since profit per worker would not change as the firm grew. These arguments suggest that self-managed firms would have less incentive to advertise so as to expand their market shares. (Vanek 1970.)
25. Moving some workers from motorbike production to bicycle production would raise the value of output on balance, since the lost motorbikes are less valued than the newly gained bicycles.
26. The entrepreneurial mechanism in self-management is beyond the scope of this chapter. A useful discussion of the topic with references to other relevant literature is Ben-Ner 1987. The successful process of launching new co-ops in the Mondragon network (referred to in section 4.4.2) is discussed by Wiener and Oakeshott 1987, among others.
27. Many countries undergoing industrialization manifest a wide gap between the level of urban wages and typical earnings in the rural, 'traditional' sector. This attracts more people to seek urban jobs than the number who can be satisfied by new job creation. Since the phenomenon occurs in many developing countries that do not practice workers' self-management, the explanation should probably be sought in institutional factors that affect both capitalist and self-managed industrial firms in such countries. Other special features of the Yugoslav economy that may limit its usefulness as a predictor of the performance of a self-managed economic system will be discussed below.
28. There is considerable empirical evidence, for example from American plywood cooperatives, to support this picture. However, it should be pointed out that self-managed firms that are free to hire temporary non-member workers, as these particular cooperatives are, are likely to do so as a buffer against unemployment of *members*, and that the job security applying to members would not tend to carry over to such hired employees. Another relevant qualification is that if self-managed firms exist in a dependency relationship wherein income shortfalls are expected to be made up for by government subsidies —in other words, Kornai's 'soft budget constraint'—the hypothesized wage flexibility may never appear. Instead, worker protection of past wage gains may

exist in the enterprise-government context much as it does in the labor-versus-management context of capitalism. This phenomenon seems to have been rather pervasive in Yugoslavia, where self-management was introduced by the government in a centralized socialist economy whose workers were accustomed to wage guarantees.

29. See Alchian and Demsetz 1972.
30. See Klein, Crawford, and Alchian 1978, and Williamson 1985.
31. See Tyson 1980, Milenkovitch 1983, Lydall 1984.
32. For some evidence, see Estrin 1983. Also Tyson 1980 and Lydall 1984.
33. While this contrasts with the Yugoslav example, we do not mean to imply that the same could not be true in a labor-managed economy *without* direct individual financing.
34. Wiener and Oakeshott 1987.
35. However, permitting a market in self-managed jobs might be rejected by some workers' management advocates because it turns the job, and arguably, then, the decision-making rights that go with it, into a commodity. To stipulate the existence of such fees could be treated as giving rise to a variant of the model of workers' self-management, distinct from the general case. Regardless of ideological acceptability, the creation of membership markets may be difficult, and their functioning imperfect, in the real world of imperfect information, risk aversion, and capital-constrained workers. For a formal analysis of the partnership deed market that abstracts from the latter issues, see Sertel 1982.
36. For a case study of Mondragon emphasizing social dynamics, see Whyte and Whyte 1988.
37. For a recent discussion of participatory management models in the United States, see Lawler 1986.
38. See Ouchi 1981.
39. A much-cited statement of this position is in Jensen and Meckling 1979.
40. See Tidrick and Chen 1987, and Walder 1989.
41. See Byrd and Lin (eds), forthcoming.
42. See Jones 1985.
43. The reader may wonder whether our more favorable assessment of workers' management with individualized financing does not amount to saying that the system will work best in its non-socialist variant. This unfortunately raises (once again; see Chapter 3, note 15) the semantic, and so largely unresolvable, question of what is meant by 'socialist'. Of course, if socialism means 'vesting of the ownership and control of the means of production, capital, land, etc., in the community as a whole' (*American College Dictionary*, 1961), the conclusion just stated seems inescapable. Yet, even in the most collectivist of existing societies, citizens are not expected to surrender all unconsumed income to the

state, and private savings instruments exist. Individualized financing might be considered to be consistent with socialism by those whose definition of the term emphasizes workers' control over production, the right of the community to regulate the usage of productive property and to alter its distribution, or the existence of reciprocal responsibilities of individuals to society and society to individuals.

Suggested Readings

Comisso, Ellen, 1979, *Workers' Control under Plan and Market*, New Haven: Yale University Press.

Horvat, Branko, 1976, *The Yugoslav Economic System: The First Labor-managed Economy in the Making*, White Plains, NY: International Arts and Sciences Press.

Jackall, Robert and Levin, Henry M. (eds), 1984, *Worker Cooperatives in America*, Berkeley: University of California Press.

Jones, Derek and Svejnar, Jan (eds), 1982, *Participatory and Self-managed Firms: Evaluating Economic Performance*, Lexington, MA: Lexington Books.

Moore, John H., 1980, *Growth with Self-management: Yugoslav Industrialization, 1952–75*, Stanford: Hoover Institution Press.

Sacks, Stephen R., 1984, *Self-management in Large Corporations: The Yugoslav Case*, London: Allen and Unwin.

Schrenk, Martin, Ardalan, Cyrus, and El Tatawy, Nawal A., 1979, *Yugoslavia: Self-management Socialism and the Challenges of Development*, Baltimore: Johns Hopkins University Press.

Stephen, Frank H. (ed.), 1982, *The Performance of Labor-managed Firms*, New York: St Martin's Press.

Vanek, Jaroslav, 1971, *The Participatory Economy: An Evolutionary Hypothesis and a Strategy for Development*, Ithaca: Cornell University Press.

Wachtel, Howard, 1974, *Workers' Management and Workers' Wages in Yugoslavia*, Ithaca: Cornell University Press.

5.
Final Considerations

Introduction

This final chapter consists of short discussions of a number of topics, reviewing and extending the themes presented in Chapters 1 to 4. In the first section, the system prototypes discussed in Chapters 2, 3, and 4 are reviewed, with an emphasis on classification and on ideological underpinnings. In the second, we look briefly at the comparative performance of economies illustrating variants of each system. In the third section, the applicability of the economic institutions with which this book is concerned to the developing economies of the Third World, and the nature of the economic institutions which those economies display, is treated.

The fourth section takes up a more theoretical question: are there alternatives to markets and planning as methods of coordinating economic activity? The fifth section deals with an equally fundamental question having both methodological and empirical import: how pervasive, in fact, is self-interest as a motive of human behavior? Related to this ultimate question about humankind is the question about its relationship to the physical world, addressed in section 5.6: how ubiquitous is scarcity? Some brief concluding remarks close the chapter and the book.

5.1 System Prototypes: A Review

Our introduction to economic systems began with a conceptualization of those systems as sets of arrangements through which people as individuals and societies are able to grasp the potential benefits of specialization while avoiding some of its costs. The need for coordinating mechanisms, and the possibly problematic distributive issues arising in complex economies, received special attention in our discussion. We argued that economic systems ought to be evaluated with a number of broad classes of objectives and effects in mind. In particular, we adopted, for examination in each of the succeeding chapters, a list of evaluative dimensions which included

195

effectiveness in meeting basic material requirements, equity, efficiency in resource allocation, effect on nonmaterial aspects of individual and social well-being, and impact on the resource base, environment, fund of technical knowledge, and capital stock handed on to future generations.

The three ideal or archetypal modern economic systems considered at length in this book were capitalism, centrally planned socialism, and workers' self-management. The first two systems could be seen as opposites in at least two major respects: the institutions of resource ownership, and the institutions that coordinate economic relations among enterprises and relations between enterprises and consumers. The third system was seen as having two classes of variants, the first making it closer to centralized socialism, the second to capitalism, in the dimension of property rights. Where inter-unit coordination is concerned, it was assumed to be a market economy, like capitalism. Modified versions of capitalism and planned socialism were also discussed.

A somewhat different and possibly more appealing way of contrasting the three pure systems would be to focus on the coordination problem alone, and to consider that that problem is solved by each of the three systems on two distinct levels: the level of coordination *within* production units, and the level of coordination of relations *among* production units. With this distinction, it becomes possible to use a single two-by-two matrix to classify the three systems as follows. With respect to coordination of relations among enterprises the basic possibilities are voluntary exchange, and planned coordination. With respect to coordination of activities within enterprises, all the systems exhibit some form of planned coordination, but in two of them, the coordinators are the owners of the capital assets employed in production, or their agents, while in the third, it is the workforce as a self-managing community.

In the resulting two-by-two grid (see Figure 5.1) capitalism would be identified as an economic system involving coordination by private capital owners at the intra-enterprise level and by the market at the inter-enterprise level; centrally planned socialism would be shown as a system marked by coordination by public capital owners at the intra-enterprise level and public planning by the same parties at the inter-enterprise level; and workers' self-management would appear as a system using coordination by workers at the intra-enterprise level and by the market at the inter-

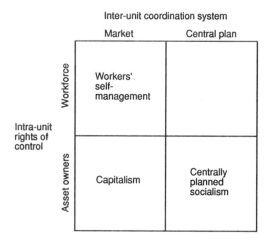

FIG. 5.1.
Classification scheme II: coordination and control rights
This two-by-two matrix includes three modern economic system prototypes,
while suppressing differences in ownership of factors of production.

enterprise level. A fourth box in this grid could be filled by a hypothetical system of intra-enterprise workers' management with inter-
enterprise public planning, but in the previous chapter we offered
some reasons why such a system might prove self-contradictory.

Historically, both centrally planned socialism and workers' self-
management have appeared partly as responses to perceived
deficiencies of capitalism. Advocates of planned socialism see
capitalism as a fundamentally inequitable and inefficient method of
using social resources to meet people's needs. They propose to
replace the market process, wherein profit-seeking producers respond
to consumers' needs where and when these are translated into
effective demand (that is, are backed by purchasing power), with a
public choice process; this would decide how resources are to be
used to satisfy needs without considering exchange value criteria
such as profit and price, except as implicit parameters of the chosen
solution. This approach runs into a basic socio-political problem,
that of the accountability of the authorities to the public, and a set of
economic and technical problems, which, in brief, might be said to
result from planning enthusiasts' underestimation of the difficulty of

mimicking the functions accomplished by markets, quite apart from improving upon them.

Advocates of self-management, at least in its market variants, would tend to see these problems of centralized socialism as difficult or impossible to rectify. At the same time, their own critique of capitalism would focus not so much on who owns the society's resources and how needs are communicated to producers, as on what social roles are thrust upon people as producers, and how their needs for dignity, satisfaction, and control over their work environments might better be satisfied while avoiding excessive concentration of economic power in the state. Self-management may be criticized from a capitalist standpoint by arguing that markets already allow workers an optimal say over the nature of their working lives since it lets them communicate their preferences over available jobs by way of their willingness to accept those jobs at offered wages. Such critics may also argue that preventing workers from entering conventional labor contracts is inefficient, and/or a violation of the general principle of liberty. Counter-arguments to these views were discussed in the last chapter.

As the last paragraph began to suggest, capitalism itself has not been without its own defenders as an ideal economic system. Not only is the market said to be efficient in allocating resources to meeting consumer demand, but it is also said to limit bureaucracy and the concentration of economic power, and to be based upon free and voluntary exchanges between juridically equal agents. While some defenders of the system would favor interventions to achieve, among other things, more equal distributions of assets and/or income, others would favor minimizing interventions, and would justify the institutions of ownership, and prevailing distributions of assets, on both incentive and desert grounds (as rewards to past effort).

5.2 The Performance of Capitalism, Centrally Planned Socialism, and Workers' Management

This book attempts to provide a conceptual introduction to the study of economic systems, leaving institutional and empirical details, as well as the nuts and bolts of analytical models and methods, to other works. Nevertheless, the concepts and evaluative criteria developed in previous chapters may strike some readers as overly abstract, without the accompaniment of at least a brief comparative assessment of the performance of the real economics embodying the system principles surveyed. Although no attempt will be made at completeness, a few observations in a comparative vein are offered in the present section.

5.2.1 Historical Overview

As already suggested, capitalist economic institutions by now have a far longer history than have the institutions of central planning or workers' management, and both of the latter are in part reactions to capitalism. It may be difficult to say precisely when capitalism as a system made its first appearance, but certainly there would be agreement that full-blown capitalism was in evidence by the mid-eighteenth century in Britain, and many would see precedents in the late medieval trading cities of northern Italy and the Netherlands. Capitalism's development is thus intertwined with the unfolding of the Industrial Revolution, and on a broader reading, with the expansion of world trade going back several centuries. Over those centuries, capitalist forms of economic organization facilitated the technological change, capital accumulation, and trade growth that have provided the bases for unprecedented increases in productivity and incomes in what are now the industrialized market economies.[1] Thus, the prima-facie case that the system is a force for economic progress and prosperity is a strong one.

There are, to be sure, reasons to be cautious in this assessment of the performance of capitalist economic arrangements. The simultaneity of the rise of capitalism with the technological developments of the Industrial Revolution means that, although such diverse witnesses as Joseph Schumpeter and Karl Marx have credited capitalism with an explosion of useful industrial knowledge,[2] it is difficult to be certain how much was causal, how much accidental, in their early links. Although a great many economic historians and interpreters of the recent comparative record would disagree, one might argue that capitalism was simply lucky in enjoying the fruits of a technological revolution whose time had come. The fact that prosperity has not followed the spread of capitalist forms with equal universality outside Western Europe and such lands of European settlement as the United States, also raises questions about the efficacy of the system versus the advantages of specific historical, cultural, and resource conditions. Certainly, proponents would argue that capitalism has been held in check by feudal and statist forces in the Third World. By the same token, since capitalism and colonialism, like capitalism and modern industry, have intertwined histories, the record of the achievements of market expansion in Asia, Africa, and the Americas is in the very least blemished, not only by political repression and economic exploitation, but also because it set the stage for later decades of economic stagnation and social instability.

The socialist alternative was supposed to follow an advanced but unstable capitalism, coordinating the complex industrial economy by means of an integrated economic plan, promoting further economic development, and ensuring that, subject to developmental requirements, the economy would be directed to meeting the needs of the population. The project got off to an uncertain start when the first opportunity to attempt it arose not in advanced north-western Europe, but in the industrially and socially underdeveloped Russian empire. The socio-political aspiration that the state act on behalf of the population was also compromised from the beginning, first by civil war, then by a diversity of policy prescriptions within ruling circles that was ended by the imposition of a totalitarian solution under a ruthless dictatorship. In the decades following 1928, the state which that dictatorship controlled succeeded in demonstrating that industrialization under state ownership and management was not impossible; industrial output in real terms grew at 20 per cent per year from 1928 to 1937, while real GNP per capita is estimated to have risen at an average rate of over 5 per cent during 1931–40, before declining during the war with Germany.[3] However, while the strategy succeeded in creating a militarily strong economy which could successfully keep at bay the military threats from the West, it did so with little or no improvement in physical living standards, over a generation, and at an enormous cost in terror and repression. Moreover, by the 1970s both its own and outside economists agreed that the system succeeded in marshalling resources to meet crude output targets, but performed poorly in terms of technological change, product quality, and allocative efficiency.[4]

Postwar Experience Broadly speaking, the Second World War was a watershed both for the capitalist West, and for the Soviet Union and the new states that joined it in the socialist world. The West had been shaken by an unprecedented depression, which spurred the creation of what in the United States was called the New Deal—a deal, in effect, between the private enterprise sector, the working population, and the government, committing the latter to a range of welfare and social insurance programs, and to efforts to promote fuller employment of labor. In many European market economies, similar social innovations preceded or followed that in the United States. The strong economic growth which marked the early post-war decades therefore took place in the setting of 'mixed economies' and 'welfare states' throughout the industrialized capitalist world.

In the Soviet Union, the war helped to justify the previous industrialization drive and to unite much of the population in a struggle to defend 'the motherland'. In its aftermath, the government began to reward the citizenry with improvements in consumption and to further routinize the use of material incentives to motivate managerial performance. Ideological barriers to charging enterprises for capital use and to using project evaluation formulas implying the costliness of time were surmounted, the importance of profit as an evaluative criterion for enterprises increased, and discussions of more fundamental reforms of a decentralizing nature took place.[5]

From 1950 to 1970, GDP per capita grew at an average rate of 3.3 per cent per annum in the western industrial nations,[6] and at 4.2 per cent per annum in the Soviet Union and Eastern Europe.[7] The 1950s and 1960s also saw the adoption by one Communist state, Yugoslavia, of an economic system of decentralized socialist workers' self-management. This economy achieved a growth rate of GDP per capita, during those decades, of 4.9 per cent per annum.[8]

By the end of the 1980s the world of the contending economic systems seemed radically different from that of the early postwar years. In the 1960s Soviet economic growth rates had surpassed those of the United States for four decades,[9] and threats that central planning and high rates of capital accumulation would allow the Soviet economy to surpass its American counterpart could be made without total implausibility. American technological superiority was the status quo in most industries, and in the less developed world, many gave credence to the notion that the only way out of underdevelopment was to break ties with the capitalist-dominated world market and follow a Soviet-type path to industrialization.

As the last decade of the century approached, however, economic growth in the Soviet Union and Eastern Europe had slowed to less

than 2 per cent,[10] and radical economic reforms were initiated, with
official declarations of the inadequacy of the traditional Soviet
model first in Hungary, then in China, and finally in the Soviet
Union itself. At the same time, American as well as European
technical supremacy had been broken by Japanese competition, and
the socialist countries felt their system to be threatened with
historical irrelevance in the face of the technological dynamism in
Japan and other market economies. Finally, the idea that development was impossible under market rules, in the less developed
countries, was deeply undermined by the rapid growth of market-
oriented economies in East and South-East Asia.

The American and European economies had serious problems of
their own in the 1970s and 1980s. The average growth rate of real
GNP per capita also slowed to under 2 per cent per annum in the
western industrial nations during 1971–87, the average rate of
unemployment rose from 3.7 per cent in 1950–69 to 6.4 per cent in
1970–86, and inflation hit an average rate of 11.2 per cent in 1980.[11]
Average hourly real wages in the United States were 2.4 per cent
lower in 1986 than in 1970, and many families felt that they were
working harder (for example, having to put a second wage-earner
into the labor force) to maintain the same standard of living.[12] Some
of these problems were related to the shock of sharp increases in the
costs of energy, due to effective action by a Middle East-led oil
cartel, OPEC, in 1973 and 1979. However, conservative analyses,
associating many difficulties with over-expansion of governmental
welfare programs and regulations, won strong political victories in
many western nations, including the United States, Great Britain,
West Germany, and even France (despite its election of a socialist
government), during the 1980s. The evolution of industrial capitalism towards a mixed welfarist system with an activist state began
to slow, and in some respects to be reversed, as the ideology of
unfettered markets and incentives gained new adherents. The mid-
to late 1980s accordingly saw successful taming of inflation, modest
economic growth with limited gains by wage-earners, widespread
deregulation of industry, more demand-stimulating military expenditure, significant increases in income and wealth inequalities,[13]
scaled-back welfare programs, and signs, for some observers, of the
emergence of a 'permanent underclass' of hard-core unemployables.

Assessments of the Yugoslav economy also changed dramatically
during these decades. In the 1960s Yugoslavia was one of the fastest

growing nations in the developing world, and its economic performance was referred to as 'the Yugoslav miracle'. Western students of the self-managed economic system also agreed that Yugoslav workers had real decision-making power in their firms, and that market forces had to a substantial degree replaced administrative decision-making as coordinators of economic activity. By the early 1980s, however, Yugoslav economic growth slowed to a crawl,[14] and the economy was racked by inflation rates averaging 52 per cent during 1980–6, and by high rates of unemployment. Analysts now noted that local bureaucratic intervention and bargaining, more than markets, were emerging as the real replacements for central planning. Observers also saw that trade and factor mobility across internal (republican) borders was greatly impeded, and that rather than being confronted by real market discipline, firms continued to experience the 'soft budget constraint' familiar in centrally planned economies.

Although the Yugoslav model of workers' management could command little admiration, examples of workers' participation, profit sharing, and co-determination proliferated in the 1970s and 1980s. Quantitative analyses by economists suggest that co-determination in West Germany has had no measurable effect on economic efficiency, and that profit sharing and participation have positive effects in worker-owned, cooperative firms, and in capital-owned firms. Among case studies showing enhanced factor productivity from worker decision-making, ownership, or profit sharing, were studies of employee-owned plywood firms in the United States, kibbutz industrial and agricultural branches in Israel, and the Mondragon cooperatives in Spain.[15]

5.2.2 From Material Needs to the Environment

Developed capitalist market economies can claim strong performance with respect to meeting the basic material needs of a relatively large fraction of citizens, but they have been faulted for failing the remaining minority. For example, in the United States in 1983 the incomes of 15.3 per cent of the population fell below a government-set poverty line, and almost 9 per cent qualified to receive government transfers (that is, food stamps) to help them reach nutritional standards they could not satisfy with their own market earnings.[16] To the extent that the poor segment of the population had difficulty improving their lot, and that public sentiment about government support for that segment was unreliable, achievement of basic needs remained problematic even in this rich capitalist society. For poorer countries, as mentioned in Chapter 3, there were indications that socialist societies performed better than others with respect to basic needs provision, although some non-socialist countries performed equally well.[17]

A large fraction of the Soviet population would have to be judged poor by American standards. While there are grounds for contrasting the Soviet system favorably with the American in terms of the distribution of basic provisions and avoidance of such manifestations of poverty as homelessness, generally lower standards of living and the failure of the system to supply even a limited range of foods and other consumer goods in a timely and reliable fashion undercut the efficacy of redistribution, and make direct comparison difficult.[18] More fundamentally, evaluation of socialism's performance with respect to provision of basic needs may turn on whether one holds the system to be responsible for slow growth of consumption. A system that guarantees a larger share of consumption to its poor but raises consumption slowly may be judged inferior, in terms of the well-being of the poor, to one with a smaller consumption share for the poor but higher consumption growth. A closely related indictment of the Soviet model is that it appears to require higher investment shares, and thus greater sacrifices of consumption, to achieve given increases in output. While we lack a clear-cut welfare standard for judging the intertemporal and intergenerational preferences implied by Soviet savings decisions, low efficiency of investment is undoubtedly not to be touted as a advantage of its economic system.

There are differing standards of equity between and among societies, and some of the issues arising in considering the equity of economic outcomes in the three systems have been discussed in earlier chapters. If simple equality of the distribution of income among households is adopted as a proxy for equity, then inter-systemic comparisons are more straightforward, although one must still choose between alternative measures, and there are serious problems surrounding the reliability of the available data. Most analyses agree, however, that income distribution in centrally planned socialist countries is more equal than that in capitalist countries, as a rule. For example, using the Gini coefficient, which ranges from a value of 0 for maximum equality to a value of 1 for maximum inequality, and choosing household income as our income concept, the average for the Soviet Union and five Eastern European countries was 0.271, while that for the United States, Canada, and four Western European countries,[19] after taxes and transfer payments, was 0.309, for various years around 1970, according to calculations by Morrisson (1984). The corresponding figure for Yugoslavia, undoubtedly influenced as much by rural–urban and regional differences as by the economic system as such, was 0.354. It is worth noting that among capitalist countries, income inequality after taxes and transfers differed widely and seemed amenable to policy interventions: hence, the Gini coefficient for Sweden (as measured by Morrisson) was 0.266, lower than those of the Soviet Union, Hungary, and Poland. Also, some observers argue that the standard measures of income distribution in the socialist countries are biased downwards by failure to account for the monetary value of benefits in kind enjoyed by political and economic elites.[20] A correction for this factor, by Morrisson, raises the average Gini coefficient for the socialist countries mentioned above from 0.271 to 0.308, indistinguishable from the average for the capitalist countries.

The conventional wisdom, supported by reform-minded leaders in socialist countries as well as by a broad spectrum of Western observers, is that capitalist market economies regularly achieve higher levels of allocative and technical efficiency than do planned socialist ones. This view is supported by studies such as one by Bergson (1987), who concludes that output per worker in the Soviet Union and East European socialist countries (including Yugoslavia) is between a third and a quarter less than that in developed capitalist countries, holding labor quality, capital, and land constant. Another study, by Desai and Martin (1983), finds that inter-industry differences in marginal rates of technical substitution between capital and labor in the Soviet Union are large, and that that country could achieve the same industrial output using between 3 and 10 per cent less input by reallocating factors among industries. On the other hand, a carefully controlled study of East and West German industrial productivity by Sturm (1977) could not discount the possibility that observed differences could be explained by nonsystemic factors, such as scale economies, and Burkett and Skegro's (1989) econometric study of factor productivity in 65 countries finds no significant productivity difference among systems.

Interestingly, Burkett and Skegro note that their evidence does not
rule out the possibility that the relative productivity of resources in
socialist versus capitalist economies is lower for countries at higher
levels of economic development, a finding that is consistent with the
widespread belief that socialist central planning is more effective in
marshalling resources for early industrialization than at using them
efficiently to meet the requirements of a sophisticated consumer-
oriented economy.[21] Even though serious misallocation of resources
in the Yugoslav economy is posited by western analysts, who stress
the effects of the country's capital market imperfections and other
institutional 'distortions', findings of improved technical efficiency
in profit sharing, participatory, and worker-owned firms in market
economies have been reported earlier in this section.

Numerous remarks regarding the social, nonmaterial dimensions
of the three economic systems, made in earlier chapters, could be
restated here. Centrally planned economies have claimed superiority
in the realm of employment security and price stability, while
industrial market economies marked by capitalist economic systems
and pluralistic political institutions have claimed superiority in the
realm of personal and political liberties. Critics of both systems see
their modes of organization as hierarchical, bureaucratic, socially
stratified, and alienating. Surveys of workers in Yugoslav enterprises
have found mixed evidence regarding the social impact of worker
participation, but numerous studies of participatory firms in market
economies suggest higher levels of job satisfaction among workers,
consistent with the rationale of participatory approaches.[22]

In comparative terms, centrally planned socialist economies have
demonstrated an ability to achieve exceptionally high rates of
saving. For example, between 1965 and 1973 the ratio of gross
domestic investment to GDP averaged around 27 per cent in the
Soviet Union and Eastern Europe, versus 21.3 per cent in the
western industrial nations during the same period.[23] Among
industrial market economies, the investment rate varied greatly,
from 18 per cent in the United States to nearly 29 per cent in
Switzerland; and it was 37.4 per cent in Japan, which is not included
in the previous figure. Yugoslavia's investment to GDP ratio was
29.5 per cent in the period. Comparisons of economic growth rates
and comments about technological change have been given above.

The tendency for industrialization to deplete nonrenewable
resources, despoil landscapes, and befoul air and water manifests

itself without regard to economic system. Private industry and individuals pollute the environment in capitalist countries, and the countervailing force of government regulations and clean-up efforts is on the one hand called into action by widespread popular sentiments, and on the other hand limited by unwillingness to pay the costs entailed, and by the related ability of industry spokesmen to influence politicians and public opinion, and to infiltrate the ranks of their regulators. The belief that state industry would internalize public concern for environmental quality, in the centrally planned socialist economies, has found little confirmation. The growth maximizing orientation of the socialist regimes, combined with their monopoly over sources of information and political expression, have allowed environmental degradation in the East to rival or exceed that in the West. There is as yet an insufficient record on which to judge the performance of workers' self-management in this regard.

It would take us beyond the limits of this short book to investigate more broadly the quality of work, community, and family life in the capitalist and socialist countries, and in Yugoslavia and communities in which cooperatives play a major role. Such issues as the economic and social status of women, the quality of child care, responses to the problems of ageing, the vitality of the arts, the frequency and severity of criminal activities and violence, and the incidence of alcoholism and drug abuse, could all be addressed with reference to the influence of economic system elements. Undoubtedly, we would find variation among countries with the same economic system label but with differences of culture and history. More interesting for our purposes would be those differences, between and within systems, attributable to variations in policies and in institutional details. The interested reader can only be urged to consult the cited sources and suggested readings, and to find other means of exploring these questions.

5.3 Economic Systems and Economic Development

Most of our illustrations of the problems of and arguments for particular economic systems have implicitly assumed the reference point of an industrialized economy. A few words about the relevance of our discussions to economies at relatively early stages of industrialization should be added before we conclude. These remarks fall under two headings. First, how should we describe the economic systems now in place in the developing or underdeveloped countries? Second, what strategies of development have been associated with each system, and what are the pluses and minuses of both the strategies and the systems themselves, from the vantage point of a less developed country?

5.3.1 Economic Systems of Developing Countries

What are the economic systems characterizing the world's developing economies today? Our remarks here will be very brief and limited to a few main points. First, there is considerable heterogeneity among developing countries, which is obvious when it is noted that they include capitalist nations such as Chile and Saudi Arabia, mixed economies as India and Zimbabwe, reforming Soviet-type economies such as China's, and imitators of the traditional Soviet model, such as North Korea. This means that 'developing economy' should almost certainly not be understood to represent another type of economic system, in the same sense as 'centrally planned socialist economy' or 'market capitalist economy'.

Some of the economic features shared by many developing countries are more structural than institutional. For example, developing countries tend to have relatively large fractions of their populations living in rural areas and engaged in agriculture, but that should probably not be seen as an 'economic system' feature, since the same observation could apply to a socialist, capitalist, or worker-managed society. On the other hand, special institutional features are sometimes attributed to developing economies. In the early stages of development, for example, it is sometimes argued that the marginal product of labor in large parts of these economies is below the income required for survival, but that people none the less subsist because families or communities share their produce, and their incomes are therefore determined by their average, not their marginal, products. Such sharing organizations, if that is a correct characterization, might be seen as a special system element. They suggest that, in other sectors of the economy operating according to conventional market principles, it may be necessary to pay wages higher than the marginal product in the sharing sectors, if people can be attracted out of those other sectors only by incomes above those that they are already used to receiving. The institutional depiction of such an economy includes the notion that it is 'dualistic', in the sense that two distinct sets of economic arrangements, sometimes called the 'traditional' and the 'modern' or 'capitalist', exist side by side.[24]

Other typical institutional elements in developing countries might include the common existence of some kind of government economic planning. However, there is little consensus on identification of a valid institutional model even for groups of similar developing countries. Perhaps most developing economies should be seen as having hybrid economic systems. They would contain sectors in which 'peasant modes of production' co-exist with 'semi-feudal' haciendas and plantations, a small-scale business sector marked by capitalist free enterprise, large enterprises existing in intimate relationship with the state (which influences many of the prices they face while controlling their access to import licenses and other essentials), and the state itself, which might be compared with its counterpart in the more interventionist mixed capitalist economies such as France. Finally, the picture of many developing economies might be considered incomplete without specification of key foreign actors, such as direct foreign investors, aid providers, and international financial institutions (for instance, the International Monetary Fund), whose participation in the economy often accounts for a substantial share of national income.

5.3.2 Development Strategies and Economic Systems

In the decades immediately after the Second World War many countries in Africa and Asia achieved independence from colonial rule, and existing less-developed countries (LDCs) in Latin America and elsewhere looked for policies to promote economic development in a new international economic environment. Competition between the western capitalist and Soviet bloc socialist nations for influence in these parts of the world also spurred the growth of theories of economic development among western economists, and the refinement of Marxist and neo-Marxist approaches to development, not only in the Soviet bloc but also in the Third World and among western radical analysts. The experience of the Soviet Union since 1917 played a role in the formulation of all of these approaches, including those of the western mainstream.

The debate over the strategy for economic development among

Soviet economists in the 1920s was a landmark in the history of ideas about industrialization. The main issues discussed were (1) the role of foreign trade, (2) the relationship between agriculture and industry, and (3) the rate of investment and its distribution among sectors. On trade, the principal question was whether Russia should continue exporting agricultural and mineral products in order to import western capital goods, or whether it should aim for greater economic self-reliance. On agriculture and industry, the main issue was whether to promote balanced development of both sectors, or to emphasize the removal or extraction of excess labor power, food and raw materials, and financial surpluses from agriculture, in order to maximize the rate of industrialization. On investment, the main question was whether to attempt a balanced expansion of the consumer and producer goods industries, so that workers and farmers would be provided with incentive goods to encourage enthusiastic work and willing sales of farm products, or to emphasize development of the producer goods industries to lay the foundation of a more industrialized economy, while keeping consumption at minimal levels over the medium term.

When western theories of economic development emerged in the post-Second World War period, one prominent idea of the Soviet industrialization debate re-appeared: the notion that agriculture was a source of surplus labor, food and raw materials, and savings, for industrial growth. However, the answers given to the three questions just posed, by western development economists and by the Soviet Union, under Stalin, were quite different. First, Stalin opted to limit trade, while western economists emphasized the concept of comparative advantage, according to which most developing countries (including Russia of that time) would be advised to export agricultural and other primary products and to import capital goods. On the second question, Stalin chose to extract as much labor, output, and savings from agriculture as he could in a short period of time, essentially by forcing peasants to join collective farms which had to sell their products to the government at low prices. Western development economists, on the other hand, generally supported the idea of keeping agricultural and industrial growth in balance.[25] On the third question, finally, Stalin imposed a high rate of savings on the Soviet population by way of the just-mentioned agricultural procurement policies, controlled wages, and limited supplies of consumer goods, and he used the savings thus obtained to finance rapid expansion of heavy (producer goods) industry. Western development economists, on the other hand, although emphasizing the need for capital accumulation, advocated financing this both through foreign capital inflows and by voluntary savings (related to unequal domestic distributions of income), and proposed no similar bias in favor of heavy industry.

In the decades following the Second World War each approach appeared to have merit. The Soviet Union had experienced economic growth of unusual rapidity between 1928 and the early 1960s.[26] Its industrial infrastructure had helped it to survive a fierce military challenge from Nazi Germany, and its decision to emphasize self-reliance and to prepare for foreign hostility had acquired some justification, in hindsight. During the 1950s and 1960s, the Soviet government was able to deliver some long-deferred improvements in its citizens' living standards, making it possible to argue that the sacrifices of the early decades of industrialization had paid off. Especially with respect to industrial infrastructure and military might, the Soviet Union had become a major world power.

Partly because of this the theory of comparative advantage fell into disrepute in much of the developing world. The logic of its refutation runs roughly as follows. The present comparative advantage of an underdeveloped country is in selling its raw materials and products using intensively its abundant unskilled labor force. But in the international division of labor, countries selling such goods would earn low returns, because of their general abundance (and, some assert, because of the low income elasticities of demand for primary products). With small earnings, it would be impossible to accumulate much capital or to finance much training of skilled labor. Over time, therefore, the comparative advantage of such countries would fail to change. They would not achieve industrialization, and they would remain underdeveloped and exploited participants in the world economy.

The planned approach to industrialization, on the other hand, rejects static comparative advantage in favor of a vision of a developed future. The country's government takes the lead in marshalling its resources not to produce what earns the highest return today, but rather to strengthen those activities seen as necessary to moving forward step by step towards industrialized status. The attraction that many developing country governments have evidenced for the Soviet approach, or for at least some use of state development planning, is partly based on this kind of reasoning.

Although their economies are far from the advanced industrial settings in which a mass of wage laborers are assumed to confront a small group of capitalists, less-developed countries (LDCs) have also been an attractive subject for Marxist-type class analysis. According to the neo-Marxist 'dependency theory' school, for example, the continuing subordination of LDCs in the world economy is facilitated by existence of indigenous elite classes socialized to the values of the advanced capitalist countries and sharing the latters' interest in exploiting the LDCs' resources to earn profits for domestic and international capitalists. Growth of output, and even some industrialization, may be fostered by this partnership, but without real development of living standards for large segments of the LDCs' populations. Inequalities of wealth, property ownership, and education and skill, translating into inequalities of income and political power, are typically far larger in LDCs than in industrialized countries, giving moral urgency to populist and radical critiques of capitalism. The linking of capitalism with centuries of colonialism and economic imperialism have also made socialism an attractive ideology to many Third World nationalists.

While the Western neoclassical approach has been able to produce theoretical arguments to show the importance of market-generated, scarcity-reflecting price signals for resource allocation in general, and of vigorous participation in world trade in particular, it is the emergence of rapid economic growth in the largely capitalist developing economies of East Asia that has done the most to restore the prestige of market-oriented approaches to economic development. It would be a mistake, to be sure, to assert that Japan, South Korea, or Taiwan, for example, had followed the path of free trade and a 'hands-off' (*laissez-faire*) government to rapid development. In each case, there were important governmental interventions, including industrial coordination of what might be viewed as business cartels, and a bias towards promotion of exports embodying increasing levels of technological sophistication. Moreover, the vast inequalities plaguing many developing countries were greatly tempered by redistribution of land and widespread access to education, in these East Asian cases.

While the East Asian success stories thus provide support for part of the argument for planning and asset redistribution, and against

passive acceptance of inequalities and of static comparative advantage, theirs are (none the less) basically market economies in which
entrepreneurship is driven by the motive of profit, and in which
individuals can accumulate and earn returns on privately owned
productive resources. Technological dynamism and rapid development of the consumer goods industries, in these countries, have also
cast doubt upon the Soviet heavy industry strategy, which is being
seriously rethought today in the Soviet Union itself, and in most
other countries having Soviet-type economies.

Workers' self-management has played only a small role in debates
about economic arrangements to promote development. A few social
thinkers have argued that both capitalist and socialist development
strategies overlook the costs of development to ordinary people, in
terms of working conditions, disrupted community and family
systems, and deferred improvements in consumption. Promotion of
cooperatives has been an element in many official development
plans. During the 1950s, 1960s, and early 1970s, Yugoslavia, as we
have seen, was among the world's fastest growing developing
countries, and its 'economic miracle' sustained claims to the effect
that workers' self-management was at least not incompatible with
economic development. However, Yugoslavia became one of many
developing countries that fell victim to international economic
turbulence in the late 1970s and 1980s, and its inability to adapt to
new conditions revealed severe structural and macro-economic
problems, all but blackening the former lustre of the 'miracle'. It
would probably be fair to say that while self-management has many
advocates and small-scale examples throughout the developing
world today, the view that workers' control is at best a luxury that
poor countries cannot afford, is widespread.

5.4 Are There Alternatives to Markets and Planning?

Arguably the most sobering message of this book, and of comparative
economic systems as a field of inquiry, is that complex economies
appear capable of being linked together only by one of two mechanisms: the market system, or state command planning. Anyone
who abhors the impersonality and frequent ruthlessness of markets
—which can, without warning, render the verdict that a valuable
skill has become obsolete, a fixed income inadequate, a commodity
produced with painstaking effort unsaleable—and who objects also

to the clumsy and rigid character of a planning hierarchy—which tends to stifle local initiative and horizontal economic relations, to respond slowly to new economic opportunities, and to inspire little love or enthusiasm from those directed by it—seems to have remaining only the doubtfully attractive option of making do without a broader social division of labor, in an economy of self-contained local economic units. How accurate is this conclusion?

One way to proceed is to try to identify some alternative co-ordinating methods. Indicative planning may come to mind. It is, of course, only a modification of a market system, and thus probably not deserving of identification as a distinct alternative. But in so far as the range of interventions that can be associated with indicative planning and with the 'mixed economy' more generally are capable of responding to many of the problems critics have with markets, noting it as an option may not be entirely inappropriate.

Another possibility that receives occasional mention is what is called 'corporatism', or the similar notion of a 'bargaining economy'. One example is Sweden, in which employers and labor belong to comprehensive federations that bargain with one another, on behalf of their members, over wages and employment. If the government joins these negotiations and extends bargaining also to cover target price and/or profit levels, many of the key parameters of the economy could end up being determined through such bargaining, with only the details being left to be decided by individual firms and their workers. The bargaining stances of each group could be said to be determined by an internal political process, including the election of the groups' leaders. The outcomes of bargaining are determined by what is called 'bargaining power' (which, among other things, reflects the ability of each side to inflict damage on the others) and by bargaining strategies and coalition formation.

Should corporatism be viewed as a coordinating mechanism on a par with markets and command planning? In the framework of the contrast in basic principles between the decentralized market system (with individualized profit- and maximum returns-seeking) and the hypothetical planned economy (in which resource allocation is directly determined by 'societal' assessments of 'use value'), corporatism, like indicative planning, seems to be basically a variant of a market economy. Organized labor is still selling a commodity—labor power—to organized employers, and the price it can obtain is constrained by labor's value to the employer in terms of its transformability into goods that can be sold to consumers.[27] It can be argued, then, that relative scarcities and individual preferences will ultimately determine resource allocation in much the same manner as in a more competitive market economy, whereas under central planning, only planners' preferences (whether representative of those of the population, or not) count. Perhaps bargaining should therefore be viewed as one extreme type of market coordination, competitive markets as another.[28]

A last alternative that might be mentioned is what has been called the 'economy of mobilization'. It is, basically, a centrally planned economy of the Soviet type, but one in which popular participation in implementing the plan is elicited through the political and ideological campaigns of a charismatic leadership, and in which the leaders may successfully convince the public that authority flows from the bottom up and that the leaders' goals are to serve the people. China under Mao Zedong has been offered as an example.[29] The question here is whether the 'economy of mobilization' is anything other than central planning with a claim of success at achieving a 'people–state identity'. To be sure, if the 'popular will' in a society did come to coalesce in a clear enough direction to dictate state policies, the nature of economic coordination would be less a matter of planning at the hierarchical apex and obedience to commands at the bottom, and more a matter of enthusiastic participation in carrying out joint aims. Even with a great similarity of objectives among the people, however, 'free-rider' problems could still exist unless there was also a high level of public-spiritedness. And if coalescence of objectives and public spiritedness were both to obtain, there would still be coordination problems to be addressed by some kind of planning process. In so far as mobilization really is capable of aligning interests and generating public spirit, it may be reasonable to list it among solutions to the economic coordination problem, but the evidence that it works is limited and subject to sharp dispute.

Local Autonomy

What of the more drastic approach of seeking self-sufficiency of local economic units, thus minimizing the need for inter-unit coordination? In Chapter 1 we extended Adam Smith's proposition that 'the division of labor is limited by the extent of the market' to allow for the possibility that planning might replace the market as a means of integrating a complex economy. Despite this modification, the Smithian idea that the productivity gains of division of labor, including those within the enterprise, require either a large market or a large sphere of integration by plan has remained unchallenged. We have held to the view, therefore, that local self-sufficiency implies a more primitive development of the division of labor, and thus lower labor productivity and living standards. Is there any possibility of questioning this characterization of local self-sufficiency?

In recent years, at least a few social visionaries have suggested that minimizing reliance on markets and plans, and maximizing local autonomy under a model of participatory local self-management, is becoming increasingly achievable without great sacrifice in living standards.[30] The technological underpinning of their argument is that the 'post-industrial' revolution of the late twentieth century differs from the industrial changes of the nineteenth century; rather than replacing dispersed cottage industries and crafts producers with ever larger and more heavily capitalized factories it encourages developments in areas such as microelectronics and biological engineering, which involve few if any economies of scale, and are knowledge- rather than capital-intensive, especially at the use (as opposed to research and manufacturing) stages. A possible complementary argument is that society will in coming decades be forced to move away from centralized generation of electrical power and its distribution over costly and scale-sensitive power grids, because of the unacceptable environmental effect of biological and nuclear fuel consumption. Intensive exploitation of solar, wind, water, and geothermal energy sources, and a shift to low-energy-consuming technologies, will thus be made necessary, and these changes will be consistent with more locally self-sufficient economic activities.

One difficulty in evaluating such approaches is that to the extent that prospective technical innovations seem insufficient to sustain the current living standards of the advanced industrial economies without substantial inter-local, inter-regional, and international trade, enthusiasts of local self-sufficiency frequently switch to suggesting that current consumption patterns represent irrational forms of material self-indulgence which are fostered by the commercial logic of the capitalist market system. Local self-reliance may be admitted to be unable to deliver the plethora of consumer goods and comforts to which middle-class consumers in the most prosperous industrial market economies are today accustomed, but it is argued that such a standard of living is in any case both ecologically unsustainable, and unnecessary either to the satisfaction of basic material needs, or to the fulfillment of human potential for community, social relationships, artistic self-expression, and so forth. In so far as this turns our attention to a critique of the preference structures that it argues are endogenous to modern market economies, it enters an area that will be touched upon in the next two sections. In so far as it represents an admission that small-scale, local production is not up to the job under prevailing preference structures, it is essentially a retraction of bolder claims. Nevertheless, since the search for optimal social arrangements can legitimately concern itself with global possibilities, rather than being limited to marginal departures from present practices, the connection between preference structure issues and coordination system issues is certainly not in itself a' reason for dismissing localistic strategies out of hand.

5.5 How Pervasive is Self-interest?

One assumption that our introduction to economic systems has shared with most of western economic analysis is that individual human beings act in the pursuit of their own self-interest, even when this clashes with the desires of others or with the needs of the groups to which they belong. The modern economic analysis of capitalism can be said to have begun with Adam Smith's famous statement, '[i]t is not from the benevolence of the butcher, the brewer, or the baker, that we expect our dinner, but from their regard to their own interest'[31] and the approach of economists has in this respect changed little since Smith's day. Unless reasons are put forward for assuming a change in the fundamentals of human behavior in the face of differing economic institutions, methodological consistency dictates that the same assumption be applied to socialism, self-management, and other economic systems, as to capitalism. But perhaps there are reasons why basic motivations would change under different institutional arrangements, or why they can be expected to change with the maturation of the human species, or with increases in income or education levels. Perhaps, too, Adam Smith's statement is wrong, or misleading, for capitalism itself, whether in his time, or in our own.

To begin with the last question, it is noteworthy that according to surveys many workers in the relatively wealthy countries say that they would continue to work even if they did not have to do so out of financial considerations; work seems to be a social activity that gives people a sense of purpose, usefulness, and identity. It has frequently been suggested that even in so far as people compete for financial rewards, they do so not so much for the sake of the money as such, but because it is a symbol of success—suggesting that if there were a social consensus replacing money with other symbols (honor or prestige, awarded for various achievements, might be possibilities), people would remain motivated to strive hard in their economic activities. Many people (teachers and health-care workers, for example) clearly choose their activities not to maximize their earnings, but to maximize their satisfaction, including that which comes from being of service to others. Still others select a career as a response to a spiritual calling, or respond to patriotic calls to military service.

Adam Smith's view of capitalism hardly requires that everyone be selfish all of the time; it only implies that most people act self-interestedly at least a good part of the time. However, Smith seems to go further than to say that there is no point in hoping that people will become selfless, that that is unrealistic. He comes close to saying that people are more likely to serve one another's interests when their immediate aim is serving themselves than when they explicitly set out to help others.[32] Perhaps his meaning was that even well-intentioned people often weaken in their resolve without some personal reward in sight. Or perhaps he meant that of all the motivations nature might have given to man, self-interest is the most useful, for there is no reliable way of communicating needs cheaply and rapidly across a complex economy composed of altruists; but such a method does exist for a complex economy of self-interested persons—namely, the price system.

Supposing that a lack of self-interest *would* be dysfunctional in a market economy, another question which could be asked is: need it be so universally? A pure communist society, in which goods are distributed according to people's needs and there are no rewards to effort, might benefit from an abatement of self-interestedness, whereas under capitalism, an increase in the propensity to cooperate might only facilitate the formation of cartels and other undesirable group behavior (including, perhaps, the worker solidarity that would spell the system's demise, following Marx's scenario). Group solidarity could be beneficial to the internal workings of self-managed firms, but the efficient functioning of a market economy composed of such firms presumes at least group-level self-interestedness.

In some of his writings, Karl Marx implied that people work only to be paid, under capitalism, because the system alienates them from work. They would, however, perceive work as the very essence of their lives, were they not cut off from the productive means with which they must work, and from the products that they create. In the higher stage of communism, wrote Marx, labor would be 'life's prime want'—that is, a good in itself. However, Marx suggested that material rewards would be necessary at least in an early stage of socialism, and elsewhere he seemed to depart from the idea that only alienation makes work unpleasant. For example, in a passage in *Capital*, he says that 'the realm of freedom actually begins only where labor which is determined by necessity . . . ceases'.[33]

Despite Marx's later view of labor, and the Soviet practice of heavy reliance on material incentives, the tradition of ascribing selfishness to capitalism and anticipating the birth of more brotherly and sisterly motivations under socialism has had many lives in radical thought and practice. In China, Mao Zedong looked towards the creation of a 'new man', called upon fellow Communists to 'serve the people', and opposed the use of large pay differentials and piece rates as encouraging a 'bourgeois' mentality. A similar although briefer episode occurred in Cuba under the influence of the charismatic revolutionary figure Che Guevara. Even the more sober V.I. Lenin, who opposed egalitarianism, referred to the desirability of rooting out habits of excessive pecuniary calculation among the working people.

A middle ground in the debates regarding self-interest, human behavior, and economic systems, would be the following. First, self-interest, narrowly construed, is only one of several important motivators of human behavior. Models or analyses that assume economic agents to behave self-interestedly are nevertheless quite often adequate as approximations to real behavior, because of the salience of selfish motivations in the context of the particular decisions involved (for example, choice of working hours and effort level, choice of savings versus consumption). A reading of twentieth-century history suggests strongly that it would be safer to build analyses of socialist and self-managed economic institutions on similar assumptions (of self-interest) than to assume that 'after the revolution, there will be a new man (or woman)'. Although human motivation is complex, and the relative importance of various components of that motivation may well be influenced by social forces and social institutions, beliefs in the likelihood of radical and rapid changes in motivation, much less the total disappearance of self-interest, are probably naïve.

Pro-market economists frequently assert that 'a decent respect for human nature as we know it' leads to an appreciation of the superiority of capitalism over its alternatives under real-world conditions.[34] Perhaps the case of those who argue that human needs and human potential would be better served by another set of economic institutions could be strengthened by showing how those alternative institutions could build upon individual self-interest, instead of presupposing its liquidation. To date, at least, economic analyses of the alternative economic institutions of planned socialism or self-management that have assumed self-interested agents, have failed to establish either that such institutions would be impossible or that they would be clearly inferior to capitalism. Building individual incentives into non-capitalist economic institutions at the design stage may turn out to serve their proponents far better than does criticizing capitalism's appeal to selfishness and demanding that people undergo a behavioral conversion as soon as attempts to build non-capitalist institutions are initiated.

5.6 Will There Always Be (Has There Always Been) Scarcity?

Economists' emphasis upon efficiency in resource allocation as a criterion for evaluating economic systems is founded on the claim that society's resources are limited and its wants large, compared with its capacity to fulfill them. If an abundance of all things wanted by men and women sprang from the ground costlessly, or were regularly produced as a by-product of their pursuits of satisfaction and self-realization, then there would be no economic barrier to letting each take according to his or her needs (Marx's communism). As long as most people still want more of some things than they can provide for themselves or society can provide for them, then economic arrangements that do not foster efficiency in production, in distribution, and in the mix of goods produced, imply losses in satisfaction. Although we have argued that the most efficient economic system is not necessarily the best, since there might be trade-offs at the margin between efficiency and other valued objectives (such as achieving an equitable distribution of income, or safeguarding human dignity), efficiency will continue to rank high among the criteria for evaluating economic arrangements so long as the degree of scarcity remains high.

It is sometimes claimed, however, that scarcity is a phenomenon specific to a particular epoch in human history. An extreme version of this claim is that there were times in the past when human beings lived without scarcity; that scarcity can be eliminated in the future; and that the existence of scarcity is actually a product of our present economic arrangements, not an objective fact helping to call those arrangements into being. These claims may be partly based on assertions about technologies and resources, but it is preferences that often play the pivotal role. Scarcity, it may be said, is a relationship between all three factors. When there are sufficient resources and sufficiently productive technologies to produce enough goods fully to satisfy the desires of all consumers (the marginal utility of each good reaches zero), there is no scarcity. Thus, scarcity can be eliminated either by increasing the resource base and/or finding a more productive technology, or on the other hand by having more modest desires for goods, or by there being fewer people.

In the past there may have been less scarcity because world population was small and the carrying capacity of the earth was great. For hundreds of thousands of years, human beings subsisted by hunting and gathering animals and plants found in nature, using simple tools. The world population before 20,000 BC is thought to have been less than five million people. Anthropologists observe today that members of hunting and gathering societies work fewer hours per week, on average, than do agriculturalists in relatively sparsely populated areas, who in turn work far fewer hours, on average, than do agriculturalists in densely populated areas, or workers in industry. Members of hunting and gathering societies who are removed from their environments and exposed for long periods to the world of modern consumer goods, hot and cold running water, modern medicine, etc., may or may not prefer their new to their old life in terms of material satisfactions. In either case, most of those who lived before the rise of sedentary agriculture, urbanization, and world population growth, might well have had difficulty understanding the idea that resources are scarce.

Future elimination of scarcity belongs to the realm of science fiction, limited only by the imagination. Among the conditions for a society in which each person takes freely according to his or her needs, Marx lists that 'the productive forces [will] have also increased . . . and all the springs of cooperative wealth [will] flow more abundantly'.[35] Perhaps Marx's expectation of such a future was in part a manifestation of the widespread optimism of the nineteenth century, an era that witnessed an historically unprecedented explosion in human productivity in the industrializing areas of the world. Such dreams are less common today. World population has quadrupled since Marx's time. Grinding poverty remains the lot of a billion human beings and not much more than subsistence that of another nearly two billion, in underdeveloped and often overpopulated nations. The environmental and climatic impacts of a century of industrial pollution are causes for alarm, and nonrenewable mineral and energy stocks are dwindling. Even in the richest countries, most people would want more of many things, if goods were free; yet it is impossible to imagine the ecological and resource costs of extending those countries' living standards to the rest of the globe. And world population is expected to double again by the end of the first third of the next century.

The prospects of scientific advance are necessarily unpredictable. New sources of energy and methods of fabricating inorganic and organic materials could give the utopia of abundance a new lease on life. But the basic problem, some would say, is not technological. It is, rather, that new wants are created even more rapidly than are the means of satisfying them. The relevance of economic system choice is that wants may be endogenous to society's economic arrangements in the sense that, rather than being given features of 'human nature', they are partly generated by economic institutions. Radical economists, for instance, argue that capitalism perpetuates itself as an economic system by fostering educational institutions that create docile workers and status-seeking managers, and by generating almost unlimited demands for goods through planned obsolesence, unnecessary changes in fashion and style, and advertising.[36] A similar judgment of capitalism comes from a leading economist of the interwar era, Frank Knight, himself pro-market, who wrote:

In organizing its value scale, the economic order does far more than select and compare wants for exchangeable goods and services; its activity extends to the formation and radical transformation, if not to the outright creation, of the wants themselves; they as well as the means of their gratification are largely products of the system.[37]

Surely there is enough evidence to show that people adjust their aspirations in accordance with what appears attainable to them. Wants do expand with the ability to satisfy them. And the producers and sellers of goods in a market economy do have an interest in creating new wants that they can successfully compete to satisfy. However, many of our desires for comfort and convenience, although perhaps not operational until the possibility of fulfillment has been demonstrated, are probably better explained by human physiology and psychology than by social events; and these desires—for pleasant and varied foods, for comfortable and season-ally appropriate clothing, for comfortably appointed and climatically adaptable housing, etc.—cannot easily be satisfied in full for all people given current resources and technologies. Moreover, even if tastes are indeed a function of social conditioning and of our responses to a variety of environmental stimuli, the question of what types of conditioning and stimuli are socially preferable is a difficult one to answer. For example, any proposal to replace the freedom of competing private firms to advertise their products with state-controlled media spreading the message that living simply is good (or patriotic, or politically correct), would require evaluation from the standpoints of political liberty, consideration of the possible misuse of such messages to inculcate docility towards political despotism or economic inefficiency, and so forth.

One important implication of the present discussion, which might be mentioned by way of conclusion, is that to the extent that tastes are endogenous to the economic system, satisfaction of wants may be a poor guide to social welfare. People may see themselves as being just as well off in a materially poor, technologically stagnant society with modest life expectancies, wherein they are conditioned to prefer simplicity, as in a richer, technologically dynamic society with longer life expectancies, in which there is constant exposure to exhortations to strive for material things, and in which people accordingly both work harder and consume more. If the 'utility functions' by which economists would ordinarily propose to measure the welfare of those affected are themselves not constant across these scenarios, then we may have to seek other ways of measuring human welfare.[38]

5.7 Economic Organization and the Human Condition: Final Remarks

We began this book by arguing that economic organization is a critical determinant of both our material standard of living and of a great many central aspects of our lives, such as our opportunities for education, the quality of our working lives, our range of personal choice regarding where to live and work, with whom to associate, and more. It can be added, without exaggeration, that what economic arrangements we adopt or devise, and how successfully they meet our objectives, will exert a great influence over such fundamental concerns as the chances of eradicating poverty in large parts of the world, the hope of building just societies, and even the likelihood of peace or war.[39]

Modern economic systems can be viewed as alternative ways of supporting a complex division of labor, that is, a situation in which each person benefits from the intricately but often invisibly inter-related actions of a myriad of other individuals, and in which no one is self-sufficient. Such a division of labor is desired because it is capable of raising productivity and thus material living standards. But along with these benefits comes the requirement of coordination, and potential problems with respect to equity and the quality of life.

Given the existence of constraints to the simultaneous satisfaction of all human wants, it may be pointless to search for an economic system that will perfectly fulfill all human material needs, achieve a high degree of equity, use resources efficiently, guarantee maximum liberty and satisfaction of nonmaterial wants, and build a still stronger foundation for future generations. Moreover, full agreement on how equity, nonmaterial wants, or even material needs, should be defined, remains elusive. This does not mean, however, that we can absolve ourselves of the responsibility of making value judgments and of identifying preferred sets of trade-offs with respect to the fulfillment of these sometimes conflicting goals. Hopes of avoiding these trade-offs by discovering a radically different alternative to markets or planning, by calling to life a better side of human nature, or by altering technology or preferences so as to eliminate the problem of scarcity, may merit some consideration as ways of softening the contradictions among conflicting ends. However, they need to be viewed cautiously, since they may well prove to be unrealistic, and they carry the danger of diverting our attention from the range of realizable possibilities which are available to human societies for the foreseeable future. That range of options is itself reasonably large, and careful, open-minded study of the variety of economic systems presently at hand, and of variants designed in a manner that is fully mindful of existing material, technological, and behavioral constraints, may facilitate sound choices and innovative improvements. The effort to build a just and prosperous world must‎ begin with an understanding of these realities.

Notes

1. Phyllis Deane (1965, p. 274) estimated an annual growth rate of about 1.5 per cent for output per capita in Britain of the early nineteenth century, and of about 2.5 per cent for the same country in the late nineteenth century. As she notes, the first rate translates into a doubling in productivity in a little under half a century, while the second implies that productivity doubled in about a generation. British economic growth in the eighteenth century was considerably slower, but accelerating, according to Deane and Cole 1962. Data provided by Mitchell 1975 implies similar growth rates, of roughly 1.5 per cent and 1.6 per cent, respectively, for Germany and Great Britain in the period 1850–1938. While lacking precedent, these rates are low compared to those achieved by late-developing countries including the Soviet Union, Japan, and South Korea, in the present century.
2. See Schumpeter 1950, chapter 11, and Marx and Engels 1978.
3. Nove 1972, Mitchell 1975.
4. Bergson 1978, Ellman 1988; Nove 1983.
5. For an overview of these trends, see Gregory and Stuart 1986, chapter 13 and sources cited therein.
6. Based on data for Australia, Belgium, Canada, France, West Germany, Italy, the Netherlands, Switzerland, the United Kingdom, and the United States, averaged by 1970 population, from World Bank 1976.
7. The latter includes Bulgaria, Czechoslovakia, East Germany, Hungary, Poland, and Romania (World Bank 1976).
8. World Bank 1980.

9. The Soviet growth rate exceeded that of the United States in every five year period from 1930 to 1975, with the exception of the war years 1940–5.

10. GNP per capita grew at an average rate of 1.92 per cent in the seven countries previously listed, weighted by 1970 population, during 1971–87, USCIA 1988.

11. Calculations based on data for the same ten nations, weighted by 1970 population. Growth data from USCIA 1988, unemployment data from ILO, various years, for 1950–69, and from OECD 1987, for 1970–86, inflation data from IMF 1988.

12. US Bureau of the Census 1987.

13. On income distribution, see Danziger, Gottschalk, and Smolensky 1989; on wealth distribution, see Wolff 1987.

14. The average growth rate of GNP per capita dropped from 4.4 per cent during 1975–80 to 0.4 per cent during 1980–5 (Gregory and Stuart 1989, p. 408).

15. On German co-determination, see Svejnar 1982; on Western cooperatives, see Estrin, Jones, and Svejnar 1987; on profit sharing in conventional firms, see FitzRoy and Kraft 1987; on the US plywood cooperatives, see Conte 1982; on the kibbutzim, see Barkai 1977; and on Mondragon, see Thomas and Logan 1980.

16. US Bureau of the Census 1987, and Reader's Digest 1986.

17. See Burkett 1985. In this study of 116 countries at varying levels of economic development, socialist countries seemed to do at least as well as others, and possibly better, when basic needs were measured by the Physical Quality of Life Index (an average of normalized life expectancy, infant mortality, and adult literacy statistics). The analysis treats the Soviet Union and its East European allies, Yugoslavia, China, and Cuba, as socialist. For a related analysis, see Cereseto and Waitzkin 1986.

18. Similar remarks might apply to Yugoslavia, except that there, state guarantees of support to households are weaker, and inter-regional differences in the extent of poverty are particularly large.

19. Denmark, Sweden, the United Kingdom, and West Germany.

20. The parallel bias resulting from the nonmonetary perks of executives and managers in western market economies is usually argued to be of less consequence, since income differentiation for such groups is already well reflected in salary figures.

21. Differences between the Burkett and Skegro and the Bergson studies include the fact that the former use data on a larger number of factor inputs and countries, and consider alternative ways of specifying the production function and handling uncertainty. The Desai and Martin study is also limited to two factor inputs. A survey of the literature on

comparative productivity under capitalist and socialist systems is found in Ellman 1989. Studies failing to show greater allocative inefficiency in the Soviet Union than in the United States are surveyed by Whitesell, forthcoming.

22. For example, Lydall 1984 concludes: 'Most Yugoslav workers in socialist "self-managed" enterprises have the same "them and us" attitude as that which prevails in other economic systems' (p. 290). On participation and job satisfaction in market economies, see Blumberg 1968, and Lawler 1986.

23. From World Bank 1976, using 1970 population weights. Figures for the socialist countries are approximations based on data provided for 1965, 1970, and 1973, only.

24. Lewis 1954. Ranis and Fei 1961. See also Georgescu-Roegen 1960.

25. Until the late 1970s, however, much foreign development assistance had a pro-industry bias. Increasing interest in agricultural development during the 1970s was partly spurred by an increasing concern of development specialists with alleviation of Third World poverty, which tended to be especially widespread in rural areas.

26. Although surpassed during certain high growth decades by countries such as Japan and South Korea, the roughly 4.9 per cent growth rate of real GNP per capita in the USSR between 1931 and 1970, excluding 1941–5, compares favorably to those of Germany and Britain during 1850 to 1938, which are reported in note 1, above. Soviet data for 1931–50, are from Mitchell 1975, and those for 1951–70 are from Gregory and Stuart 1986.

27. This may raise the question of whether something similar could not be said of a centrally planned socialist economy, since in it a single organized entity (the state) faces the entire population of unorganized consumers and sellers of labor. The difference is that in theory such a state can assess its options without initial reference to economic data such as prices, because, while consumer preferences and purchasing power will determine what final goods it can sell at what prices, *purchasing power*, and thus the level of state capital accumulation versus consumption, is itself a variable under state control.

28. Similar to the idea of bargaining as an alternative coordinating mechanism is the concept of 'relational contracting'. The idea here is that market exchange refers to what might be once-only interactions between random buyers and random sellers, on terms determined by neither of the individual parties, but only by aggregate demand and supply. Under planning, 'exchange' is superseded by authority and command. 'Relational contracting' refers to a third form of interaction, in which specific parties deal with each other on a long-term basis, establishing relations of trust or at least mutual recognition, in which

the flows of goods, services, and so on need not be perfectly balanced at any given moment. Examples include long-term contractual relations between a particular parts supplier and a specific buyer. Proponents of this view, such as Oliver Williamson, Victor Goldberg, and G. B. Richardson, see industrial market economies as exhibiting all three types of coordinating mechanisms: planning or hierarchy within firms, relational contracting in ongoing long-term exchange relationships, and market exchange in transactions without those characteristics. See Williamson 1985, Goldberg 1980, and Richardson 1972.

29. See Ward 1967.
30. See Bookchin 1982, Henderson 1981.
31. Smith 1985, p. 16.
32. '[B]y directing that industry in such a manner as its produce may be of the greatest value, he intends only his own gain, and he is in this, as in many other cases, led by an invisible hand to promote an end which was no part of his intention. Nor is it always the worse for the society that it was no part of it. By pursuing his own interest he frequently promotes that of society more effectually than when he really intends to promote it. I have never known much good done by those who affected to trade for the public good.' Smith 1985, p. 225.
33. Marx 1967*b*, p. 820. The statement appears to be neutral to the economic system.
34. Knight 1965, p. 270, quoted in Williamson 1975.
35. Marx 1978, p. 531.
36. See Bowles and Gintis 1977 and Baran and Sweezy 1969.
37. Knight 1935, p. 46.
38. For one recent effort in this direction, see Sen 1987.
39. The prosperity of Germany, following the Second World War, is often cited as a basis of European peace, whereas its economic troubles after the First World War are thought to have been a major contributor to starting the Second. In a similar vein, desires to achieve faster economic development appear to have led to less aggressive foreign policies on the parts of China and the Soviet Union in the late 1980s. To the extent that economic arrangements underlie relative poverty or prosperity, they will be directly linked to such trends.

Suggested Readings

Bornstein, Morris (ed.), 1985, *Comparative Economic Systems: Models and Cases* (5th edn), Homewood, IL: Richard D. Irwin.
Davies, R. W., 1980, *The Industrialization of Soviet Russia (Vols. I and II)*, New York: Macmillan.
Dobb, Maurice, 1966, *Soviet Economic Development since 1917*, London:

Routledge and Kegan Paul.

Erlich, Alexander, 1960, *The Soviet Industrialization Debate, 1924–28*, Cambridge: Harvard University Press.

Gillis, Malcolm, Perkins, Dwight, Roemer, Michael, and Snodgrass, Donald, 1987, *Economics of Development*, (2nd edn), New York: W. W. Norton.

Gruchy, Allan G., 1977, *Comparative Economic Systems: Competing Ways to Stability, Growth, and Welfare*, Boston: Houghton Mifflin.

Meier, Gerald (ed.), 1984, *Leading Issues in Economic Development* (4th edn), New York: Oxford University Press.

Pryor, Frederic, 1973, *Property and Industrial Organization in Communist and Capitalist Nations*, Bloomington: Indiana University Press.

―― 1985, *A Guidebook to the Comparative Study of Economic Systems*, Englewood Cliffs, NJ: Prentice-Hall.

Riskin, Carl, 1975, 'Maoism and Motivation: Work Incentives in China', in V. Nee and J. Peck (eds), *China's Uninterrupted Revolution*, New York: Pantheon.

Schumacher, E. F., 1973, *Small is Beautiful: Economics as if People Mattered*, New York: Harper and Row.

Wheelwright, E. L. and McFarlane, Bruce, 1970, *The Chinese Road to Socialism: Economics of the Cultural Revolution*, New York: Monthly Review Press.

Wilber, Charles (ed.), 1988, *The Political Economy of Development and Under-Development* (4th edn), New York: Random House.

Wiles, Peter J. D., 1977, *Economic Institutions Compared*, New York: Halsted Press.

Zimbalist, Andrew (ed.), 1983, *Comparative Economic Systems: An Assessment of Knowledge, Method, and Theory*, Boston: Kluwer-Nijhoff.

―― and Sherman, Howard J., 1988, *Comparing Economic Systems: A Political-Economic Approach* (2nd edn), New York: Harcourt Brace Jovanovich.

This list includes general sources on comparative economic systems not specifically cited in the References or listed among the suggested readings of other chapters.

Appendix

In this appendix we briefly introduce the formal apparatus used to expound the concepts of efficiency in production, efficiency in distribution, and efficiency in product mix (see Chapter 1, section 1.4.2).

Productive Efficiency

Consider a good, x, which is produced using two inputs, i and j. If we graph the quantity of i used to produce x on the vertical axis, and the quantity of j used to produce x on the horizontal axis of a diagram such as Figure A.1, the quantity of x produced should increase as we move from the origin in a north-easterly direction. Suppose that in a third dimension, rising above the plane of the figure, we were to depict the level of output. Its elevation would increase as we moved from the origin to the north-east, along any ray, and also as we moved to the east from the vertical axis or to the north from the horizontal axis. The information shown by such a third dimension can be represented, instead, in the two dimensions of the figure, by a set of contour lines, each of which identifies a set of input combinations that yields a certain fixed output level. These contour lines are called *isoquants*, and the output levels that they indicate are increasing as one moves away from the origin. The diagram as a whole is referred to as an isoquant map.

The shape of the isoquants shown in Figure A.1 is based on the assumption that rather than having to be provided in fixed proportions, inputs i and j can be combined in varying proportions to produce the product x. The amount of i that can be withdrawn when a given amount of j is added, leaving the output of x constant, is called the *marginal rate of technical substitution* (MRTS) of j for i, and is equal to the slope of the isoquant at any given point. Although substitution is possible, in general it is imperfect, in the sense that it takes more j to make up for a given sacrifice of i as less i is used. This causes the MRTS to decrease in absolute terms as i declines. Declining MRTS means that isoquants become less steep as one moves clockwise in Figure A.1; therefore, isoquants are convex with respect to the origin, as shown.

Suppose, now, that an economy has only two inputs, which we may continue to call i and j, and that these two inputs can be used to produce only two products, x and y. If the ways in which i and j can be combined to produce y obey the same laws as does the technology for producing x, then we can also display an isoquant map for the y industry in the ij space. Isoquants for y will also be convex to the origin, and will denote increasing levels of y for increasing levels of i and j.

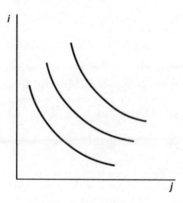

FIG. A.1.

Now, if the economy contains a finite amount of i and j, the production possibilities for the two goods, x and y, can be fully described by combining the isoquant maps for the two industries into a single diagram, called the Edgeworth box.[1] In Figure A.2, which may be interpreted as an Edgeworth box for a two-goods economy, the isoquant map of the x industry has its origin in the south-west corner of the box, as in Figure A.1, but the isoquant map for the y industry is drawn with its origin in the north-east corner. The height of the box represents the total available quantity of input i, while the length represents the total quantity of input j. A point in the box therefore indicates the amount of i used in the x industry, by height measured from the bottom, the amount of i used in the y industry, by height measured from the top, the amount of j used in the x industry, by length measured from the left, and the amount of j used in the y industry, by length measured from the right, with available i and j thus exactly used up between the two industries. Each point in the box also lies on both an isoquant of the x industry, convex to the south-west origin, and an isoquant of the y industry, convex to the north-east origin.[2]

In most cases, the two isoquants passing through a point, such as R, intersect at that point; but there is one set of points in the box, including S and T, that mark tangencies between isoquants of the two industries. These points of tangency, which together comprise the *production contract curve*, can be shown to be allocations of inputs i and j to industries x and y that have the property of *efficiency in production* (see Chapter 1). For example, consider point R, at which x' units of x and y' units of y are produced. If a few units of i are shifted from the x to the y industry, while a few units of j are shifted from the y to the x industry, output of both x and y can be increased, as indicated by movement towards higher isoquants for both industries. Thus,

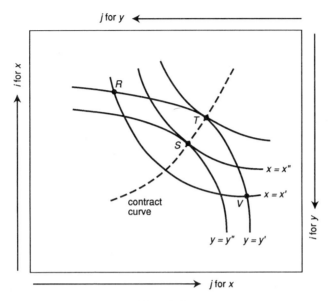

Fɪɢ. A.2.

the economy is not *allocatively efficient* at R; it has not allocated its resources in a manner consistent with achieving maximum output of each good subject to the output of the other good, the availability of resources, and the known production technologies summarized by the isoquant maps. Suppose, however, that the reallocation of i and j between the two industries moves them to point S, at which their isoquants are tangent. Now $x'' > x'$ and $y'' > y'$ units of the goods are produced, but it is impossible to produce any more of x or y without producing less of the other. That is, if i and j are reallocated back in the direction of R, or onwards towards V, output of both x and y will decline, relative to their levels at S. On the other hand, if more of both inputs are allocated to the x industry, as at point T, then it is possible to increase the output of x, but only at a corresponding loss of output for y.

Distributive Efficiency

The exposition of efficiency in distribution parallels that of efficiency in production so closely that the same diagrams can be used, after a simple relabeling. Thus, in Figure A.1, let i and j now be understood to be two consumption goods, and let the axes measure the level of consumption of the goods by a certain consumer, whom we can call x. It is conventional to assume that for most goods and consumers, welfare, satisfaction, or 'utility' increases with the amount of each good consumed. If we were to substitute the level of utility for the level of output as the imagined third dimension of Figure A.1, it would have the same general shape: namely, height would be greater further from the origin along any ray, and further from either axis along any perpendicular to it. The height information in this third dimension could again be represented as a set of contour lines in the two dimensions, i and j, and these would have the same convex shape as did the isoquants, this time indicating that the quantity of j that must be obtained by the consumer to compensate for a given loss of i is increasing as i declines. The contour lines are in the present case called *indifference curves*. The rate at which j can be substituted for i without loss of utility is called the *marginal rate of (indifferent) substitution* (MRS), and is equal to the slope of the indifference curve, which is declining in absolute value with falling i or rising j.

The Edgeworth box for production can now be reinterpreted as an Edgeworth box for distribution or consumption. For this purpose, it is convenient to consider the case in which there are exactly two consumers, x and y, and fixed total quantities of two goods, i and j. Then Figure A.2 can be understood as having its height determined by the total quantity of good i available, and its length determined by the total quantity of good j available. The lower left corner can be interpreted as the consumption origin for consumer x, and the curves convex to that origin as the indifference curves of that consumer, with utility increasing towards the north-east. The upper right corner is the zero consumption point of consumer y, and the curves convex to it are y's indifference curves, with utility increasing towards the south-west. As with productive efficiency, *efficiency in distribution* (see again section 1.4.2) turns out to occur on a *contract curve*, along which the indifference curves of the two consumers are tangent. For example, let x and y be allocated bundles of i and j which place them at point R. If x trades some of his i for some of y's j, both can move to higher indifference curves. But if they arrive at distribution point S, on the contract curve, x can become still better off only at the expense of the y, and vice versa.[3]

Efficiency in the Product Mix

Return to the interpretation of i and j as inputs, and of Figure A.2 as the Edgeworth box for production of products x and y. Notice, now, that as the allocation of inputs shifts along the contract curve, for example from S to T, output of one good increases while that of the other falls. This relationship can be captured in another diagram, Figure A.3, in which the two

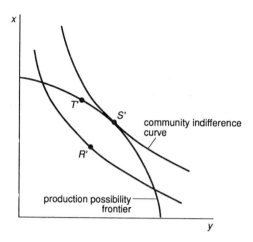

Fig. A.3.

dimensions are quantities of the products x and y. Suppose, for example, that S′ graphs the quantities of x and y that are produced using input allocations S. Then the point in the product space of Figure A.3 corresponding to input allocation T in Figure A.2 must lie somewhere to the north-west of S′ (which is where we place point T′) since T is on a higher isoquant for the x industry, but a lower one for the y industry. The rest of the contract curve in Figure A.2 can be similarly translated into the terms of Figure A.3, generating the concave curve on which S′ and T′ lie. This curve is known as the *production possibility frontier* (PPF) because it shows the maximum amount of x that can be produced subject to the amount of y that is being produced, assuming complete efficiency in production. Points to the south-west of the PPF, such as R′, correspond to inefficient input allocations, such as R in Figure A.2. Compared with such points, it is possible to produce more of both goods through a better allocation of the inputs.[4] Points to the north-east of the PPF are assumed to be unattainable using the presently available resources and presently known production methods. The PPF is shown as a concave curve because the economy's resources are assumed to be not equally well suited to use in both industries. As the inputs most suitable for x production are used up, more x can be produced only by withdrawing from the y industry some inputs that are very suitable for y production but less so for x production; hence, the cost, in lost y, gets higher and higher, while the gain, in added x, becomes smaller and smaller, as the transfer process proceeds.[5]

Just as there are a large number of points on the contract curve in Figure
A.2, each of which satisfies the requirements of efficiency in production, so
there are a large number of points on the PPF in Figure A.3, all of which
also satisfy those requirements. The third efficiency property, *efficiency in
product mix* (see again section 1.4.2), makes reference to the idea that not all
points on the PPF are equally good in the eyes of consumers.[6] For example,
suppose that x is food and y is health care. Consumers will probably want to
have quantities of both goods, so as x approaches zero, the amount of y
needed to make them indifferent to giving up another unit of x becomes
extremely large. To simplify, imagine that the preferences of all consumers,
in the aggregate, can be represented by one set of indifference curves, which
have the same properties as those of an individual consumer: convexity to
the origin and increasing satisfaction as one moves away from the origin or
from an axis. Then the community's preferences among the points in Figure
A.3 are such that combination S', at which a community indifference curve
is tangent to the PPF, is clearly superior to all others that are feasible (that
is, within or on the production possibility frontier). While the economy is
efficient in production if it attains any of the infinity of points located on the
PPF, efficiency in the output mix is therefore attained only at S'.

Notes

1. After the nineteenth-century British economist Francis Y. Edgeworth.
2. Output is assumed to expand continuously as inputs increase, so there
   must be a new isoquant passing through each point encountered as one
   proceeds along any ray from the origin of an isoquant map. Only a few
   isoquants are actually drawn in our figure, however, for purposes of
   illustration.
3. The term 'contract curve' is used because beneficial trades can be made
   from points off the curve to points on the curve.
4. Alternatively, a point like R' may be attained not because inputs are
   misallocated among industries, but because they are used in a technically
   inefficient way, for example, wastefully, within each industry. Ordinarily, neoclassical economic theory assumes that technical efficiency is
   achieved, owing to the desire of producers to maximize the returns from
   scarce resources, but this assumption may not be entirely reasonable, in
   reality.
5. The slope of the PPF is known as the *rate of product transformation* and can
   be shown to equal the ratio of the marginal costs of production of y and x.
   (See Table 1 in Chapter 2 section 2.2.2.)
6. In Chapter 3 we consider the possibility that it is social planners, rather
   than consumers, whose preferences count.

References

Alchian, Armen and Demsetz, Harold, 1972, 'Production, Information Costs, and Economic Organization', *American Economic Review* 62: 777–95.

Avineri, Shlomo 1968, *The Social and Political Thought of Karl Marx*, London: Cambridge University Press.

Baren, Paul and Sweezy, Paul, 1969, *Monopoly Capital: An Essay on the American Economic and Social Order*, New York: Monthly Review Press.

Barber, William, 1967, *History of Economic Thought*, Harmondsworth: Penguin.

Barkai, Haim, 1977, *Growth Patterns of the Kibbutz Economy*, Amsterdam: North-Holland.

Ben-Ner, Avner, 1987, 'Producer Cooperatives: Why Do They Exist in Capitalist Economies?', in W. Powell (ed.), *The Nonprofit Sector: a Research Handbook*, New Haven: Yale University Press.

—— 1988, 'The Life Cycle of Worker-owned Firms in Market Economies: a Theoretical Analysis', *Journal of Economic Behavior and Organization* 10: 287–313.

Bergson, Abram, 1978, *Productivity and the Social System: The USSR and the West*, Cambridge, Mass. Harvard University Press.

Bergson, Abram, 1987, 'Comparative Productivity: the USSR, Eastern Europe, and the West', *American Economic Review* 77: 342–57.

Bettelheim, Charles, 1975, *Economic Calculations and Forms of Property*, translated by John Taylor, New York: Monthly Review Press.

Blaug, Mark, 1978, *Economic Theory in Retrospect*, 3rd edn, Cambridge: Cambridge University Press.

Blumberg, Paul, 1968, *Industrial Democracy: the Sociology of Participation*, New York: Schocken Books.

Bonin, John P. and Putterman, Louis, 1987, *Economics of Cooperation and the Labor-Managed Economy (Fundamentals of Pure and Applied Economics, vol. 14)*, London: Harwood Academic Publishers.

Bookchin, Murray, 1982, *The Ecology of Freedom: the Emergence and Dissolution of Hierarchy*, Palo Alto, CA: Cheshire Books.

Bowles, Samuel, 1985, 'The Production Process in a Competitive Economy: Walrasian, Marxian and Neo-Hobbesian Models', *American Economic Review* 75: 16–36.

—— and Gintis, Herbert, 1977, *Schooling in Capitalist America*, New York: Basic Books.

Burkett, John P., 1985, 'Systemic Influences on the Physical Quality of Life: a Bayesian Analysis of Cross-Sectional Data', *Journal of Comparative Economics* 9: 145–63.

—— and Skegro, Borislav, 1989, 'Capitalism, Socialism, and Productivity: an Econometric Analysis of CES and Translog Functions', *European Economic Review* 33: 1115–33.

Byrd, William and Lin Qingsong, (eds), 1990, *China's Rural Industry: Structure, Development, and Reform* New York: Oxford University Press.

Cave, Martin, 1980, *Computers and Economic Planning: the Soviet Experience*, Cambridge: Cambridge University Press.

Cereseto, Shirley and Waitzkin, Howard, 1986, 'Economic Development, Political-Economic System, and the Physical Quality of Life', *American Journal of Public Health* 76: 661–6.

Clark, John Bates, 1899, *The Distribution of Wealth: a Theory of Wages, Interest and Profits*, London: Macmillan.

Coase, Ronald, 1937, 'The Nature of the Firm', *Economica* IV: 386–405.

Conte, Michael, 1982, 'Participation and Performance in U.S. Labor-Managed Firms', in Derek Jones and Jan Svejnar (eds), *Participatory and Labor-Managed Firms: Evaluating Economic Performance*, Lexington, Mass: Lexington Books: 213–37.

Cooter, Robert and Rappaport, Peter, 1984, 'Were the Ordinalists Wrong About Welfare Economics?', *Journal of Economic Literature* 22: 507–30.

Dahl, Robert, 1985, *A Preface to Economic Democracy*, Berkeley: University of California Press.

Danziger, Sheldon, Gottschalk, Peter, and Smolenski, Eugene, 1989, 'American Income Inequality: How the Rich Have Fared, 1973–87', *American Economic Review (Papers and Proceedings)* 79: 310–14.

Deane, Phyllis, 1965, *The First Industrial Revolution*, Cambridge: Cambridge University Press.

—— and Cole, W.A., 1962, *British Economic Growth 1688–1959: Trends and Structure*, Cambridge: Cambridge University Press.

Desai, Padma and Martin, Ricardo, 1983, 'Efficiency Loss from Resource Misallocation in Soviet Industry', *Quarterly Journal of Economics* 98: 441–56.

Domar, Evsey, 1957, *Essays in the Theory of Economic Growth*, New York: Oxford University Press.

Dorfman, Robert, 1953, 'Mathematical, or Linear, Programming: a Non-mathematical Exposition', *American Economic Review* 43: 797–825.

Dreze, Jacques H., 1976, 'Some Theory of Labor Management and Participation', *Econometrica* 44: 1125–40.

Ellerman, David, 1986, 'Property Appropriation and Economic Theory', in Philip Mirowski (ed.), *The Reconstruction of Economic Theory*, Boston: Kluwer-Nijhoff Publishing: 41–92.

Ellman, Michael, 1989, *Socialist Economic Planning*, 2nd edn, Cambridge: Cambridge University Press.

Engels, Frederick, 1978 [1872], 'On Authority', in Robert Tucker (ed.), *The*

Marx-Engels Reader, 2nd edn, New York: W. W. Norton: 730–3.

Estrin, Saul, 1983, *Self-management: Economic Theory and Yugoslav Practice*, Cambridge: Cambridge University Press.

——— Jones, Derek, and Svejnar, Jan, 1987, 'The Productivity Effects of Worker Participation: Producer Cooperatives in Western Economies', *Journal of Comparative Economics* 11: 40–61.

Feldman, Allan, 1980, *Welfare Economics and Social Choice Theory*, Boston: Martinus Nijhoff Publishing.

FitzRoy, Felix and Kraft, Kornelius, 1987, 'Cooperation, Productivity and Profit-Sharing', *Quarterly Journal of Economics* 102: 23–35.

Friedman, Milton, 1962, *Capitalism and Freedom*, Chicago: University of Chicago Press.

Furubotn, Eirik G. and Pejovich, Svetozar, 1970, 'Property Rights and the Behavior of the Firm in a Socialist State: the Example of Yugoslavia', *Zeitschrift fur Nationalokonomie* 30: 431–54.

——— and ——— (eds), 1974, *The Economics of Property Rights*, Cambridge, Mass.: Ballinger Publishing Co.

Georgescu-Roegen, Nicholas, 1960, 'Economic Theory and Agrarian Economics', *Oxford Economic Papers* 12: 1–40.

Gintis, Herbert, 1972, 'A Radical Analysis of Welfare Economics and Individual Development', *Quarterly Journal of Economics* 86: 572–99.

Goldberg, Victor, 1980, 'Relational Exchange: Economics and Complex Contracts', *American Behavioral Scientist* 23: 337–52.

Gregory, Paul R. and Stuart, Robert C., 1986, *Soviet Economic Structure and Performance*, 3rd edn, New York: Harper and Row.

——— and ———, 1989, *Comparative Economic Systems* (3rd edn), Boston: Houghton Mifflin.

Hardt, John P. (ed.), 1967, *Mathematics and Computers in Soviet Economic Planning*, New Haven: Yale University Press.

Hare, Paul, Radice, H., and Swain, N. (eds), 1981, *Hungary: a Decade of Economic Reform*, London: Allen and Unwin.

Harrod, Roy, 1948, *Towards a Dynamic Economics*, New York: St Martin's Press.

Hayek, Friedrich A. (ed.), 1935, *Collectivist Economic Planning*, London: Routledge and Kegan Paul.

——— 1945, 'The Use of Knowledge in Society', *American Economic Review* 35: 519–30.

——— 1973, 1976, 1979, *Law, Legislation, and Liberty* (Vols 1–3), Chicago: University of Chicago Press.

Henderson, Hazel, 1981, *The Politics of the Solar Age: Alternatives to Economics*, Garden City, NY: Anchor Press.

Hewett, Edward, 1981, 'The Hungarian Economy: Lessons of the 1970s and Prospects for the 1980s', in US Congress Joint Economic Committee, *East*

European Economic Assessment, Part 1, Washington: US Government Printing Office.

Hirschman, Albert, 1970, *Exit, Voice and Loyalty: Responses to Decline in Firms, Organizations, and States*, Cambridge, Mass.: Harvard University Press.

Holmstrom, Bengt, 1982, 'Moral Hazard in Teams', *Bell Journal of Economics* 13: 324–40.

Hurwicz, Leonid, 1971, 'Centralization and Decentralization in Economic Processes', in Alexander Eckstein (ed.), *Comparison of Economic Systems*, Berkeley: University of California Press: 79–102.

International Labor Office (ILO), 1956, 1965, 1970, *Yearbook of Labor Statistics*, Geneva: International Labor Office.

International Monetary Fund (IMF), 1988, *International Financial Statistics Yearbook 1988*, Washington DC: IMF.

Ireland, Norman J. and Law, Peter J., 1982, *The Economics of Labor-Managed Enterprises*, New York: St Martin's Press.

Jensen, Michael and Meckling, William, 1979, 'Rights and Production Functions: an Application to Labor-Managed Firms and Codetermination', *Journal of Business* 52: 469–506.

Jones, Derek C., 1985, 'The Economic Performance of Producer Cooperatives Within Command Economies: Evidence for the Case of Poland', *Cambridge Journal of Economics* 9: 111–26.

Klein, Benjamin, Crawford, Robert, and Alchian, Armen, 1978, 'Vertical Integration, Appropriable Rents and the Competitive Contracting Process', *Journal of Law and Economics* 21: 297–326.

Knight, Frank H., 1935 [1922], 'The Ethics of Competition', *Quarterly Journal of Economics* 36: 454–81, reprinted in Frank Knight, *The Ethics of Competition and Other Essays*, New York: Harper and Brothers.

—— 1965, *Risk, Uncertainty and Profit*, New York: Harper and Row.

Knight, Peter and Roca, Santiago, 1975, 'Synthesis of the Principal Conclusions of the Workshop on Implementation of Self-managed Systems in the Third World (Cornell University, June 9–27, 1975)', *Economic Analysis and Workers' Management* 9: 368–84.

Kohler, Heinz, 1989, *Comparative Economic Systems*, Glenview, IL: Scott, Foresman and Co.

Kornai, Janos, 1980, *Economics of Shortage*, Amsterdam: North-Holland.

Kuznets, Simon, 1965, *Economic Growth and Structure*, New York: Norton.

Lange, Oskar, 1964 [1938], 'On the Economic Theory of Socialism', in Benjamin E. Lippincott (ed.), *On the Economic Theory of Socialism*, New York: McGraw-Hill: 57–143.

Lawler, Edward, 1986, *High Involvement Management*, San Francisco: Jossey-Bass Publishers.

Lerner, Abba P., 1944, *The Economics of Control: Principles of Welfare Economics*, New York: Macmillan.

Levine, Herbert S., 1959, 'The Centralized Planning of Supply in the Soviet Union', in Joint Economic Committee, *Comparisons of the United States and Soviet Economies*, Washington, DC: US Government Printing Office: 151–76.

Lewis, W. Arthur, 1954, 'Development with Unlimited Supplies of Labour', *The Manchester School* 22: 139–92.

Lindbeck, Assar (ed.), 1977, *The Political Economy of the New Left: an Outsider's View*, 2nd edn, New York: New York University Press.

Lydall, Harold, 1984, *Yugoslav Socialism: Theory and Practice*, Oxford: Clarendon Press.

Malthus, Thomas R., 1970 [1798], *An Essay on the Principle of Population*, Harmondsworth: Penguin.

Marglin, Stephen A., 1974, 'What Do Bosses Do? the Origins of Hierarchy in Capitalist Production', *Review of Radical Political Economics* 6: 60–112.

Marschack, Jacob and Radner, Roy, 1972, *Economic Theory of Teams*, New Haven: Yale University Press.

Marx, Karl, 1967*a* [1867], *Capital: An Analysis of Capitalist Production*, vol. I, New York: International Publishers.

—— 1967*b* [1894], *Capital: The Process of Capitalist Production as a Whole*, vol. III, New York: International Publishers.

—— 1978 [1875], 'Critique of the Gotha Program', in Robert C. Tucker (ed.), *The Marx-Engels Reader*, New York: W. W. Norton: 525–41.

—— and Frederick Engels, 1978 [1848], 'Manifesto of the Communist Party', in Robert C. Tucker (ed.), *The Marx-Engels Reader*, New York: W. W. Norton: 473–500.

Milenkovitch, Deborah D., 1983, 'Self-Management and Thirty Years of Yugoslav Experience', *Association for Comparative Economic Studies Bulletin* 25 (3): 1–26.

Mill, John Stuart, 1936 [1852], *Principles of Political Economy*, Book IV, Chapter VII, 'On the Probable Futurity of the Labouring Classes', London: Longmans, Green and Co.

Mises, Ludwig von, 1981 [1933], *Epistemological Problems of Economics*, New York: New York University Press.

—— 1951, *Socialism: an Economic and Sociological Analysis*, New Haven: Yale University Press.

Mitchell, B. R., 1975, *European Historical Statistics: 1750–1970*, New York: Columbia University Press.

Montias, John Michael, 1976, *The Structure of Economic Systems*, New Haven: Yale University Press.

Morishima, Michio, 1973, *Marx's Economics*, Cambridge: Cambridge University Press.

Morrisson, Christian, 1984, 'Income Distribution in East European and Western Countries', *Journal of Comparative Economics* 8: 121–38.

Myrdal, Gunnar, 1961, *The Political Element in the Development of Economic Theory*, translated from the German by Paul Streeten, Cambridge: Harvard University Press.

Nalbantian, Haig R. (ed.), 1987, *Incentives, Cooperation, and Risk Sharing: Economic and Psychological Perspectives on Employment Contracts*, Totowa, NJ: Rowman and Littlefield.

Nemchinov, V.S. (ed.), 1964, *The Use of Mathematics in Economics*, [Russian edn, 1959], English translation with an introduction by Alec Nove, Edinburgh: Oliver and Boyd.

Network of Solidarity Organizations in Leading Factories (Poland), 1981, 'Position on Social and Economic Reform of the Country', Solidarność (Gdańsk) Nr 29/59/81.

Neuberger, Egon and Duffy, William, 1976, *Comparative Economic Systems: a Decision-Making Approach*, Boston: Allyn and Bacon.

Nove, Alec, 1962 [1958], 'The Problem of "Success Indicators" in Soviet Industry', *Economica* 97: 1–13, reprinted in F. Holzman (ed.), *Readings on the Soviet Economy*, Chicago: Rand McNally.

—— 1972, *An Economic History of the U.S.S.R.*, revised edn, New York: Penguin.

—— 1983, *The Economics of Feasible Socialism*, Boston: Allen and Unwin.

Organization for Economic Cooperation and Development (OECD), 1987, *OECD Labor Force Statistics*, Paris: Organization for Economic Cooperation and Development.

Ouchi, William G., 1981, *Theory Z: How American Business Can Meet the Japanese Challenge*, Reading, MA: Addison-Wesley.

Pagano, Ugo, 1985, *Work and Welfare in Economic Theory*, New York: Basil Blackwell.

Pateman, Carole, 1970, *Participation and Economic Theory*, Cambridge: Cambridge University Press.

Pejovich, Svetozar, 1969, 'The Firm, Monetary Policy, and Property Rights in a Planned Economy', *Western Economic Journal* 7: 193–200.

—— (ed.), 1978, *The Codetermination Movement in the West*, Lexington, MA: Lexington Books.

Polanyi, Karl, 1957, 'The Economy as Instituted Process', in K. Polanyi, C. Arensberg, and H. Pearson (eds), *Trade and Market in the Early Empires*, Glencoe, IL: Free Press: 243–70.

—— 1970, *The Great Transformation*, Boston: Beacon.

Prasnikar, Janez and Svejnar, Jan, 1988, 'Economic Behavior of Yugoslav Enterprises', in Derek Jones and Jan Svejnar (eds), *Advances in the Economic Analysis of Participatory and Labor-Managed Firms*, vol. 3, Greenwich, CT: JAI Press: 237–311.

Pratt, John and Zeckhauser, Richard (eds), 1985, *Principles and Agents: the Structure of Business*, Boston: Harvard Business School Press.

Putterman, Louis, 1984, 'On Some Recent Explanations of Why Capital Hires Labor', *Economic Inquiry* 22: 171–87.

—— (ed.), 1986, *The Economic Nature of the Firm: a Reader*, New York: Cambridge University Press.

—— 1988, 'The Firm as Association versus the Firm as Commodity: Efficiency, Rights, and Ownership', *Economics and Philosophy* 4: 243–66.

Ranis, Gustav and Fei, John C. H., 1961, 'A Theory of Economic Development', *American Economic Review* 51: 533–65.

Reader's Digest, 1986, *Reader's Digest Almanac: 1987*, Pleasantville, NY: Reader's Digest Association.

Reynolds, Bruce (ed.), 1987, 'Chinese Economic Reform: How Far, How Fast?, *Journal of Comparative Economics* special issue, vol. 11, no. 3.

Ricardo, David, 1951 [1815], *Essay on Profits*, in Piéro Sraffa (ed.), *The Works and Correspondence of David Ricardo*, vol. IV, Cambridge: Cambridge University Press: 1–41.

Richardson, G.B., 1972, 'The Organization of Industry', *Economic Journal* 82: 883–96.

Robbins, Lionel, 1932, *An Essay on the Nature and Significance of Economic Science*, London: Macmillan.

Roemer, John, 1982, *A General Theory of Exploitation and Class*, Cambridge: Harvard University Press.

—— 1988, *Free to Lose: an Introduction to Marxist Economic Philosophy*, Cambridge: Harvard University Press.

Rosefield, Steven, 1981, 'Knowledge and Socialism: Deciphering the Soviet Experience', in S. Rosefielde (ed.), *Economic Welfare and the Economics of Soviet Socialism: Essays in Honor of Abram Bergson*, Cambridge: Cambridge University Press: 5–23.

Scherer, F.M., 1966, 'General Equilibrium and Economic Efficiency', *The American Economist* X(1): 1–17.

Schumpeter, Joseph, 1949, *The Theory of Economic Development: an Inquiry into Profits, Capital, Credit, Interest and the Business Cycle*, translated from the German by Reduers Opie, Cambridge: Harvard University Press.

—— 1950, *Capitalism, Socialism, and Democracy*, New York: Harper and Row.

—— 1955, *History of Economic Analysis*, New York: Oxford University Press.

Schweickart, David, 1980, *Capitalism or Worker Control? An Ethical and Economic Appraisal*, New York: Praeger.

Scott, James, 1976, *The Moral Economy of the Peasant*, New Haven: Yale University Press.

Sen, Amartya K., 1967, 'Isolation, Assurance, and the Social Rate of Discount', *Quarterly Journal of Economics* 81: 112–24.

—— 1974, 'Informational Bases of Alternative Welfare Approaches: Aggregation and Income Distribution', *Journal of Public Economics* 3: 387–403.

—— 1987, *The Standard of Living*, Cambridge: Cambridge University Press.

Sertel, Murat, 1982, *Workers and Incentives*, Amsterdam: North-Holland.

Seton, Francis, 1977, 'The Question of Ideological Obstacles to Rational Price Setting in Communist Countries', in Alan Abouchar (ed.), *The Socialist Price Mechanism*, Durham, NC: Duke University Press: 10–39.

Shapiro, Carl and Stiglitz, Joseph, 1984, 'Equilibrium Unemployment as a Worker Discipline Device', *American Economic Review* 74: 433–44.

Simon, Herbert, 1957, *Models of Man*, New York: John Wiley and Sons.

Smith, Adam, 1985 [1776], *An Inquiry into the Nature and Causes of the Wealth of Nations*, New York: The Modern Library.

Sturm, Peter H., 1977, 'The System Component in Differences in per Capita Output between East and West Germany', *Journal of Comparative Economics* 1: 5–24.

Svejnar, Jan, 1982, 'Codetermination and Productivity: Empirical Evidence from the Federal Republic of Germany', in Derek Jones and Jan Svejnar (eds), *Participatory and Self-Managed Firms: Evaluating Economic Performance*, Lexington, Mass: Lexington Books: 199–212.

Tidrick, Gene, and Chen, Jiyuan, (eds), 1987, *China's Industrial Reform*, New York: Oxford University Press.

Thomas, Hendrik and Logan, C., 1980, *Mondragon Producer Cooperatives*, The Hague, Netherlands: Institute of Social Studies.

Todaro, Michael, 1989, *Economic Development in the Third World*, 4th edn, New York: Longman.

Tyson, Laura D'Andrea, 1980, *The Yugoslav Economic System and its Performance in the 1970s*, Berkeley: Institute of International Studies, University of California.

US Bureau of the Census, 1987, *Statistical Abstract of the United States, 1988*, Washington DC: Government Printing Office.

US Central Intelligence Agency (USCIA), 1988, *Handbook of Economic Statistics*, Washington DC: National Foreign Assessment Center.

Vanek, Jaroslav, 1970, *The General Theory of Labor-Managed Market Economies*, Ithaca, NY: Cornell University Press.

Walder, Andrew, 1989, 'Factory and Manager in an Era of Reform', *China Quarterly*, 118: 242–64.

Ward, Benjamin, 1958, 'The Firm in Illyria: Market Syndicalism', *American Economic Review* 68: 566–89.

—— 1967, *The Socialist Economy: a Study of Organizational Alternatives*, New York: Random House.

Whitesell, Robert S., forthcoming, 'Why Does the Soviet Economy Appear to be Allocatively Efficient?, *Soviet Studies*.

Whyte, William F. and Whyte, Kathleen K., 1988, *Making Mondragon: the Growth and Dynamics of the Worker Cooperative Complex*, Ithaca, NY: ILR Press, Cornell University.

Wiener, Hans with Oakeshott, Robert, 1987, *Worker-Owners: Mondragon Revisited*, London: Anglo-German Foundation for the Study of Industrial Society.

Williamson, Oliver E., 1975, *Markets and Hierarchies: Analysis and Antitrust Implications*, New York: Free Press.

—— 1980, 'The Organization of Work: a Comparative Institutional Assessment', *Journal of Economic Behavior and Organization* 1: 5–38.

—— 1985, *The Economic Institutions of Capitalism: Firms, Markets, Relational Contracting*, New York: The Free Press.

Wolff, Edward N., 1987, 'Estimates of Household Wealth Inequality in the U.S., 1962–1983', *Review of Income and Wealth*, Series 33, September: 231–56.

Wood, Allen, 1972, 'The Marxian Critique of Justice', *Philosophy and Public Affairs* 1: 244–82.

World Bank, 1976, *World Tables, 1976*, Baltimore: Johns Hopkins University Press.

—— 1980, *World Tables*, (2nd edn), Baltimore: Johns Hopkins University Press.

—— 1988, *World Development Report 1988*, New York: Oxford University Press.

Index